One Hundred Dogs & Counting

One Woman, Ten Thousand Miles, and
a Journey into the Heart of Shelters and Rescues

Cara Sue Achterberg

PEGASUS BOOKS
NEW YORK LONDON

ONE HUNDRED DOGS & COUNTING

Pegasus Books Ltd.
148 W 37th Street, 13th Floor
New York, NY 10018

First Pegasus Books cloth edition July 2020

Interior design by Maria Fernandez

ISBN: 978-1-64313-412-3

10 9 8 7 6 5 4 3 2 1

Printed in the United States of America
Distributed by Simon & Schuster
www.pegasusbooks.us

For Frankie, the dog of my heart.
In the end, I couldn't save you, so I will try to save the others.

Awareness is like the sun. When it shines on things, they are transformed.

—Thich Nhat Hanh

Contents

Introduction

Our family has fostered 162 dogs for an all-breed, foster-based rescue that saves dogs from southern shelters, moving them north to be adopted. By the time you read this, that number will probably be over two hundred. We continue to commit to dog after dog, seeing each one through to its eventual forever home and then immediately picking up another. The dogs live with us, as our own dogs, as part of our family. We teach them how to be a family pet, sometimes offering the first indoor accommodations they've ever experienced. With that comes the fun of house-training, crate-training, and leash-training. But we also teach them about belly rubs and squeaky toys and the comfort of snuggling on the couch to watch football. There have been plenty of moments when I've laughed myself silly or cried in frustration, swearing off this particular addiction, but mostly I am struck time and again by the capacity of these marvelous four-legged individuals to trust and to forgive. They are always a lesson in love and perhaps a bigger lesson in patience.

Fostering is not for the faint of heart. We love these dogs, and then we let them go so we can love another. Those good-byes used to seem like the hardest part. Now I know better. I have met the dogs still in shelters and dog pounds who never make it on a transport, the ones who don't know safety and yet wait patiently for a home they may never get.

After *Another Good Dog: One Family and Fifty Foster Dogs* was published, the drumbeat began: "When's the next book?" But I hesitated, wondering if there was an audience for endless foster dog stories. I'd be the first to say that every foster dog that comes to us brings a whole new experience—"boring" is not a word I would ever use to describe fostering—but really just how many times does a reader want to hear about another stuffed animal mauling or counter raid? How many puppies have to be born in my mudroom before readers become like my own children and complain about the smell and the work, completely missing the cuteness?

On the heels of my most difficult foster dog to date, and a few months before the publication of *Another Good Dog*, I was struck with the realization that the stream of dogs was not abating. If anything, it was growing, and the fostering requests felt more desperate. If fostering was helping, why wasn't that stream slowing at least?

I've always been a person who would rather look at the cause of an injury than simply put on a Band-Aid. I have no patience for doing the same thing over and over to no effect.* If fostering one hundred dogs in our home hadn't made a dent in the problem, then why were we even bothering? After all, our carpet was ruined, our front hall had turned into an adoption center, and visitors had to navigate two baby gates to get from our kitchen table to the bathroom. As our social lives became intertwined with the lives of other "crazy dog people"† and swirled around the endless needs of homeless dogs, I thought for certain we were making a difference. So certain, I wrote a book about it!

And then just before the book came out, I had a mini-crisis, doubting that all the work and dogs and heartbreak were making any difference. Sure, I could see it in the individual lives of the dogs that came through our home and the families that adopted those dogs, but were we making a dent in the larger problem? How was it that the pleas for foster homes to save dogs destined to be euthanized in shelters never slowed, never lessened, no matter how many we rescued?

I needed to see the situation for myself. So, I hijacked my book tour and turned it into a shelter/book tour. What I saw changed the trajectory of my life.

---

* And yet I have mucked stalls out daily for years.

† My husband's term.

I had always thought rescue dog fostering was an interim in my life—foster some dogs, write about it, the situation improves—then I go back to my real life writing novels, pulling weeds, hiking in the woods, and worrying about my (now adult) children. Instead, I can't seem to stay with a story long enough to see it through to publication, my gardens have been plowed under, my hiking boots sit idle, and the kids are traipsing all over the globe without the protection of my nonstop nagging. I am too distracted by these dogs and the people who fight for them.

After visiting the shelters, I had to do something. This book is the first something. I was, and still am, convinced that if people knew what was happening in the rural southern shelters, they would not stand for it. They, like me, would be moved, they would get involved, they would help. I can't say it enough—it's not that people don't care, it's that they don't know.

So let me tell you . . .

NOTE: Throughout this book, you will read the term "pit bull." I want to be clear here that there is no such breed as a pit bull. You might as well call them unicorns. "Pit bull" is an umbrella term for dogs with a muscular build, large head, tiny ears, and hearts of gold. They may or may not have American Staffordshire Terrier or American Bull Dog Terrier or any number of terriers or bulldogs in their heritage. There is so much I could say about the misinformation, biased press, and complete nonsense that surrounds these dogs. They are near and dear to my heart, and I struggled with how to label them in this book. I considered putting the term in quotes, but it became confusing and awkward. So, suffice it to say, that while I use the term "pit bull" I don't believe in it, and I am fully aware that no such "breed" exists. I truly hope that someday everyone is lucky enough to know the love of a dog erroneously labeled "pit bull."

1

Loose Dog

Gala got out!" Brady yelled.

It was a postcard-worthy summer day in south-central Pennsylvania, the kind that almost makes the cold, gray winters worth it. I was at my desk, shades drawn, deep into a dreaded edit of a novel in progress.

My first reaction was fury. My son Brady and his friends had taken over our kitchen, reuniting over Mountain Dew and memories, trading notes about their second year of college. The last time I'd seen Gala, our foster dog, she was contentedly hanging out on the Frank bed* in the kitchen enjoying their antics.

So what was she doing outside? And why weren't all those able-bodied young men out there tracking her down? Their laughter and loud music would have drowned out my questions if there'd been time to ask them. Having

---

* The Frank bed was an enormous dog bed monogrammed with the word "Frank." It was the most sought-after spot (for dogs) in our kitchen. Previous adopters gave it to us when they returned a foster dog named Frank, and since then it had been the prize lounging spot for countless foster dogs and the background for hundreds of pictures.

recently returned from college, Brady hadn't lived with Gala long enough to know that a loose Gala was an all-out emergency.

I sprang from my ergonomically correct desk chair in such a panic that my feet tangled in the folded metal. I landed in a fuming heap, kicked the chair off me, and dashed out the door. Gala was sprinting across the pasture in search of the horses. Her long, brown form galloped back and forth across the hillside, her clever mind sifting through her options.

It wasn't the first time Gala had escaped. The last few times, she'd also run after the horses, chasing them from one end of the pasture to the other, ignoring my pleas to "come right now!" She only heeded them when she caught a hoof to her side from my elderly mare Cocoa, who abided no fools—and certainly not canine ones.

This particular afternoon, though, the horses were shut in their stalls out of the heat, except for Cocoa, who was in the paddock with a run-in shed for shade. Cocoa is a strong-willed creature, not unlike Gala, and won't tolerate being closed inside a stall. About the same time Gala spotted her, I saw Ian, my fifteen-year-old son, running across the grass, trying to put himself between Gala and the fence that separated the pasture from the paddock.

Gala ran toward him but then made a quick dodge around him before ducking underneath the bottom fence board into the paddock. The delight on her face was obvious. Gala set her sights on Cocoa, barking with abandon, darting toward her and then dashing away each time Cocoa turned her hind end at her.

Ian yelled for her, but Gala only increased her frenzy. Cocoa sprinted around the tiny paddock in a panic, using her quarter horse acceleration to stay out of Gala's reach. Gala couldn't be deterred by my yelling or any of the treats I held up.

Minutes felt like hours as we watched, helpless to stop the inevitable. Having now had time to replay the events in my head too many times to count, I wish I had thought to tell Ian to open the gate so Cocoa could have outrun her. If I'd done that, perhaps this tale would have turned out differently.

Eventually, Cocoa ran out of steam and patience and retreated to the run-in shed. Triumphant, Gala ran in after her. A moment later, I heard the unmistakable thud and then a yelp. Gala slunk out of the shed and crept toward Ian, who was waiting on the other side of the fence. When I reached them, I hooked a leash on Gala and led her to the house.

"Is she okay?" Ian asked.

"I don't know," I told him, but I was pretty sure she wasn't. The funny angled way she held her head and the missing hair on one side of her face made it clear that Cocoa had gotten her good. Once inside, Gala stood frozen, her mouth half-open and her tail between her legs as I tried to examine her. I called my veterinarian, who also happens to be my neighbor and friend. Dr. Chris's receptionist said to bring her over and they would fit her in.

X-rays confirmed that Gala's jaw was broken.

Great. Now what? We'd been fostering Gala for Operation Paws for Homes (OPH), an all-breed, foster-based rescue, for over three months. Before Gala, we'd successfully fostered over seventy-five dogs. Most arrived late on a Friday night or early on a Saturday morning on a transport van from a shelter in the rural South. All kinds of dogs and even pregnant dogs and puppies had journeyed to our home, where we nurtured them and prepared them to be adopted into forever homes. It was rewarding, if messy and sometimes heart-breaking work that we'd stumbled into quite by accident two years ago when we began searching for a new dog.

The plan had always been to foster until we found our dog, but once I learned how many dogs would die in southern rural shelters if not for rescues like OPH, I couldn't stop. Thankfully, my husband, Nick, and our three teens had all adjusted to this new normal of living with dog after dog after dog.

To date, Gala had not been an easy foster. She arrived skinny and heart-worm positive; she did well with treatment, gained weight and confidence, but as she recovered her health, she began to challenge my other foster dogs and particularly our personal dog, Gracie.

All attempts to keep Gala contained failed. She leaped easily over baby gates, dashed out any door left ajar, and dove off our deck, trailing the leash she usually wore 24/7 (so we could catch her when she inevitably got loose). She scaled the side of a six-foot outdoor kennel we thought would be the answer, pausing on the top like a bird on a wire before leaping to the other side and dashing off in victory. If anyone left the lever-handle kitchen door unlocked she was out in a flash. The same thing happened whenever someone failed to shut the storm door and left only the screen door between Gala and a freedom run.

This was bound to happen. In the two and a half years we'd been fostering, this had been one of my greatest fears. I'd watched my horses throw warning kicks at neighboring dogs, occasionally making contact. Most dogs learn quickly to stay away.

Not Gala, apparently.

During her wild chase before she trapped Cocoa in the run-in shed, Cocoa had already run over Gala . . . twice. Each time, I thought, "Okay, now she knows."

But no, Gala had blossomed into a determined and confident girl. Her heart was much bigger than her head. I'd asked the rescue to move her to another foster home away from the siren call of the horses, but Gala's reputation preceded her and there were no takers. I couldn't bear the idea of putting Gala in a boarding facility indefinitely, so she'd remained with us—and we did our best to keep her contained and safe. Only now it was clear our best was certainly not enough.

For all her antics, she was a sensitive and loving dog. I enjoyed her as a running partner, and all of us had fallen for her silly personality and effervescent love. She was that rascally kid you couldn't help but root for, even as she drove you nuts.

And now her jaw was broken. It was a relatively clean break, and because she'd gotten help so quickly it hadn't had the chance to shift. Dr. Chris used medical tape to fashion a muzzle to hold her jaw in place. He pumped her with antibiotics and pain meds, and we spent the weekend trying to keep her quiet and still and medicated while we waited for OPH to find a surgeon to look at the X-rays and make an expensive decision.

All weekend I fretted. In my time as a foster, I'd made more than my share of mistakes. I took comfort in the fact that the dog's options were to remain in a shelter and possibly/probably be killed or come to my house and be subjected to the best I could do. Granted, I did think the best I could do was getting better.

But Gala's predicament took away all the confidence I had so carefully crafted. A million "should-have"s rotated through the playlist in my head. There was no point in blaming anyone else anyway. That summer there were too many available culprits, as the plethora of young adults in our house changed daily.

My oldest son, Brady, was home for the summer working second shift at a local publishing company. As he was a creative writing major, it was good life experience, not only learning the reality of minimum wage and shift work but also exactly how a book was physically put together. The monotonous work gave his fertile mind plenty of playtime, as he was always working on a story or two, and the night hours left his days free to hang out with friends.

This meant that during the day our house was regularly infiltrated with young adults who parked all over our lawn and stayed for daylong games of Dungeons and Dragons. These brilliant young men and women could understand complex, elaborate games and debate just about any topic or recount Greek myths, but they simply could not remember to lock the door behind them.* Gala had quickly figured out the lever-handle door was her key to freedom and the pursuit of horses.

My eighteen-year-old daughter, Addie, had recently graduated from high school and was in constant motion that summer—working as a barista at Starbucks, playing Belle in a local community production of Beauty and the Beast, and preparing to leave for her freshman year of college at Rowan University. She loved Gala dearly but was rarely home, and when she was, locking the door behind her was the last thing on her mind.

Only fifteen-year-old Ian, my rule-following kid, who had borne witness to plenty of Gala's escapes and several fights between Gala and Gracie, knew the importance of containing the dog. Ian had been my best assistant through countless fostering adventures, loving the dogs and sacrificing plenty of personal time (and shoes) to help care for them.

---

* To be fair, until this point, we had never locked our door. Security was not a concern in our hollow on the outskirts of our tiny town, and we don't even own enough keys to the house for everyone to have one. There had never been a reason to lock the door before.

Sunday night, having nursed Gala through the weekend, Nick and I talked about what would happen next. When it came to my "dog habit," Nick had been a willing, if not enthusiastic, partner enabling me to take on more and more with the rescue. He generally launched an obligatory protest at my plans, but once the dogs were in the house, he was always on board. His problem-solving skills and engineering prowess had come to the rescue time and again. He'd built, fixed, and designed all kinds of contraptions to keep puppies in, keep dogs out, and even teach a swimmer puppy to walk. Basically, he was my hero. But he couldn't fix this.

Gala's jaw was broken, but that weekend it felt more like it was her spirit that broke. Watching her lie sadly on the Frank bed in the kitchen, uncharacteristically still and silent, Nick said, "Every time a dog gets loose and you panic and say, 'We have to catch it before it gets its head kicked in,' I think you're exaggerating. I didn't really think it would happen."

2
Dogs Are Expensive

By the time I loaded Gala up that Monday morning for the two-hour drive to a vet in Virginia, the "if-only"s had dragged me to the lowest point in my fostering career.

If only I'd crated her that afternoon while so many kids were at our house.

If only I'd gotten to her faster.

If only I'd thought to open the big gate to the pasture.

If only she'd come when we called.

If only someone else would have agreed to foster her.

If only I were better at this.

If only, if only, if only. They were stacked up in my heart as I drove in silence, Gala quiet in the crate in the back. I desperately wanted to rewind the tape and get a different outcome. One that didn't leave this sweet dog in such agony. I was worn out from worrying over Gala even before this episode. My heart felt bruised like Gala's head. Even if the vet fixed Gala's jaw, what then? Who's to say she'd learned anything? What if she got out again?

Between her rescue, heartworm treatment, months of foster care, and now the broken jaw, this dog was costing some serious money. Why did we pour all this money into a stray dog from South Carolina? She was just one dog and a difficult one at that. There were thousands in need of rescue, and the need never lessened.

If you separated the emotions and looked at this objectively, we could save a dozen dogs for the same amount OPH had already spent on Gala—and now this. I had to remind myself: it's just money. The same thing I told myself as we negotiated the cost of college or we lost money on something stupid or needed an expensive repair on the car or the house. Because it was just money. And doing right by this dog was far more important than money.

A noble thought, but it wouldn't pay her bill. She wasn't the most expensive dog OPH had rescued, not by far. I'd watched more expensive efforts be made by the organization to save a life. Not that they threw money around willy-nilly; they certainly considered each penny before it was spent, and they'd made more than a few hard decisions. It was rare, though, that money was the only consideration.

Dogs are expensive. That's a fact that seems to slip the minds of plenty of people. And for whatever reason—ignorance or arrogance—there are plenty of people out there who don't think a rescue dog should cost a lot. After all, a purebred dog could cost hundreds or even thousands of dollars. More than once, I'd come up against the mindset that since a person was saving a dog no one wanted or a dog someone threw away, the dog should be free or at least cheap.

OPH's adoption fee was somewhere in the middle range for adoption fees for shelters and rescues. By the time a dog is adopted, OPH has paid for spay or neuter surgery, vaccines, deworming (with puppies this can be six times or more), flea/tick preventatives, heartworm preventative, and a microchip, not to mention the original health screening, transportation, and food. And with many dogs, there were other expenses. Just that week, Dug, the puppy we were also fostering, had to visit the vet to be treated for Demodex mange.*

---

* And before you freak out at the word "mange," rest assured that Demodex mange is non-contagious. Many times it is caused by stress. For example, being starved could induce stress. When Dug arrived two weeks prior, he weighed eleven pounds, now he weighed almost twenty pounds.

The adoption fee even for a healthy dog who didn't get kicked in the head by a horse or develop Demodex mange didn't begin to cover the cost of saving that dog.

As I pulled into the vet's parking lot, I said a prayer that Gala was fixable. And if God was in the mood for miracles, that it could be a relatively inexpensive miracle, since Nick and I had decided we would pay for Gala's treatment, whatever that would be. Two kids in college didn't leave much money lying around, but I couldn't stomach asking the rescue to pay the cost of my negligence.*

Dr. Walker took additional X-rays and examined Gala and decided it might be possible to avoid surgery if Gala would tolerate being crated while wearing a muzzle and a cone 24/7. Because Chris had put a "tape muzzle" on her so soon after the accident, the bones hadn't shifted despite multiple fractures.

Dr. Walker wanted to avoid surgery if at all possible, not just because of the expense, but also because Gala had been treated for heartworm just two months prior and putting her compromised heart under anesthesia would be a risk she might not survive. He would keep her for three days to be sure she would tolerate the conditions without jarring her jaw. If all went well, I would troop back down to Virginia to pick her up later in the week.

OPH lent us an enormous crate so Gala's confinement wouldn't feel so confining. On the night before I picked up Gala, Nick assembled it in the living room next to Gracie's crate; we figured it might help them bond, and Gala would like a room with entertainment.† When Nick finished setting up the crate, he yelled, "When's the baby elephant arriving?"

---

* We only ended up paying for half of Gala's expenses—readers of my blog pitched in with generous donations.

† She'd be able to debate politics with Gracie and binge watch *Parks and Recreation*, *The Office*, and *Jane the Virgin* with Addie.

The crate was huge. I would be able to sit inside it with Gala. In fact, several of us would be able to sit inside with Gala.* Gracie watched the empty crate warily, sniffing around its edges. Gracie was our eight-year-old hound mix whom we loved despite the hours of sleep we'd all lost to her loud, insistent nightly barking and her hair-trigger reaction to any noise or smell. She had proven untrainable in the eight years since we brought her home from a different foster home as an adorable puppy. She was a bit of a bully with other dogs but could rarely back up that bluster. Deliverymen and strangers at the door were another story.

Gala was the first foster dog to call Gracie's bluff and raise her, so my days were spent negotiating the peace between the two dogs. Gracie knew that crate meant another dog, but whether she realized Gala would become her roommate, I didn't know. She sniffed it indignantly and then curled up in her own crate.

Driving to pick up Gala, I promised myself we would help her heal up and then we would insist she leave. It was clear we could not keep her safe at our house.

Gala moved home and took her sentence in stride. She ate her slurry† and tried very hard to be calm on the leash, eventually learning to avoid battering me with the edges of her cone as we walked. She spent long days lying in her ginormous crate looking very forlorn. Sometimes Ian or I would climb inside with her and read a book or sit with her to watch a television program.

As I weaned her off her pain meds, she became more determined to get the muzzle and cone off, but each time she tried I held her still and explained about the Frankensteinish surgery involving screws coming out of her face and wires connecting them that Dr. Walker had explained would be required if she didn't let her head heal.

---

* Even the baby elephant.

† "Slurry" sounds like a yummy treat from Dairy Queen but is actually watered-down canned dog food mashed to a runny consistency.

We watched her confidence leak out that month until she was only a shadow of her former self. She walked slowly on the leash, occasionally standing frozen for minutes at a time. I wasn't sure if the pain was overwhelming her or if she was lost in thought or if the kick to her head also shook up her brain. My poor girl.

She lost much of the weight we'd helped her put on in the previous months. The morning before her escape I remember watching her on our run and thinking how gorgeous she looked—healthy and strong and beautiful. The shaved spots from her heartworm treatment had almost disappeared.* She looked so different from the skinny, sick dog who arrived at our house three months prior.

About midway through Gala's recovery, Dug left with an understanding adopter who wasn't afraid of a mouthy puppy with an oversize appetite and the recovery from Demodex mange. She could see past these temporary issues to the amazing dog Dug would become. It was a happy ending for a wonderful pup whose story could have been over before it started without rescue.

With Dug gone and needing a distraction from the agony of watching Gala, I agreed to foster a litter of puppies from North Carolina who were found on the side of a road beside their dead mother. They would be on an emergency transport flight arriving the next day at a small airport outside Warrenton, Virginia. I was braced for the worst, but the only bad part about the Highway Pups† was the horrendous drive south to get them.

I tried to avoid the rush hour traffic by driving the back roads, but it seemed everyone had that same plan, plus every construction vehicle owned by the states of Maryland and Virginia had somewhere to be and was getting paid by the hour. It had never taken me so long to get to Fauquier County. The drive back was mercifully quick, which was a good thing, as the car was perfumed with the combined scent of puppy poop and barf.

---

* Heartworm treatment requires shots given in a dog's back, and the dogs come home with two neat shaven squares where the treatment was administered.

† All OPH litters get an official litter name; these would be the "Highway Pups" because "Highway Litter" didn't sound very good.

The pups were in surprisingly good shape, which told me they weren't strays. If they'd been strays for any length of time, they'd have been much thinner and full of worms and fleas, and likely wouldn't love people so much. Instead, they were a healthy weight, had shiny coats with no sign of fleas or worms, and LOVED people.

So if they weren't strays, what were they doing on the side of a highway? I've mentioned before that people are horrible. (Not you, but people.)

Rather than taking mom and pups to a shelter, I could only guess that some remarkable individual simply opened the car door and threw them out like litter. I always tried not to think too much about where my dogs came from and focused instead on where they were going. I had no doubt these beautiful pups that resembled yellow labs would be adopted quickly. The applications poured in.

As we approached the end of her confinement, Gala grew more depressed. It was as if she'd given up. She would curl in a tight ball, facing the back of the crate, and didn't react when people came into the room. If I opened the crate, she didn't move. She had to be coaxed, and sometimes dragged out, to go for potty walks. She didn't even get up when her food was served. Eventually she ate it, but it was no longer the highlight of her day.

Other times, she whined and repeatedly bashed her cone against the sides of the crate. When I took her out at those times, she lunged and pulled and wagged her tail, happy to be out. She swung back and forth between these two states all day long like a bipolar prisoner.

Personally, if I was forced to be still and quiet for a month in a comfy bed and everyone was taking care of all my needs and stopping by frequently for visits, I think I might enjoy it.* All that lounging and catching up on my reading and dining on food someone else prepared and cleaned up—what's not to like?

---

* Except Addie's endless streaming of *Parks and Rec*; that might make me feel as Gala did.

Nick worried about her so much that he bent the rules and brought her out and coaxed her up on the couch to be with us to watch the Phillies. But even then she only lay still. No Gala play. No Gala curiosity. No Gala snuggles. Not very Gala at all.

Gala was a smart dog, maybe the smartest we'd fostered, so I knew this confinement was harder on her mentally than it was physically. I tried to tell her it was just two more days until we would go to the vet for our follow-up. I was ever hopeful Dr. Walker would allow us to at least take off the muzzle and cone, even if she must still take it easy. She was breaking all our hearts. I wanted to believe that in just a few weeks, or even sooner, old Gala would be back—jumping over furniture, scaling fences, teasing the cat, and making us laugh.

She did always brighten when I allowed her to stop to see the puppies—they touched noses through the puppy-pen fence, and the puppies shrieked for her like she was a rock star.

On a Wednesday, I drove Gala back to Purcellville, Virginia, for her follow-up visit. I had a dozen questions ready for the doctor if his verdict was more muzzle/cone/crate time. I'd wanted to break the rules these last few weeks, but I hadn't because I was committed to doing what was best for Gala, even if it killed me. But staying in that dang crate wearing a muzzle/cone for much longer was going to kill her, so if that was the verdict there would have to be some modification. I was ready to press my case, even as I trusted Dr. Walker to know what was necessary to help her heal correctly.

The waiting room was bustling with people and their pets. I walked a subdued Gala to a bench and sat with her at my feet, a hand on her collar. A healthy Gala would have wanted to greet every person and dog we passed, but my current Gala only watched silently.

A young woman with a blue pit bull sat crying on the bench across from us. The dog growled and snarled at anyone who approached. A vet tech stood nearby talking quietly. He handed her a muzzle and she tried to put it on her frightened dog as the tears streamed down her face. The dog's eyes flashed as the door opened and a man walked in with an elderly Golden Retriever. The pit bull's loud barking echoed through the waiting room, silencing conversations.

My heart went out to her, but I was helpless. I couldn't leave Gala's side. I wanted to walk over, reassure her or at least catch her eye, but I had to stay focused on Gala. Gala could be that dog in a different circumstance. Vet's offices are scary places for a lot of dogs, but when a pit bull acts frightened, people read it differently.

A moment later, Dr. Walker appeared. "Here's my girl. Let's have a look," he said, reaching for Gala's leash.

Gala eyed him warily and refused to leave my side to go with him. "Guess you'll have to lead the way," said Dr. Walker, handing me the leash. I led her back to the work area for X-rays and then was shooed back to the lobby to wait and worry.

When Dr. Walker reappeared, he gave me a grin and declared, "The muzzle worked! She's all healed up!" He told me Gala's jaw had "knit itself back together." She was cleared for all activities—running, playing, even eating regular dog food!

A few moments later, Gala came bounding out dragging a tech behind her and launched herself on me. The tech handed me the muzzle and cone "just in case." I nodded through my happy tears and thanked them.

Back at home, Gala was beside herself, leaping into the arms of everyone, licking legs, rolling on the floor, tossing toys. Our happy girl was BACK!

My relief didn't last though, because with Gala back at full speed, all my worries prior to the broken jaw came rushing back. There were still no adoption applications for her. Another suitable foster home had not been found. Either she had to stay with me or OPH would pay to put her in a boarding facility. Because she didn't get along with other dogs and could climb fences, she wouldn't get to be out in the play yard. She would essentially live in her kennel, occasionally taken for walks if OPH volunteers came to visit her. I couldn't bear the idea of Gala living as she had for the last month, so there seemed to be no choice but to continue to foster her.

To keep Gala (and Gracie) safe, though, we had to restrict her activity. She was back in the crate much more than she'd have liked, but with a houseful of teenagers and their assorted friends, it was impossible to ensure her safety otherwise. Now I knew too well what could happen. During the times she was loose in the house, we continued to leave a leash on her so if she were to escape, we had a better chance at catching her on her way to the horses.*

Five months from when she'd arrived, we were back at square one. Reinforcing manners and retraining her to walk nicely on the leash. Gala's days were regimented—crate time, walk time, office time, walk time, crate time, walk time. I longed to toss a ball and watch her sprint across a field after it, but, at our house at least, that could never happen. None of us wanted her to get loose again, afraid this time one of the horses might kill her.

We all loved Gala, truly.† She had stolen our hearts, but we were winded physically and emotionally from the constant effort of managing her. It was time for Gala's people to come for her. It was time she started her real life with her real people. We'd never had a foster dog this long; most stayed only a few weeks. It had been five months. Why was it taking so long this time?

One by one, all the Highway Puppies left. What a joy they had been right when I needed joy most. They were loving and sweet and healthy and beautiful. How different their stories might have ended if a good soul hadn't rescued them from the side of that highway in North Carolina. As I rubbed their fat bellies and accepted their endless kisses, I tried not to imagine what could have been for them and what might still be for Gala.

---

* Which was really laughable because Gala could outrun a cheetah.

† Except Gracie, they still had not made peace.

3

Wearing Out Your Welcome

Soon after the Highway Puppies departed, Yin and Yang arrived. Two border collie puppies in constant motion—uncomplicated, happy, and always, always ready to play. My "puppy-blurs," as a friend called them, were tail-waggingly thrilled to see visitors. Like overwrought teenagers at a rock concert, they leaped on the puppy-pen fence at the sight of anyone, throwing themselves in your general direction and then falling to the ground in ecstasy if you reached in to touch them.

"Why do we have more puppies?" Nick asked.

"Because I need them," I told him.

"But we have Gala."

"And we might always have Gala. These puppies needed a place to go."

"And, somehow, that's always our place."

There were times when I wished my husband didn't have to be Eeyore. I wished he was as enthusiastic about fostering dogs as I was, but he wasn't. In fact, if I were to suffer an untimely death, I'm pretty sure another foster dog would never darken our doorway. But the thing about Nick is, while he might not love fostering dogs, he does love me. And he's been around long enough[*] to know when I'm passionate about something, I go all in, which means it's almost always better to get on board than to get in the way.

Sometimes that's a good thing, like when I went organic and learned to bake bread and make yogurt or when I wanted a third kid and nine months later there was Ian, but occasionally it could go awry, like when I planned to order a dozen chicks through a mail-order catalog and thanks to a weather mishap,[†] we ended up with fifty-six.[‡] Or when I brought home a "free" beautiful sixteen-hand registered quarter horse who turned out to not only be unbroken but to have endless mysterious soundness issues and a penchant for dumping me on my butt. So, puppies? He could handle puppies, but he felt obligated to complain. Lucky for both of us, Eeyore is my favorite Winnie-the-Pooh character.

After being dragged by Gala through countless daily walks, Nick attached a metal snap to a seventy-five-foot heavy-duty rope. We held one end of the line (braced around a waist or firmly in gloved hands) and Gala could finally run at full speed all over the hillside. It didn't take her long to figure out when to put on the brakes to avoid the sudden forced stops, and it was great to see her joy and grace as she finally ran uninhibited by that pesky leash.

One afternoon, Gala kept me company in my office, which lately looked like the aftermath of a toddler's birthday party. In some kind of lucky-streak-curse-avoiding weird decision, I'd decided not to vacuum up the mess she had made (and continued to add to) until she was adopted (or a houseguest arrived), so the floor was covered by a gazillion tiny white pellets from an exploded Beanie Baby, shreds of my old leather sandals, several outgrown

---

*   Twenty-five years and counting.

†   There was a twenty-four chick minimum (to keep them warm while shipping) and then I added six more to get the free shipping (what's thirty when you already have twenty-four?) and then the company added three "bonus" chicks. They arrived at our post office on a Sunday when the temperature was well below zero and after sitting overnight, ten of them died. When I reported this to the company, instead of replacing the ones that didn't survive the freeze, they replaced the entire order.

‡   I'm here to tell you no one needs fifty-six chickens (no one needs thirty-three either).

sneakers pulled to pieces, and countless ravaged dog toys. She loved to lounge among the ruins, chewing on the one Kong toy she hadn't been able to destroy, creating an endless soundtrack of sneakers on the gym floor as she worked the rubber with her tireless jaw.

Nothing particularly exciting was happening outside that day, but Gala spent a long time staring out the office window. I didn't think much of it, figuring she could see things I couldn't. Rather than watching for squirrels, she must have been taking note of how the screen was secured in the window because very quietly, with no fanfare, she simply pushed the screen out with her nose and took off out the window.

I leaped from my desk to sound the alarm. Nick ran for the paddock to keep her away from the horses. They were in stalls, but once again Cocoa was shut in the paddock. Addie and Brady followed Gala into the pasture. I called for her, but she ignored me, galloping all over the pasture, occasionally challenging Nick for access to the paddock.

Finally, she stopped to sample a pile of horse poop.* Addie and Brady walked slowly toward her from different directions. I could see her glance at them, but she continued her snack. Brady got to her first, calmly saying things like, "That looks tasty, Gala. Yummy horse poop. You enjoying that?" Gala, feeling no threat,† continued to nosh. Brady grabbed the leash and just like that—crisis averted!

I shut her in her crate since not only did she pig out on horse poop, she'd also rolled in it. A bath would be in her very near future. Maybe it was time to vacuum the office. Maybe leaving the mess was having the reverse effect. Maybe if I finally cleaned it up, Gala's people would come for her.

That evening, after bathing Gala, I sat on the hillside watching the sun set and wondered how her story would end. For the life of me, I couldn't understand why no one even applied for her. She was beautiful. Sure, she had

---

* Dogs love horse poop—just ask Gracie.

† Brady was rarely the person to put a leash on her, preferring to play the role of the indulgent uncle, slipping her treats and letting her lick his face. Sometimes when she jumped up on him, he'd take her paws and dance with her around the kitchen.

a lot of energy and was prone to escape, but with the right person, she would settle down.

Nothing was going particularly well for me that summer. Normally, I loved this time of year—for gardening, riding, hanging out with friends on our porch—but this year was different. My gardens were weed-infested, the horses hadn't been ridden in weeks, and we rarely invited anyone over. Maybe some of it had to do with Gala. Inviting people over meant crating Gala or managing her introductions and then vigilantly watching that she didn't slip out when someone came or went through the porch door. And, lately, she had growled at some of Brady's friends, so there was that, too. I didn't know what caused Gala to find one person threatening and another not.

Managing Gala was a full-time gig for me. Unless she was securely locked in her crate, it was impossible for me to relax. The kids did their best, but I didn't want to depend on them to keep Gala safe.

And then there was Gracie. Gala and Gracie had been adversaries ever since Gala arrived. Gracie was a sweet but chicken-hearted dog. Gala may have known this, or maybe not, because Gracie growled at Gala nearly as much as Gala growled at Gracie. If only I spoke dog! I had no idea what they were saying to each other, I only knew that when both dogs were in the house, I had to contain Gala. Seemingly for no reason, she would leap over a baby gate separating the two dogs and go after Gracie. Again and again, I had to break up fights, separate them, put Gracie outside or Gala in a crate. Month after month, their feelings never abated, and while they didn't seem to do any real damage, just the intensity and sound of their fights would leave me shaking for an hour.

One of my favorite summer activities was riding with Nick. The only way I ever got him on a horse anymore was if I suggested we ride over to Gunpowder Falls Brewing for a beer. It was a gorgeous ride through our woods and across a few fields to the brewery, where we would have a beer in the parking lot, sharing it with the horses in cupped palms, and then wonder on the way home if it was illegal to drink and ride.* That summer, though, my horse True

---

* For the record, we were never drunk as we rode home, but we still wondered about the legal ramifications.

had begun attempting to buck me off in earnest. Maybe he suspected I was distracted, which I probably was, but it left me avoiding the idea of a ride and certain I shouldn't ride him after having a beer.

My writing, like my riding, had lost some of its joy, too, as I wrestled with yet another rewrite for a novel I'd been working on for over seven years. My agent, Carly, pushed me to dig deeper and infuse it with more mystery and suspense, but I'm not a mystery or suspense writer, I protested to myself each time I sat down to work on it.

So, I distracted myself with my blogs or freelance articles that rarely paid much if anything. I had my fingers crossed that Carly would sell the memoir I was working on—it told the story of our first fifty foster dogs. She had helped me polish the proposal and was currently shopping it, but with every rejection, my hopes dimmed more.

Thank goodness for the puppies. They were a constant source of distraction and joy, two things I needed sorely, as nothing else in my world seemed to be going according to plan.

Most people had stopped asking about Gala. They knew the news was never good, and if you opened up that jar, you were likely to be subjected to my long list of frustrations about Gala, my unsold writing, my filthy house, my forgotten gardens, my bucking horse, and even the awful hot weather.

The thing about Gala, though, was that deep down I knew she was a good dog. She wanted nothing more than to please us; she loved with a devotion that was clear and true. Her eyes shown with intelligence, and at times I was certain she could read my mind. So, did she know I was afraid for her? Did she sense that I worried she'd never find her home? Or had she already decided this was her home and that was the real reason she challenged Gracie and threatened visitors?

"This isn't your house, Gala," I told her as I got up to go back inside. "You can't be our dog, you know that, right?"

4

Full-on Life

F or more than two weeks I'd been quietly negotiating Gala's move, afraid
to mention it out loud or on my blog for fear I would jinx it.* One thing
or another had delayed it again and again, but finally, she was set to move
to another foster home about an hour north of us. We weren't sure yet if the
move would be temporary or not. It would depend on Gala.

Shannon and her boyfriend were young and active; had two big, friendly,
well-trained dogs and a fenced yard; and had volunteered to work with Gala.
They had successfully trained another difficult-to-adopt-out OPH dog,
helping her find her forever family after many months in foster care. I was
hopeful that they could take Gala the next step, too.

After six months with us, we'd reached the end of what we thought we
could do for Gala. I couldn't say what, if anything, we'd done to help her, but
I did know she needed structure and direction. She still pulled on the leash
terribly, jumped up on people, and only came when called if it was in her

---

* Gala seemed to bring out the superstitions in me.

best interest. She needed to learn boundaries and how to get along with other dogs,* two things we couldn't teach her here. And she really needed to learn that she wasn't our dog. She'd grown much too attached to us, especially me.

In a quieter house, I was hopeful that Gala would settle. She was an extremely sensitive and smart dog, and our crowded, busy household with its stream of teenage guests and new dogs made her anxious and excitable. I hoped a calm setting with a regular schedule and two well-behaved dogs would enable Gala to thrive; her confidence could grow and her ability to trust with it.

Gala loved Shannon on sight and happily jumped in her car, always ready for an adventure. Shannon was smart and kind and eager to take on the challenge of Gala. We'd agreed that I would take Gala back if she couldn't adapt to her new setting, but both Shannon and I were hopeful that she would.

I was glad for the extra emotional bandwidth. In another week, Addie would leave for her freshman year of college in New Jersey, and soon after that Brady would fly across the Atlantic to study in Cyprus for the semester. Sending Gala to Shannon's was kind of a tiny test run for my heart. I had to trust that Gala (and my kids) would be successful without me and accept that it was the best thing for them.

Addie was more than ready to be out of the nest. In fact, she'd been clamoring for her independence since she was two years old when she threw a tantrum on the sidewalk outside her preschool insisting that I not walk her in on her first day. That independent streak was a source of strife throughout her early years. All she ever wanted was to be in charge of her life.

Her high school path had not been smooth. While she was smart, in fact, certified "gifted" by the state of Pennsylvania, her grades rarely reflected that. Teenage drama and fads were lost on her. She spent her lunch periods in the library, befriending the librarian, reading her way through the back issues of *Psychology Today* and writing *Les Miserables* fan fiction. By the end of sophomore year, it was clear traditional high school wasn't working for her, so for Addie's junior year we divvied up her classes between "brick and mortar" school and cyber school. Senior year she went to the school for two

---

* Or at least to not attack them upon introduction.

classes, worked an internship for the Democratic Party of York, took a course at a local college, and became a barista at Starbucks, working nearly full-time.

I had no doubts my fiercely independent daughter could handle college. I just hoped she'd be happy. Sometimes I worried that she wasn't. She pushed herself hard and held sky-high expectations not just for herself but for others, who couldn't help but disappoint her. She was not your average teen, and while that was her choice, I think sometimes it was a lonely choice. The hardest part of parenting is not when your kids are in your house making a mess and testing your patience; it's when they are out of your sight and beyond your reach. In less than a week, I would no longer know her daily struggles, and even if I did, I would be powerless to help.

I began spending a lot of time with Yang, the longer legged of my two border collie puppies. Yin had been adopted, but Yang was still around. We'd been forced to install her in the kitchen ever since she jumped over the puppy room gate. It's pretty difficult to be sad or preoccupied in the presence of a puppy. Yang was the definition of happiness. She was sweet beyond measure, sauntering across the grass with a happy gait, an ever-present smile on her face. She never ran out of kisses and loved every person she met with an unconditional immediacy that is often missing in our world. Addie gravitated toward her too. As we prepared for her departure, maybe we both needed Yang's happy company.

Without Gala, the energy in our house was different. The first night she was gone I dreamt about her. I woke at 3 A.M. with an uneasy feeling. I lay there imagining what she was thinking, worrying about her tender heart, and sending up silent prayers that she would blossom in her new setting. Was she missing me? I told myself that Gala and I had been through so much, that was the reason for my worries. That and it was a distraction from my real worries about saying good-bye to my children.

Three days after Gala left, my cell phone rang. It was Shannon. I expected she was calling to give me another happy report that Gala was doing great.

I'd already seen her post on Facebook of Gala playing in a river alongside her two dogs. It shocked but delighted me. I answered happily expecting another excellent report.

"I've been bitten!" Shannon cried in a panicked voice.

"Are you okay? What happened?" She recounted the story in bursts, most of it unclear to me. I asked how badly she was hurt and which dog bit her.

"I don't know which dog it was! I'm hurt. Can you come get Gala?"

This was not the same calm, confident young woman who picked up Gala. She was obviously in shock, but instead of seeking medical help she was worrying about Gala.

"Where is Gala now?"

"She's in her crate."

"Are you going to the doctor?"

"Do you think I should?"

"Yes, if the skin is broken, you should."

It was late in the afternoon, but I told Shannon I would leave to come to get Gala as soon as I could. By the time I was able to get to her house, it was dark and pouring rain. Shannon was calm and had a bandage on her arm. She told me again that she didn't know which dog bit her and confessed that she'd done the absolute worst thing you can do when breaking up a dog fight—she had reached in and put herself between them.

Having broken up more than a few fights between Gala and various foster dogs or Gracie, I knew better. I'd used bar stools, brooms, books, and a floor lamp (which paid the ultimate price) to separate them.*

Gala was happy to see me. I ran my hand over her, and she flinched as I felt the bite marks on her back from Shannon's dog. Driving home through the pouring rain on back road after back road, all I thought was, Now Gala will never be adopted.

---

* Never, EVER, use your hands or feet to break up a dog fight. Use whatever is handy, or if you have water (or any liquid) handy, dump that on them. If you have nothing else, make a loud noise to distract them.

Because Shannon didn't know which dog bit her, Gala would have a "bite addendum"* on her adoption contract. She hadn't had any adoption applications yet, and a bite addendum would ensure that she might never.

There were four distinct punctures on Gala's back from where Shannon's dog had gotten a serious bite of Gala, but Shannon's dog was, per Shannon, "fine." They had cleaned Gala's wound and there was no blood by the time I saw her, but clearly Gala had gotten the worse end of the fight.

Her back was sore, but she seemed okay, until the following afternoon when out of the blue she began growling. It was just the two of us in the office. I looked out the window. No cars. I looked at Gala. She appeared frozen, her posture upright, her eyes unfocused; she emitted a low growl. I touched her and she winced, growled more. Something was seriously wrong. I put a muzzle on her and drove her to Cape Horn, a vet that gave reduced rates to OPH for our foster dogs.

Upon examination, the vet told me the puncture wounds went into her muscle and she was experiencing shock. They would need to sedate her and clean them out, and then put her on an antibiotic. So, once again, I left Gala with a vet and went home to worry.

I called Nick to tell him what was going on. "She just can't catch a break," I told him. That's what it felt like. Whatever could go wrong did go wrong for this dog. As I watched her sleep off her sedative, I wondered if Gala's stream of mishaps and misfortunes had more to do with how fully she lived her life than any kind of black cloud hovering over her.

My little brother was the same way. He had broken at least five bones (maybe more, I lost count) when we were kids—falling out of a treehouse, taking a header over an unexpected wall, pretending to be Evel Knievel. It seemed like every summer he had a plastic bread bag over his casted arm as we

---

* A bite addendum is an extra contract that adopters must sign that says they know the dog they are adopting may have bitten someone in the past.

swam at the beach. As a teen, he totaled at least three cars. He later became a fighter pilot in the US Air Force, flying F-15s all over the world, including in Korea, Iraq, and Afghanistan. Day to day, even now that he was retired from the air force, he still lived his life full-on, taking big chances and making big gestures. His wife, Sherry, told me, "Life is never dull with Tom."

That was how Gala lived. She had an exuberance for life that sometimes led her into trouble but made everyone around her smile. I loved this dog; life with her would never be boring. Antibiotics and pain meds worked their magic, and she was almost at full strength only a week after the fight. But now what? Who would ever adopt this dog?

She became my leggy brown shadow, following me everywhere and whining for me when I left her to tend to the horses or Gracie. She barely gave the cat the time of day and even walked calmly past the horses on the other side of the fence. I imagined she was thinking, I better stick close and behave myself or who knows what kind of major hurt will come next.

I was absolutely certain that she would make the very best friend for some lucky adopter, but she would need an adopter who was as devoted to her as she would be to them. Then again, every dog deserved that. Gala had some powerful love to give. But would anyone ever give her a chance?

5

Lost Dog

Yang found her people, and much to my family's disappointment it wasn't us. Everyone, even Gracie, wanted to keep that special pup, so I was very happy that she wasn't leaving our lives entirely. She was adopted by a wonderful family who lived nearby and who had become our friends after they adopted Millie (aka Estelle), my very first pregnant foster dog.

Estelle had arrived here the previous Christmas with a belly full of puppies. Until that point, I had only fostered already-born puppies. This time they were arriving still in their mama's belly! Estelle was only eight months old, which meant she'd gotten pregnant on her first heat cycle—a relatively common occurrence for dogs in the rural South. When she went into labor, she had no idea what was happening. She kept trying to drag me outside so that she could try to poop. On the third trip outside, it dawned on me that she might be in labor.

I called Chris, another OPH foster who is my unofficial mentor. I'd watched her help Lily, a previous foster dog, bring ten puppies into the world almost exactly a year prior. I explained what was happening and she calmly said, "Yup. Sounds like this is it. We're on our way." Chris and her daughter, Caitlyn, arrived within the hour.

The first puppy arrived butt first, and Chris coached me as Estelle struggled. When we finally freed the humongous puppy, Estelle realized what was going on and commenced growling at anyone except me. Chris and Caitlyn backed out of the room. They hung around a little longer, but it was clear that Estelle did not want an audience, so like it or not, she was stuck with my novice midwifing efforts. Lucky for all of us, dogs rarely need any help delivering their babies, and Estelle didn't need my help bringing her other three puppies into the world.

Christmas came and went, and at three weeks of age, three of the puppies were up and walking, wrestling, and playing, but one of the puppies, Fruitcake, resembled a starfish more than a puppy. He couldn't stand or walk. He grew fatter and fatter, flattening out. Eventually, he could pull his front end up and drag his hind legs, but something was clearly wrong. A vet confirmed what we'd already guessed—Fruitcake was a swimmer puppy.*

I read everything I could and studied the therapies that had worked with other puppies. If Fruitcake would ever walk, we needed to act fast. I recruited people for "Team Fruitcake," a gang of volunteers comprised of other OPH volunteers and some of my friends and neighbors.

Nick built "runs" for Fruitcake out of two-by-fours—narrow chutes that kept his limbs from slipping sideways, effectively forcing him upright. The first time we put Fruitcake in the chute, he stood dazed and unmoving for several minutes, then collapsed with his limbs stuck out in front of him and went to sleep. With encouragement from plenty of cheerleaders, he was soon marching up and back in his chute. In between therapy sessions, he charmed volunteers, nestling in their arms for naps or belly rubs.

---

* An uncommon developmental deformity of newborn dogs (and cats) in which the limbs, primarily the hind limbs, are splayed laterally, making it impossible for the pup to stand or walk. Instead they "swim"—paddling laterally and going nowhere. Without early intervention the pup will likely never walk and could likely die of congestive heart failure or similar afflictions because of the flattened chest and weight bearing down on their heart and lungs.

Dr. Chris stopped by and worked his medical tape magic, creating hobbles for Fruitcake's back legs that would keep them from splaying. With hobbles on his legs and lots of donated yoga mats covering the surface of our puppy pen to help his grip, soon Fruitcake was awkwardly walking without the aid of the chutes. He still couldn't keep up with his siblings, but he was mobile! Sometimes, when the others were running and playing, he'd sit down in a huff, paw at the air, and whine. He knew he should be able to run like them and didn't understand why his legs weren't cooperating. Eventually, Fruitcake learned to walk and run and play like every other puppy, and if you met him today, you'd never know that he was once a swimmer puppy.

After all I'd been through with Estelle's delivery and then Fruitcake's rehabilitation, I was happy when Estelle was adopted by Mara and her family, who lived just a few miles away over the state line in Maryland. Mara, Chris, and Galit quickly became our friends. Mara brought Galit, an independently minded, smart fourth grader,[*] to visit often, especially when there were puppies in the house.

When they adopted Yang, they named her Lucy, not knowing that Yin's adopters had chosen the same name. That alone was cool, but if you knew my history, you'd also know that I began this entire fostering adventure after my beloved dog Lucy died. Lucy had been my best friend and companion for seventeen years—through three babies and two moves and some dark, lonely days on our hillside farm in Pennsylvania. She'd trained for a marathon with me and kept my garden free of rabbits. When she passed, it shook my world. Unable to find a dog who measured up, I launched our family into fostering dogs, and the rest, as they say, is history.

A few days after we'd moved Addie into her dorm in New Jersey, Gala was gone again.

This time I thought she was gone for good. I watched her disappear through the woods in pursuit of a herd of deer headed in the general direction of

---

[*] Galit reminded me of another fiercely independent young woman I know . . .

Maryland, and I was pretty sure she would make it. We were about a mile and a half away from home on our regular run when several deer ran across the road in front of us. Gala did what she usually did—leaped in the air after them.

I ran with Gala on an Easy Walk harness,* which meant that whenever she reached the end of her lead, the harness forced her to do a pirouette in midair and land facing me again.

At that point, I'd say, "Leave it!" in my firm, take-no-prisoners voice, and then she would not leave it. Most days it took three or four pirouettes and reminders before she gave up and simply pranced for a quarter mile or so.

On Friday, she had done about four pirouettes when she went airborne for a fifth. This time, though, when she landed, the leash inexplicably unhooked and she was gone like a flash. I was left yelling her name in vain. I looked at the end of the leash and wondered how on earth she'd broken it. It looked fine, completely intact.

Somehow, and heaven knows it could only happen with Gala, she had twisted just right and forced the leash to release. This was a brand-new leash. Because we kept leashes on Gala 24/7, she had been steadily chewing through every leash I owned, and OPH had thoughtfully sent me a package of brand-new leashes. The leash I'd chosen to use that morning was a sturdy pink lead with a rubber grip handle. Of late, we'd been running with a reflective orange leash that had three knots tied in it where Gala had gnawed partway through the nylon. When I'd clipped the new leash on her that morning, I noticed the different type of snap, a lobster claw type, but thought nothing of it; I was just happy to have such a nice, intact leash.

I ran after Gala for a few hundred yards, but the brush in the woods was thick, and in only minutes there was no sight or sound of her. I trooped back to the road to get a better cell signal and called Chris since she was the OPH foster closest to me and always seemed to know what to do. I told her what happened, and she said she'd contact OPH Lost Dog volunteers and post Gala's picture on the local Facebook pages.

---

* With a front-leading harness the leash attaches to a ring in the center of the dog's chest. It's especially effective with dogs that pull.

Gala had too much of a lead on me. I needed to get home and get in my car, so I called Brady. He had one week left before he would leave for Cyprus. Brady can sleep through anything, so after four attempts, I gave up and called a neighbor, who said she'd send her husband to fetch me. I pulled up the Nextdoor* website on my phone. After I posted a description and my best guess at Gala's whereabouts, I sprinted toward home. My neighbor picked me up about a half mile from my house and drove me the rest of the way. He offered to help, but I knew the sight of a stranger would send Gala running, so I thanked him and then grabbed a better leash and a package of hot dogs and jumped in my car.

For the next hour, I drove around yelling out my window for Gala, creeping up the long gravel driveways of my few and far between neighbors, leaving notes and numbers everywhere. I was headed home to warm up when my phone buzzed with a text from Donna, a woman who had seen my post on Nextdoor. She was out looking for her dog, a little white Westie who'd been missing for three months. She still drove around daily looking for him.† She said she'd look for Gala, so I zoomed home to get warmer clothes, my hiking shoes, and my son.

Brady and I were gathering essentials when Donna called to say she'd spotted Gala. She was on the road a mile or so away, following our running route, headed toward home. Donna said she'd follow her, and Brady and I jumped in the car.

We were almost there when Gala was spooked by a man on foot, reversed course, and sprinted east toward Stewartstown. Donna stayed with her, and when Gala darted into a driveway, she drove past the driveway, turned around, and effectively blocked the road with her van. When Gala emerged from the

---

* Nextdoor is a micro social media site specific to your immediate area. It's great for letting neighbors know about emergencies, road closures, suspicious book salesmen knocking on doors, as well as selling/giving away unwanted items and finding house sitters. It's also excellent for finding lost dogs.

† As far as I know, she never did find him, but it wasn't for lack of trying or devotion. That entire year there were signs posted all over town and her blue minivan was emblazoned with white windshield paint declaring "LOST LITTLE WHITE DOG" with her phone number painted beneath the words.

driveway, Donna's presence forced her to reverse direction again and head back toward us. I stopped the car and Brady jumped out.

Gala was running full speed at us, and I could see the terror in her eyes. Her tail was tucked between her legs, and it was clear that she was running blind as she zipped past Brady and our car. I jumped out and crouched down on the road. I clapped my hands and called her. She was probably a hundred feet away from us by then, but she stopped and looked back. I patted the ground and kept calling her, using my puppy voice and smiling at her. The moment she realized it was me, relief flooded her face and she bounded back toward me, practically bowling me over in happiness before leaping into the car.

Donna pulled up in her van and I thanked her and told her I looked for her dog every day on my runs. We were both teary. "I'm just so glad you got her back," she said. I'd only lost Gala for ninety minutes. I can't imagine what it was like for Donna to have lost her dog for months.

As another friend said that weekend, Gala seemed to have nine lives, but she was burning through them quickly.

Here are a few things I learned that Friday in the hours that Gala was missing:

1. Don't ever use a leash with a lobster claw clip. I threw mine out.
2. The moment your dog is missing, get the word out. Don't wait until you've searched for hours and can't find her. Don't worry about troubling people or overreacting. If you don't find the dog quickly, you may never catch it. Gala was clearly in another mode when we saw her. She loved Brady but ran right past him in her panic. OPH's Lost Dog volunteers had already generated a flyer to hand out and had volunteers prepared to drive to my area within the hour. If not for Donna, we would have needed all their help.
3. If you have Nextdoor or another site like it in your area, you should join even if you're social media averse. It's more effective

than Facebook at getting the word out to your immediate neighbors.

4. Be sure your dog is microchipped and wearing a collar with tags. If someone finds your dog, it's much easier to get it back if it's chipped, and even faster if it has a tag. Gala is chipped, but she lost her tags months ago. I ordered more that day.
5. I have awesome neighbors.

6

Projecting

I yammered about our latest batch of puppies as we drove Brady to the airport for his flight to Cyprus to start his junior year of college. He was excited, but my worry for him had ratcheted up to an entirely new level. Looking back now, maybe that was why I agreed to yet another litter, this time six-week-old Catahoula puppies. I certainly didn't need to bring in more puppies; Gala was going nowhere fast, and I had yet to finish rewriting my latest manuscript.

Nick quizzed Brady on his plan—finding his gate, boarding the aircraft, making his connection at Heathrow (gasp), meeting up with Jackson (his friend also studying in Cyprus), and getting from the airport to the college. Brady had good answers for all Nick's questions. He'd come up with this study abroad plan on his own, and perhaps in an effort to show his meddling, doubtful parents that he could handle it, he'd kept most of the details to himself.

Over the summer when we'd pressed him for information, he'd been dismissive, assuring us he had it under control. He would turn twenty-one while he was in Cyprus. It was time we let him handle his own life. This was not easy for parents who had witnessed his previous twenty years, during which details, homework, driver's licenses, wallets, and books were lost regularly; deadlines rarely observed; and most of his days spent daydreaming or writing in a world we knew nothing about. For better or worse, we'd rescued him time and again, but now the safety net of our love would be on the other side of the ocean. I couldn't make the phone call, show up with the forgotten item, or be sure he remembered to eat and to wear sunscreen.

We all knew this experience would be good for all of us, but that didn't mean it would be easy (at least for me). I tried to keep things light, distracting them both with talk of the new puppies—an overly active colorful batch that loved to be snuggled and slept in a pile—but we rode most of the way in silence.

I could hardly see through my tears when we dropped him at the check-in area. Brady smiled and let me hug him for a really long time, then he waved and disappeared up the escalator. Nick reached for my hand and led me out of the airport. I felt numb, terrified, but in a strange way proud.

Stuck in traffic on the way home, I persuaded Nick to stop at a little tavern not too far from the airport for a snack. I wasn't really hungry, but it was a good excuse to delay going home. I wanted to stay close to Brady until the plane took off. You never know, I unreasonably thought. He might need me.

There wasn't much time to worry about Brady as I prepared all my puppies to be adopted and Ian for the start of the school year. Luckily, Brady adapted to the relaxed atmosphere of Cyprus easily and bonded with the other American roommates who would share his apartment for the next three months.

On the first day of Ian's sophomore year, he left for school without a hat. Not an oddity for the average kid, but my kid was anything but average. In fact, he's part of the 1 percent of alopecia areata patients who lose every hair on their body. Ian once had beautiful curly red hair—so soft and so pretty that in the small town where we lived, elderly women often paused to pet his head and hairdressers told me his hair was the color everyone wanted.

And then one day in December when he was four, I noticed a small spot on the back of his head that was completely bald. Smooth like plastic, about the size of a quarter. As a four-year-old, Ian was unconcerned, but then as days went by, the spot grew and hair began to disappear from the rest of his head, thinning like his grandfather's. We made a rushed appointment with our pediatrician, who said, "Don't worry. Happens all the time. It's alopecia areata. By the next time I see Ian, it will have all grown back."

Only everything I had read (which the doctor admitted was probably more than he had read about this rare condition) said it probably wouldn't grow back in this case.* So we took Ian to see dermatologists at Johns Hopkins Hospital and also Hershey Medical Center, two of the finest medical facilities in the country, both less than an hour from us.

At that point, Ian was completely bald. It had only been two months since I first noticed the spot. We learned that alopecia areata universalis, the rare form of alopecia that Ian had, was not treatable. And no one knew what caused it. Not long after that his eyebrows and eyelashes fell out. As a young mom with a vivid imagination, I was distraught. My emotions ran so close to the surface that a simple "Hi, how are you?" could make me sob.

But my little boy was unfazed. When you are four, hair is not very important. In fact, not having hair meant you didn't have to wash it, brush it, or have it cut—three things Ian had never enjoyed, as his unruly curls took a lot to tame.

I took Ian to an "alternative" doctor whose office was in a dark basement apartment in a nondescript building in downtown Lancaster. He did a lot of odd noninvasive tests and charged me a small fortune, promising to fix Ian's alopecia with vitamins and supplements and a completely different diet. I left the office with my head spinning but clinging to one thing the doctor told me—"The human body is miraculous. If you put the right things in it, it will fix itself."

---

* The American Academy of Dermatology says that when there is total hair loss, like in Ian's case, it is much less likely to grow back. Although technically the hair follicles are still healthy, it is the immune system malfunction that is causing the white blood cells to attack the hair follicles and push the hair out. I do believe that someday when scientists figure out the autoimmune puzzle, there will be a cure for alopecia.

I went home and cleared every toxic substance out of our house, instead filling my cleaning closet with vinegar, lemon juice, baking soda, hydrogen peroxide, and old-fashioned Murphy Oil Soap. Next, I took to the cupboards and removed everything with chemicals, preservatives, food colorings, and additives I didn't recognize or couldn't validate. I learned to make yogurt, bread, ice cream, cereal, crackers, and cheese.

I'd already been an avid gardener, but that spring we more than doubled the size of our gardens, digging terraced beds into our hilly property. And then we got chickens! Over the course of a year, our lives became completely organic.

The kids and I battled over the virtues and dangers of Cheez-Its, Aunt Jemima syrup, and soda. In the end, Ian's diagnosis changed all our lives. Brady's asthma improved to the point that he didn't need daily meds. Nick's cholesterol, which had been hovering right around the danger mark, dropped so low the doctor took back everything he'd said about drugs and diets. My moods improved, and Addie did not need her ADHD medicine.

I hadn't noticed, but at the kids' yearly physicals, the doctor said, "Hey, I haven't seen you since the last well visit." We were all healthier, but Ian's hair did not grow back. It was something we learned to live with—and truthfully, in many ways, we are better for it.

When Ian entered elementary school, he became self-conscious about his baldness, and rather than explain it, he chose to wear an Under Armour skullcap whenever he went out. At home, with good friends, or when we were on vacation, though, he never wore it.

When we traveled with our bald preschooler, many people assumed Ian had cancer. We got the royal treatment and unasked-for favors everywhere we went. People are nice to kids with cancer. At one point, I confessed to another parent of a child with alopecia that I felt guilty about taking the occasional free meal, the prize at the boardwalk arcade, the kind gestures and random gifts (like the one-pound chocolate bar Ian received from a security guard at Hershey Park), and she said, "You know, having alopecia sucks, so I think our kids deserve a few niceties. Plus, if you tell the strangers he doesn't have cancer, they'll just feel awkward and Ian will be embarrassed. They feel good about doing a nice thing for a kid with cancer—let them have that."

And she was right. I stopped trying to explain Ian's bald head to strangers. Most everyone in our town got used to the sight of my kid who had no hair, and a few even learned to pronounce alopecia areata. Ian played sports year-round, so in our small community, just about every kid had been on a sports team with Ian. They knew he had alopecia. The elementary school principal waived the hat rule for him, and eventually the district granted him a 504 plan, which legally labeled Ian as handicapped and gave him the right to wear a hat at school, which he did every day all the way through ninth grade.

But on the first day of tenth grade, he went to school with no hat on. The only other time he'd done that had been an accident in first grade. He'd somehow forgotten his hat. The bus driver pulled over and called me because Ian was so distraught. I drove a hat to the school, in tears myself, and from that day on, his teacher kept a spare for him in her desk.

My heart was in my throat all day imagining the stunned looks of Ian's classmates as he arrived with no hat. Gala and the puppies were an excellent distraction. I texted Ian at lunchtime, Everything okay? He typed back, Fine. Ian has never wanted a big deal made about him. He doesn't share his sister's love of the stage. In fact, he is adamant about not being late for practice, school, meetings, etc., because he never wants to walk in late and "have everyone look at me." I've never known if this is because of growing up with alopecia and having everyone stare at him or if it's just the way he is and would have been even if he'd never developed alopecia.

Today, I was certain, that everyone was staring at him. And it made my heart hurt. When he got home from school, I wanted to pull him into my arms and hear all about his day, but at six foot two and two hundred pounds, that was impossible, even if he did want to talk about it. Which he didn't. He never has. He told me once back in elementary school that he wore a hat so that he didn't have to talk about it. He's never wanted his life to be about having alopecia.

When he came home, I asked how it went.

"I could see kids staring, but that's their problem."

I want to believe he feels that way. I try not to project my own fears and insecurities on him or any of my kids, but I'm not a professional parent and I'm sure they seep out.

I feared the same thing was happening with Gala. I was certain she would react badly toward a new dog or person, and then she did. Was she reading my fear? Had we crossed some line between helping her and hurting her? Maybe I was the reason she was increasingly aggressive toward people who came to the house. Maybe Gracie's continued threats were only increasing Gala's negative reaction toward other dogs. I tried to remember Gala when she first came to us—hadn't she loved everyone she met back then?

Well, that wasn't completely true. When Brady had first come home from college, Gala growled and lunged at him. We'd had to crate her just so he could walk in the kitchen. It took her a few days. Days in which I had e-mailed anyone and everyone at OPH—She has to move, she can't stay here. But then Gala decided Brady was okay. In fact, he was not just okay, he was her favorite person most days. She would jump up on him in greeting and he would waltz her around the kitchen.

We'd gotten used to Gala, adapted to her and managed her around everyone she met—people and dogs. But was that enabling her? Legitimizing her fears?

When I wrote about fostering on my blog, I tried to be positive and helpful and inspiring. But lately, it was hard to find that positive note. For the first time, fostering was decidedly not fun. It was heartbreaking and messy and well beyond frustrating. I couldn't go to adoption events because of Gala, so I rarely saw other fosters. I watched the OPH Facebook page and saw dog after dog being adopted, and still no one even applied to adopt Gala. Unfairly, maybe, I began to feel forgotten, isolated, angry. No one wanted Gala and no one wanted to hear me say once again that I needed her to be moved.

When we set off on our fostering adventure, my biggest fear was that we would get a dog that would never be adopted. And now here we were.

7

Is She Ever Leaving?

L ots of readers were following Gala's saga on my blog, and a few suggested that I try to write more about the positive qualities of Gala instead of only her misadventures. Maybe that would encourage someone to adopt her. Truthfully, there were so many times a day when Gala made me smile, many more than when she made me scold her. Her misadventures were simply more interesting.

But there were plenty of positive experiences, too. Every morning, our run took us alongside a weed-infested culvert that edged a farmer's field. In that culvert were thousands of crickets. As we made our way beside the field, Gala pounced on the crickets, like a cat or a puppy with both paws extended and a big smile on her face. The crickets magically disappeared right out from under her and she wiggled her body and wagged her tail excitedly only to pounce again a few feet later. I'd slow to a walk to allow Gala to try to catch crickets.

The rescue road had been too long for Gala. She needed to find her family. A picture is many times the key to finding an adopter. People fall in love with a dog online, and sometimes that pull is strong enough to get the dog adopted.

So I invited my friend Nancy, a local photographer, to come and take pictures. Nancy adopted my fiftieth foster dog, Edith Wharton, the previous fall and had become a regular volunteer with OPH, donating countless hours photographing dogs and editing the pictures. I put Gala on her seventy-five-foot lead, and Nancy captured her radiant personality in full-speed Technicolor. I uploaded the shots to her profile hoping they would attract equally full-speed Technicolor adopters.

A week after her pictures were taken, Gala had an interested adopter who seemed like a real possibility. The couple lived on a large property and had an active but quiet life. The husband was away on business at the time, but the wife came to meet Gala. We took a walk together around the pasture. Gala was on her best behavior, and I answered the woman's questions as honestly as I could.

"My teenage son is with us on some weekends, how do you think she'll do with that?"

"She'll need a slow introduction to him, but once she accepts him, she should be fine."

"What if he brings friends?"

"You might want to crate Gala when that happens."

"Do you think she can be loose outside?"

"Probably not, at least not without some real training. She'll chase deer."

"Does she always pull like this?" Gala was straining against the leash at the sound of the neighbor's dogs across the cornfield.

I shrugged, trying to downplay it. "She's just excited. She does better with a front-leading harness."

In the end, Gala was more than the woman felt she could handle. So many people want a "turnkey" dog, one that requires very little of them. A dog who is housebroken, crate-trained, good on a leash, loves everyone, listens perfectly, doesn't chase cats or deer or squirrels. One that, effectively, doesn't act like a regular dog. Turnkey dogs are rare. And they don't happen without a lot of work. Would Gala ever be a turnkey dog? Unlikely.

"When is she leaving?" asked Nick after stepping through the baby gate into the kitchen and negotiating around the vacuum cleaner I had placed in front of the gate. Gala was terrified of the vacuum—crying out in agony if I turned it on. This became yet another excuse for me not to clean my house, but it also served as a guard to keep Gala from leaping the baby gate that kept her shut in the kitchen away from Gracie.

"She's not. They passed," I said, rubbing Gala's head in apology. I wondered if she had any idea what had transpired that afternoon. At this point, she was probably pretty sure she was our dog.

"We can't keep doing this forever," said Nick as he frowned at Gala.

The Gala situation was a perfect illustration of our relationship. Nick grumbled, but did things to help, like install baby gates and create a longline for Gala to run on, while I painted a prettier picture, coming up with plan after plan—the vacuum will keep her in the kitchen; I'll take her for walks on the rail trail so she can meet people; I'll set a schedule for crate time; maybe if I increase our run distances she'll settle more. I wrote and wrote and wrote about her, ever hopeful that each next tactic would help her get adopted. Nick listened to all my ideas and didn't express any doubt verbally, even though I knew inside he was saying, "Right, uh-huh, here we go again, another brilliant plan that won't work." Sometimes I thought he felt it was his duty to counter my Pollyanna with his Eeyore.

That's why we were such a good couple—we were just different enough to complement one another. I was ideas and he was action. I can't imagine another person who could not only tolerate my endless ideas and blind optimism, but also help me wholeheartedly, despite his own skepticism. He might grumble,* but he'd also go get his power tools or his sketch pad or a new attitude and help me make it happen. So, while he was sick of Gala, tired of the gates and the heartache, he soldiered on, cursing her one moment and snuggling on the couch with her the next.

---

* Actually, he would grumble.

As Gala languished at our house, I worried that her non-breed designation was hindering her chances of finding an adopter. On the website, she was listed as a retriever mix.

"What's a retriever mix?" I asked anyone who would listen. "That's not a breed. No one searches Petfinder for a 'retriever mix.'"

I knew most of the dogs we fostered were true mutts, but I was certain Gala would be more appealing if she was listed as a boxer or maybe vizsla, two breeds I'd speculated she could have in her DNA. I began lobbying the powers that be at OPH to change her breed listing but was told that we were not allowed to change the breed listed by the vet who evaluated her in South Carolina before she came north. Who doesn't allow it, I wondered? The police? Animal Control? I didn't know, and nobody I asked knew either, but it seemed like yet again another affront against Gala, one more thing keeping her trapped at our house.*

After combing through her original records, which were buried among many layers of records accumulated since being rescued by OPH, I found a vet in South Carolina who originally labeled her a "yellow Labrador retriever." Aha! A real breed! A popular breed! But, from my intimate experience with Gala, definitely not her breed.

That evening Gala morphed from a retriever to a yellow Labrador retriever, at least on the OPH website. Would this help her find her people? I had no idea, but at that point, I felt compelled to do something.

I was told that as her foster, I could give her a secondary breed. So I listed her secondary breed† as boxer. I thought her coloring, her athleticism, her intensity, and her habit of using her paws like hands lent credence to this idea.

---

* Later I learned that OPH keeps the breed label given by the examining vet at the shelter to avoid subjective labeling to get a dog adopted—a practice some rescues (and shelters) use to try to attract adopters. People are much more inclined to adopt a black Lab mix than a pit bull mix, as I would learn eventually firsthand.

† Which is many times simply the foster's best guess.

Here's what the AKC website says about boxers:

> Boxers move like the athletes they are named for: smooth and graceful, with a powerful forward thrust. Boxers are upbeat and playful. Their patience and protective nature have earned them a reputation as a great dog with children. They take the jobs of watchdog and family guardian seriously and will meet threats fearlessly.*

That described Gala perfectly.

My other guess was vizsla. They were known for their speed, energy, hunting abilities, and love of people. Gala was more or less the color of a vizsla. She had speed, energy, and hunting abilities in spades. And, wow, was she devoted to her people. She could very likely be vizsla.

But maybe breed descriptions were sort of like your horoscope—depending how you interpreted it, it could apply to anyone or any dog. Further reading revealed Gala could be Dalmatian or whippet or Weimaraner. The truth was, she could be any breed.

And why, people, was that so very important? What would knowing her breed tell you, that I couldn't tell you after six very eventful months living with this dog?

Gala was a dog.

Who knew what breeds created her, and even if we knew those breeds, we couldn't possibly know which characteristics came along for the ride. If Gala was a Lab, well, she certainly didn't get the easygoing nature, but she did get the joyful eating habits, affinity for water, and the ability to monopolize the couch.

For whatever reason, this world needs to label everyone and everything. Why that is has always confounded me. We do it with people as well as dogs. As a writer, I like to have the right word for something, too, but a label is too confining. Anyone who has raised a child (or fostered a dog) knows there are very few absolutes in life, in people, or in dogs.

---

* www.akc.org/dog-breeds/boxer

Much too often, we worry over our labels and our assumptions instead of looking at the dog in front of us. As a dog. Another good dog.

As if to underline my point, I received a call from one of the adopters of my litter of Catahoulas. Her vet had told her in no uncertain terms that the sweet puppy she'd adopted was not a Catahoula at all, but a pit bull. Certain he was wrong, she'd paid to have a DNA analysis done on her pup. Turns out that adorable, colorful, snuggly litter we'd fostered were 100 percent American Staffordshire Terrier.

And I wondered if we'd known and we'd labeled them as such, would they have gotten adopted quite so quickly? Or would they still be here, lingering in my puppy room, keeping Gala company?

8

A Web of Enablers

The Sunday before I had to head to Ohio for a book festival, I was itching for a foster dog. Gala was Gala, nothing had changed, but who knew how long she would be here. Watching the list of dogs in need of fosters circulated online made me sad. How many lives had I not saved because Gala took up so much of our world? I didn't want to think of it that way. I couldn't resent Gala, It wasn't her fault. Or maybe it was. Why couldn't she be more "adoptable"?

The high energy was one thing, but the bigger concern was her increasingly unpredictable reactions to strangers at our house and anywhere we went. To be fair, I didn't take her many places, so maybe that wasn't helping. Between promoting my books, writing the blog, managing our little "farm," and making sure Gala got her four-and-a-half-mile romp every morning, I didn't have a lot of time for field trips. So, another foster dog made no sense.

Except I wanted one.

One night, while snuggling on the couch with Nick and Gracie, I said quietly, "I think I'm going to get another foster." It seemed the perfect time to bring it up, as Nick was three beers into an Eagles inevitable win.

"But you're going away," he said without taking his eyes off the screen.

"I won't get a whole litter, just one puppy."

He got up to go make popcorn, and I took that as a yes.

I scanned the list of available foster dogs and chose Buford. He was about five months old and twenty-five pounds. Perfect! Buford was currently in another foster home in North Carolina, and conveniently, his current foster had already managed to rid him of his flea infestation and worms. Even more perfect!

Reports from shelters are often sketchy. They come from people who are juggling a hundred or more dogs, and not only do they not have the time to write down details, but much of their information is outdated, as it comes from the dog's intake, which could be weeks prior to their arrival with OPH.

Reading the notes provided by Buford's foster made it clear that he was not only a stellar pup, but he'd gotten excellent care and plenty of love. He was nearly crate-trained and housebroken, loved people, was good with children, didn't overreact to a cat, and had a little experience on a leash. Having spent the last few months with Gala and/or a mob of puppies, this one felt like a walk in the park.

The only problem was that with me traveling to Ohio, I couldn't meet Buford's transport, and I couldn't ask my husband to not only look after Gracie and Gala, do the barn chores, and drive Ian to and from soccer, but also meet a late-night transport to bring home a new puppy.[*]

But that was the thing about rescue—we are a community of enablers. We would always go above and beyond to save a dog or to help someone who wanted to save a dog but had to travel to Ohio (in the pouring rain) to sign books.

Tim agreed to pick up Buford and hold him for the weekend until I could get him after I returned home on Sunday. He even sent me pictures of my gorgeous new foster puppy while I was busy being an author in Cincinnati.

The network of foster homes created by OPH meant that help was almost always at the ready. Other volunteers not only were available for advice,

---

[*] Although part of me wanted to point out that is exactly what I would be doing if I weren't traveling to Ohio, and I would still manage to pick up the new foster dog.

sympathy, supplies, and hands-on help, but they also foster-sat for us when we were on vacation and transported dogs to vet appointments and adoption events.

Reading the report on Buford, it occurred to me that there were people fostering dogs all over our country connected by an invisible web spun from our shared passion. As I walked with Gala the morning before I left, I imagined that Kristin, Buford's foster mom in North Carolina, might have been walking Buford at that very moment, watching the sun come up, smiling as the puppy on the end of her leash chased down a flying leaf or paused to watch a squirrel scramble up a tree.

All these dog-hearted people, working together, that was the only way it was possible to save so many lives. So, as alone as I'd been feeling lately, trapped on my hillside with Gala, the dog no one wanted, I really wasn't alone. And that was pretty much what made not only fostering dogs, but life, doable.

After a long weekend of driving in the rain and being on my feet talking to strangers (and trying to be charming), it was nice to be surrounded by dogs once again. They were very honest about what they wanted from me—food, squeaky toys, belly rubs, and nice long walks.

Buford was a bull terrier with the classic bulbous-shaped nose* and plenty of happy energy. He loved me on sight and followed me like a little black-and-white shadow. He was too small for Gala's big energy, but she squealed whenever she caught sight of him. Gracie, on the other hand, gave him her usual greeting—growling and snarling whenever he ventured toward her. Buford was not a particularly brave little guy, so that was always enough to deter his attentions.

Upon meeting any new dog, Gracie's assumption has always been that this new animal is a lethal threat to her well-being (or at least the Frank bed). For her, they were all horrible until proven otherwise. Never mind

---

* Think Spuds MacKenzie.

that with very few exceptions, the previous ninety-four dogs had not harmed her, and quite a few of them she had come to enjoy, or at least tolerate nicely.

I didn't know what we did to raise such a grumpy, unfriendly dog, but she felt the same way about the milkman, mailwoman, UPS driver, and any stranger who happened upon our doorstep. I warned all my kids to put Gracie in her crate when people came to our door before opening the door. At least in Pennsylvania, the dangerous dog laws made keeping a dog that had a bite history nearly impossible. It was a very real fear for me. Some people met Gracie and experienced her bluster and her mostly chicken heart, and some (like my kids) couldn't imagine Gracie biting anyone. I, however, knew all too well, having stepped in the path of her lunge for the UPS guy and felt her teeth in my thigh.

When we adopted Gracie as a sweet little puppy, I had high hopes, but whether it was the state of my overwhelmed life or the capacity of Gracie's wee little brain, none of them materialized. I did manage to teach her to sit and offer a paw, but she never mastered lay down, stay, don't-roll-in-horse-poop, or come when called. She barked at the horses, the neighbors, the birds, every passing car, trees blowing in the wind, and everything her little mind could concoct. Which meant she barked ALL DAY, and on the nights when she wouldn't come in, ALL NIGHT.

I was pretty certain my neighbors hated her with a vengeance. They probably ran as many box fans as we did at night to muffle her sound. I worried that someday one of them would reach a breaking point and shoot her. Seriously. They all have guns. We live on a road that winds through a hollow alongside a creek lined by train tracks that haven't been used in years. Houses are few and far between. In fact, many of my neighbors still have dial-up internet because the cable company won't run cable any farther up our road than the pole at the end of my driveway* because there are too few houses.

---

* And why they've run it that far is rumored to be solely because the neighbor across the street from me is a very convincing person (and a gifted lawyer). I ask no questions, just gratefully use my internet.

I absolutely love my quirky Gracie,* but she is not always an easy dog to live with, and having tried and failed to train her in any way, I'd given up and let her be who she was—Gracie, an independent, mildly insecure pup who loves us in her own way. Sometimes people ask me why I keep bringing in foster dogs if Gracie doesn't like them. Maybe I'm naively optimistic, but I think they are helping her become a friendlier dog. In fact, as the years go by, she is mellowing, especially at the door when visitors come by. I'd guess she assumes that Gala and whatever other dogs happen to be bunking with us at the moment are enough security detail and she doesn't have to handle it all on her own. After all, Gracie never showed this ferocious streak until our first dog, Lucy, passed. It was then that she decided she had to step up and protect us.

Buford was only with us a few weeks before being adopted, which was good because it was time to get ready for our upcoming trip across the Atlantic to visit our baby boy, who turned twenty-one that week in Cyprus, where other than one serious virus that landed him in a hospital,† he was thriving. I was excited to see him, but there were a million details to tie up before we could get on that plane.

I didn't hold out much hope for finding anyone to foster-sit Gala, but I posted on the OPH family Facebook page for fosters and volunteers anyway, pleading for someone to take Gala while we were gone so that she wouldn't have to go to a boarding facility. I knew the noise and chaos of a boarding facility would overwhelm her, and because of her bite history, she would get very little handling.

---

* I do love Gracie, contrary to what a few readers of my first book insinuated. Gracie is Gracie, for better or worse, and I take full responsibility for her behaviors. While she can, on occasion, drive me bonkers, I love her, warts and all. She has beautiful, big brown eyes that give her a perennially puppy appearance, a quirky personality only a mother could love, and our undying commitment all of her days.

† About which he neglected to tell his mother until it was over!

That very day, a foster I'd never met, who lived in Maryland, volunteered to take Gala. Pam seemed to understand what she was getting into, but that didn't stop me from worrying about her and her son and also Gala, who I feared might feel deserted and be a little depressed. She was completely bonded with us by that point and surely thought she was our dog. Pam didn't have a personal dog, so at least Gala wouldn't have to deal with meeting a dog.

With Gala all set, and a house sitter for Gracie, the cats, and the horses, we were ready for Cyprus! Just before we left, I took Gala for her follow-up heartworm test* and she was negative! Finally, a little good news for our girl.

---

* Given seven months after she completed heartworm treatment to see if the treatment worked.

9
Going Abroad

This was my first trip across the Atlantic Ocean. Ian's too. For much of the trip, I felt a strange uneasiness. I've never been a person who loves to travel. I like my routines and the familiarity of home. We stopped in London on our way and spent a few days in Windsor before Addie met us to fly on to Cyprus. Windsor was magical, the buildings and streets infused with history and the castle bells ringing out our arrival. Actually, it sounded more like a preschooler had been let loose in the bell tower with bells crashing one after the other endlessly. We eventually learned that we'd arrived on the queen's anniversary.

The one thing I truly loved about England in our brief stay, besides the scones, was that, at least in Windsor, people brought their dogs with them to the local pub and no one batted an eye. In the States, dogs are prohibited in establishments that serve food, and I've never understood why. I see having dogs in a restaurant as a kind of win-win. Seeing dogs at the next table when we were out was comforting to me.

The days in Cyprus passed too quickly, but it was lovely, as were its people. Watching Brady negotiate his new world, deciphering menus in Greek and explaining the customs, I realized that I never should have worried. In my mind's eye he's still a child—a tow-headed, sparkling eyed, distractible, innocent, sweet dreamer, but seeing him in Cyprus, it was clear he was an adult who was eating a lot more vegetables, occasionally did shots of ouzo, and was more than capable of surviving without me in the world.

I picked up Gala the day after we returned. She'd done well with Pam, and for a few days after we brought her home, she seemed calmer and more content. This only further convinced me that living at our house was not the best situation for Gala. She needed a calmer life.

Gala still had no adoption applications. I'd tried to stay upbeat about it—Yes, yes, I told myself and everyone else, Gala's family will come. They always do. But as December began, it didn't seem even remotely possible. She'd had exactly one potential adopter make the trek to our house to meet her in the entire nine months that we'd had her. Our house was a maze of baby gates that kept her separated from Gracie. She spent long hours in her crate because it was the only way to keep her safe and not punish the animals (and people) who lived here.

She was always quiet in her crate, watching us with her sad, expressive eyes. All she really wanted was to be near us; well, that and to get outside to chase horses or deer or anything that ran from her. When someone new came to the house, I couldn't risk her being loose—she loved people, but she needed slow introductions. She had to learn they hadn't come to harm her. I didn't believe she deserved the bite addendum attached to her foster contract. Shannon never was sure which dog bit her, but I was sure it wasn't Gala, so I didn't want her to end up with a legit bite addendum because I hadn't managed her well. Not that I thought she'd ever bite anyone—her growling threats were just that—threats. And they were born of fear, not aggression. If she were going to aggressively bite someone, I was convinced she would have done it by now.

I watched the e-mails begging fosters to take dogs out of boarding or off transport and my frustration increased. So many dogs in need. I wanted to help, but until someone helped me with Gala, there was little I could do. Gala couldn't handle more dogs coming and going. So we said no to helping another dog because we so desperately wanted to help Gala.

I didn't know what happened to Gala prior to coming to rescue, but I knew it was powerful. Powerful enough that the echoes of that tragedy were obvious in her reaction to sudden noises and movements, unfamiliar people and dogs. She needed someone who was determined to love her and give her a chance. Someone who would not expect her to be the dog she could not be.

"Eventually, it'll happen," Nick assured me. The fact that he was the one taking the positive tack should have been a clue to how close I was to my breaking point.

"No, it won't. Why would anyone pick her?" I asked, my voice growing strained and shrill. Gala retreated to the other couch. We were sitting in the living room, enjoying the warmth from the woodstove. Gracie was outside barking at the neighbors. "Why would anyone want her, when there are so many nice dogs they could pick? Easy dogs, dogs who don't attack their friends or require a fifty-point harness* just to go for a walk."

"Then we'll just keep her and stop fostering," he said.

This was a threat he pulled out when he had no other defense against my frustration. He knew how much I loved fostering, and this comment would almost always turn the tide.

"No. We'll find her a home. Her family must be out there somewhere. We are not her family."

On cue, Gala sighed, rolled over, and offered her belly for Nick to scratch.

Determined to get Gala adopted before the new year, I refreshed her pictures and description on her OPH page and was rewarded with a real application! A family who lived just north of us was interested in Gala as well as several

---

* We'd been using a new harness on Gala, and I was flummoxed by it nearly every time I attempted to put it on her, sometimes requiring my engineer husband's assistance.

other dogs. I took Gala to an adoption event that Sunday to meet the family. It was the first event I'd taken her to since the previous spring, before the broken jaw, when Gala had only recently recovered from heartworm treatment.

The event last spring was at a pet store in a busy shopping center. She reacted badly to the other dogs, so we'd stood outside the entrance to Jersey Mike's Subs, while the rest of the OPH crowd gathered in front of the Pet Valu next door. We'd been there about an hour when a large pickup truck stopped in front of the store and three people got out. A woman and a teenage girl headed for the OPH table, and the driver, a large man with plenty of tattoos and a beer belly, ambled toward Gala and me.

Up until that point Gala had enthusiastically (perhaps too enthusiastically) greeted all the humans she'd met—tail wagging, big smiles, happy to give kisses and hugs—but as this man approached us, she lowered her head and the hair on her back stood up in a ridge. When he reached toward her she began a steady growl. Surprised, I pulled her back to me.

He said, "Oh, she's a meanie! I like meanies, I got two at home." He proceeded to tell me about his two "purebred" pit bulls* who were so ferocious, no one but he could handle them. He told me he hadn't had either the male or the female fixed because the vet said that would only make them more aggressive.

I swallowed all the things I wanted to say and instead told him that I'd never heard a vet say anything like that; in fact, to the contrary, all the vets I knew would say the opposite—that spaying and neutering can make a dog less aggressive. He seemed proud that he had raised two vicious dogs. When I asked if he planned to breed them, he said, "Oh, I wouldn't breed my girl because then she'd have those droopy boobies. That looks disgusting."

Thankfully, about that time, his passengers were ready to go and I was saved from responding to this horrific comment. During our entire exchange, Gala kept up a steady growl. As they pulled away, the man rolled down his window and yelled, "Bye, Meanie!" The woman riding with him laughed and called, "He likes 'em mean!"

---

* An oxymoron since there is no such thing as a purebred pit bull, "pit bulls" not being a breed but rather a catchall term for dogs with wide foreheads, tiny ears, muscular builds, and possible Staffordshire terrier or bulldog heritage.

As soon as the truck was gone, Gala relaxed and resumed her happy greetings. In fact, moments later a family with a toddler approached and helped their daughter pet Gala gently. My nerves were still up from the previous exchange, but Gala had obviously let it go. Remarkably, she dialed back her energy for the little girl, giving her a gentle kiss on the cheek.

Yeah, what a meanie, I thought. But that was more than six months ago. And not long after that event was when Gala had her tragic encounter with our horse, and after that commenced reacting negatively to not just dogs, but people. We hadn't been to an event since, but maybe I was the one with the problem. Maybe Gala would be just fine. She'd calmed and settled and been through a lot since those first months with us. And the Pet Valu was only a mile or so from our home, so I figured I could bail if she didn't do well.

Mostly, I took her because sometimes it felt like no one would ever pick her and I naively hoped she'd find her family there. Her people were certainly not finding her online or at our house.

Gala was anxious but quiet when we arrived, nervously greeting the potential adopters. She was sweet with the young children, but as she interacted with the adults, she was anxious, taut, ready to defend herself. Or maybe I imagined that. I was certainly feeling anxious and defensive. I watched Gala, my stomach in my throat, picturing her recent lunge toward one of Brady's friends in our kitchen just a few days earlier. When another new foster dog arrived who was bouncy and friendly, the family quickly gravitated to her and quietly made it clear that Gala was not the dog for them. Would she ever be the dog for anybody?

As I stood with her outside, away from the other dogs, she became unpredictably explosive. Friendly with one person, erupting in growls and snaps the next. When she let out a string of threats to a woman and child, I decided it was time to leave.

I drove Gala home frustrated and saddened, convinced no one would ever pick her (why would they?) and that we were only making her less adoptable. Her behavior was much worse than that first adoption event so long ago. My mind spun with thoughts: What will become of her? Are we doing more harm than good? Is she like this because of me? Is she mirroring my anxiety and sadness?

I wanted to believe that Gala's family was out there somewhere, but that day it was hard. My heart broke for our sweet, loving, intense, frightened dog. But it mostly broke because that was the day I realized I couldn't save her. No matter how much I loved her, or maybe because of how much I loved her, she would never find her family as long as I was on the other end of her leash.

10

Breaking Point

rying to distract myself, a few weeks before Christmas, I took in four
twelve-week-old terrier puppies. They were beautiful brindle pups with
tiger stripes. Four little girls with no names because the right to name
them had been given to donors in exchange for a hefty donation to OPH
during their Giving Tuesday campaign. As I got to know them and waited
for names, I called them Pink Collar, Blue Collar, Purple Collar, and Brownie
(the only solid brown pup). Their joyous, busy activity was the perfect distraction as I prepared for Brady and Addie to return home and fretted about
how Gala would handle the chaos of a crowded holiday house and visiting
puppy adopters.

Luckily, Gala didn't have to handle it, because Pam offered to take Gala for
Christmas. Pam was now Gala's Adoption Coordinator and her biggest fan.
At times she was my lifeline. She listened to my frustration and validated my
feelings. She said, "You're right, it sucks," which was maybe all I needed and
all anyone could say, but Pam actually said it. She reached out to me again
and again to check how I was, how Gala was doing, or to share a new idea to

help Gala. While she didn't have the answer, it did feel like she had my (and Gala's) back.

I loved OPH and was dedicated to their mission, but that cold, dark December, I felt abandoned and forgotten. Pam's presence reminded me that I wasn't, but still, I questioned everything about Gala's situation and my ability to find her a home. That list of questions was long, starting with why Gala had to have a bite addendum, something that made her adoption not just difficult but nearly impossible. There was no proof she had ever bitten anyone. The bite addendum seemed unfair and became my catchall for everything that had gone wrong with Gala. Why did OPH let me just move Gala to Shannon's last August? What qualifications did Shannon have? None. Just like me. None of us had qualifications; we were all just making it up as we went along, banking on our good intentions and the fact that we were better than the other option for many of these dogs.

But that seemed slipshod. The dogs deserved better. How had it come to this? In a country as rich and wasteful and sentimental and animal-loving as ours, how was it we were still killing dogs, forcing rescues like OPH to be the stopgap in a system that our government should have fixed a long time ago?

I looked up Gala's history. She was a stray from South Carolina. She turned up at the shelter heartworm positive and having recently had puppies. Most likely those puppies were adorable. Someone probably kept the puppies and threw away the mama. In too many cultures, dogs are disposable. Are they disposable here, too? Large, heartworm positive, with a possible bully breed heritage, Gala should have died in that shelter. In light of all that she had been through with me in the past year, would that have been better for her, I wondered? She would have never gone through the painful heartworm treatment, broken jaw, punctured back, and a life restricted to crates as much as eighteen hours a day. Which was worse? And who was I to say?

I carried these questions with me as the new year approached and enjoyed the peace of two weeks without Gala as a daily reminder of my heartbreak.

The puppies attracted not only plenty of adopters, but also a new visitor that December. A red fox began serenading them just outside our front door. It was mating season for foxes and likely all that terrier yipping (they were VERY vocal pups) had attracted a potential suitor. Even when I went outside to do barn chores, the fox didn't leave, just backed away to the edge of the woods. He hung around for over a week and we got postcard-worthy pictures of him.

One of the puppies' regular visitors was Susan, who came for "puppy therapy" many nights on her way home from work. She'd been a regular ever since the winter before when tragedy struck in my puppy room.

Darlin' was an older Shar-pei/shepherd mix who arrived pregnant the previous February and delivered her puppies over the course of a sad, cold weekend. My best guess was the puppies were premature; five of the nine puppies perished within hours or days as I desperately tried to keep them alive. Another lived three weeks before succumbing to congestive heart failure, effectively suffocating himself with his own weight because he was still too weak to stand. With the help of many, many volunteers we were able to save the last three puppies.

Susan had been a regular here with those puppies and every litter that followed, and we'd formed a friendship. I respected her outspoken manner and honesty. She lived about ten miles away from us in Loganville with her cat, who was the reason she didn't foster dogs along with the fact that she worked long days at a hospital in Maryland.

Over the course of the year and lots of puppy therapy, Susan and I had bonded, but she'd also fallen for Gala. Maybe she identified with Gala's strong will and independent streak. I began to wonder if maybe Susan would be the answer to Gala's predicament.

The time with my kids and the break from Gala renewed my energy, and I started the new year hopeful. Carly had sold the manuscript for *Another Good Dog: One Family and Fifty Foster Dogs* to Pegasus Books, and I was excited to polish it and get it ready for publication. More than that, I was excited to spread the message of fostering. For all my frustration with Gala's situation, I did still believe that fostering reduced the number of healthy adoptable dogs being euthanized. Telling my story, the messy, hard, joyful truth of it, might encourage others to try fostering. And that, in turn, would save more dogs.

I had worked hard to promote my novels and still enjoyed having the opportunity to talk to readers about my stories, but this book was different. This book would expose my family. It would be filled with fact, not fiction, an altogether different beast.

When Gala returned, so did the stress of living with her. There were no applications and I was pretty much all out of hope for her ever being adopted. We'd tried everything, but the real problem to me was clear—Gala was beyond my help, too difficult, too complicated, and much too bonded with me. I imagined her reactions before they happened, unable to stop my mind from envisioning her attacking every person who reached for her. I began to believe I was the one responsible when she growled at a friendly visitor or lunged at one of Brady's friends. I clung to the fact that while she'd had opportunities to attack someone, she never had. She warned them away with a growl, and if that wasn't effective, she lunged and retreated, but never made contact.

I didn't want to have a house where people were afraid to stop by for fear of being bitten. I didn't want the parents of my kids' friends to worry about their safety when they were here. And more than anything, I didn't want Gala to actually hurt someone. I couldn't do this any longer.

"I'm done," I told Nick. "If someone else won't take her, she can go to boarding. I can't keep doing this. It's not fair to her and it's not fair to us."

I shared Gala's situation on the blog and it triggered an avalanche of reaction. Suggestions for trainers, meds, herbal supplements, and special harnesses and collars poured in. And more than that—lots of support and encouragement, which is maybe what I needed most. Sadly, it did not trigger any adoption applications or offers of other foster homes.

OPH offered to send her to a board and train facility when a spot opened up, but that was more than a month away. Dogs stayed with this trainer for two weeks or longer while he sorted out what their issues were and came up with a plan for managing them. Then the foster would meet with him and he would teach them the plan. Meanwhile, they suggested that I speak with the trainer from that facility.

I was game. I called the trainer. Like many dog professionals I'd met, he was opinionated and confident in that opinion. Perhaps not unlike an alpha dog. I explained Gala's history—the condensed version. When I was finished he tossed out a few ideas before dropping his bomb.

In his professional opinion, it sounded like the best thing for everyone involved was to euthanize Gala. He said it in a matter-of-fact way as if it were a legitimate plan.

"But you haven't even met her," I protested.

He said, "I don't need to meet her. I've met her before, or dogs exactly like her."

He went on to say that rescues are misguided to think they can save every dog, and in his opinion they took advantage of fosters like me, leaving us with a difficult and dangerous dog. Then he said he was still willing to take Gala and work with me, but not until the weather improved. It had been snowing for what seemed like months already that January and the temperatures were painfully cold. I hung up frustrated and sad, but mostly furious at him, at me, at OPH, at pretty much everyone and everything.

The idea of euthanizing Gala was suggested from other directions—well-meaning, experienced dog rescue people, frustrated OPH volunteers, and, most painfully, by other people who had put down a dog like Gala. Sometimes, their reasoning made absolute sense, right up until the minute I looked at Gala. She'd never hurt anyone. Maybe I was the monster here. Her intelligent eyes watched my every move. There were moments when I thought she could read my mind.

I wanted nothing more than for Gala to go—to training, to another foster home, to boarding if that was the only option. She needed training. I knew that. Someone with a lot more knowledge than me, who could reprogram her. She was not a lost cause, of that I was certain. But until someone else volunteered to foster her after training, we were right back where we started, with Gala stuck here indefinitely. I knew I couldn't take her back after her training. I knew that no matter how much Gala learned or improved, my anxiousness would handicap her. I would see the "old" Gala and she would read my heart. No, I said, on my blog and to anyone who would listen, I cannot do this anymore.

Let me take a second here to be sure you know that I am not a quitter. I don't quit on people—I'm that friend—the one you can count on to show up even when everyone else won't. I thrive on complicated problems.* Despite literally hundreds of rejections, I have pursued my writing career doggedly. My kids know better than to think I'll give up on them just because they've slammed the door in my face, ignored my directions, or refused to eat kale salad; I persist in loving them even when they can't stand the sight of me. I still prune and shape my nectarine and plum trees, handpicking off pests, even though I've yet to see a real harvest after ten years of effort. There is a horse in my pasture who bucks whenever ridden, cribs on my fence, and once put a dear friend in the hospital with an unexplained kick, and yet I will be hauling hay out to him until the day he dies. I desperately did not want to give up on Gala; it went against the grain of my very soul.

I tried to explain to Gala, who might be the one dog who would understand, that I wasn't giving up. I was choosing to do what was best for her by handing her over to someone who hadn't been sitting in the front row for the past year—someone who wouldn't have images seared in her mind of Gala snarling at teenagers, chasing horses, attacking her dog. Someone whose heart rate wouldn't skyrocket every time a new person approached Gala, every muscle tensed and ready to pull back on the leash should Gala react negatively. I knew that Gala sensed my every emotion, and, yet, it was impossible to push my fears aside and feign calm, confidence.

It was time. My family had been more than patient. And Gracie. Oh, the guilt I felt about Gracie. She was not safe in her own home. She had a torn ear and a timid step to show for it. She was cautious in the house, walking slowly into any room, scanning it for Gala. When she heard the familiar sound of Gala scaling a baby gate, she hid under the coffee table or in her crate or under my desk. How could I have done this to my sweet dog?

---

* I do a Sudoku puzzle every morning in ink!

Every time they'd tussled, we made an adjustment. Of late Gala was in her crate more hours than out of it, and Gracie was outdoors a good part of the day. The house wasn't big enough for the both of them. In the beginning, the fights were started as much by Gracie as by Gala, but somewhere along the way, Gala had gotten the upper hand. Perhaps that was evidence of how her confidence had grown. But that was probably not something to mention to potential adopters. It had become a daily challenge to keep Gracie safe. And that was not fair. Gracie was my dog, so Gala had to go. If no one would take her, she would have to go to boarding. I even put a deadline on it—March 1. That would be just about a year since she'd arrived from South Carolina.

Although I suggested it subtly and then directly, Pam couldn't take her. It just wasn't something she could handle in her life at that moment. I respected that and was more than grateful for all that Pam had done for Gala and me to date. She worked tirelessly on her behalf. Her efforts were a big reason why Gala would be going to training, but Pam could not become her foster.

Luckily, Gala did have one other fan: Susan, whose regular presence here had enabled Gala to trust her. Susan had actually been the first person to fall for Gala when she picked her up from the original transport nearly a year ago and took her to boarding, where I picked her up a few weeks later. Susan had borne witness to all my misadventures with Gala, and yet she said she would be willing to try fostering her. But first, we had to have a test run.

11

Lessons Learned

I t was possibly Gala's last week with us, I told people. Possibly? Yes, I assured them, possibly. We'd been here before. Time and again, we'd had a plan for Gala and it did not come to fruition. My family rolled their eyes at me each time I told them Gala was leaving on [insert fairy-tale date].

This time felt more certain. Maybe it was because Susan had done so much to prepare for Gala's arrival. Along with the two trial runs they'd already had together, she'd had extensive conversations with the trainer who would be helping her. Gala wouldn't go to board and train; instead, she and Susan would go to training sessions together and then come home and practice.

Susan lived alone with only one cat. The cat had been one of her concerns, but Gala was good with cats. She wasn't a true threat—just curious about them. I was certain she would give the cat a wide berth as long as it did the same for her.

Living with one person in a quiet home would be good for Gala. Only one person to take direction from. Only one person to love on. Only one person to worry over. I hoped her stress level would plummet and the worry lines on her forehead would finally ease.

And Susan was a smart and competent person. I was certain that she would capitalize on the training help and be diligent about working with Gala on all that they learned.

I grew up with dogs but had no recollection of ever having to house-train a dog or teach it to come or sit or walk on a leash.* We never owned a crate; the dog just slept in the laundry room. When the dog wanted to go out, you opened the door, or, if it was summer, he used the dog door. The dog roamed the neighborhood and came back when it was hungry.

When one died, we got another. Mostly, we ended up with strays or dogs someone else didn't want anymore. I don't remember that we ever went to the pound or the pet store; the dogs just found their way into our lives—Spot, Candy, Scamp, Meeko, and finally Fluffy, a devoted cockapoo who helped me through young adulthood.

Prior to Gala, we'd had pretty straightforward foster dogs and a lot of puppies. Fostering didn't seem that difficult. I had lots of questions, but there were plenty of people with answers. I made mistakes but more or less bumbled along doing the best I could. I would never claim to be a dog expert; in fact, I'd say I'm closer to the other end of the spectrum. Mostly, what I am is a dog lover. I'm good at loving them; I'm not good at making them behave.

Gala adapted as best she could to our gates and rules and crates, but it did not still her soul. Instead, she'd grown more anxious and more reactive to people and dogs. Despite all the love and affection we poured on Gala, her fears had grown during her year with us.

While we'd done the best we could, it wasn't enough and most likely it never would have been. There were simply too many people, animals, activity, and frequent visitors in our house for Gala, many more than her heart could manage.

When Gala returned from her test runs at Susan's house, I saw a marked difference in her. For the first few hours, she seemed like a different dog—relaxed and calm, and instead of inspecting the house, she lay down on the Frank bed for a good twenty minutes.

---

* I'd never even picked up dog poop in a bag until I had a foster dog.

But then the house got busy, and she went back to work—protecting all of us, monitoring our activities, her brow wrinkled and worried. It was only when the two of us went for a walk around the pasture that I saw the puppy hidden inside her. She pounced and ran and smiled.

I'd spent countless hours trying to figure out what was going on inside that beautiful head of hers. She was a conundrum made up of biology and a history I would never know. No doubt her year with us added to that history. How much of her anxiousness was nature and how much was nurture was hard to guess.

I didn't know what the future would hold for Gala. I'd already shed plenty of tears over our inability to help her find her forever home, but being a person who finds it important to learn from failure, I thought a lot about what she'd taught me in our almost year together.

She had certainly taught me that love was not always enough. I loved that dog fiercely, still did, but my love may have actually been an obstacle. I should have called for help much sooner; I should have loved her enough to refuse to continue fostering her, even if it meant she went to boarding.

I also learned, once again, that I didn't know that much about dogs. Dogs, particularly shelter dogs, can be more complicated than I'd ever believed. Sometimes it was enough to love them and feed them and give them a warm, safe place, but sometimes it wasn't. Like people, they were individuals with their own stories. Best intentions and big hearts would not always be enough. Knowledge and experience and the ability to say uncle were also important.

Looking back now, I realized I should have trusted my instincts. I knew I was in over my head back in May, the day I took Gala to that adoption event and the scary guy who loved the "meanies" laughed in my face while Gala growled at him. I remember the dark feeling he left me with and how Gala had changed in his presence. That was the first time I heard her growl, the first time I was aware that she was capable of threatening others. It scared me and I drove home thinking she was too much for me to manage.

I've gone through life pretending I know more than I do, thinking I can handle situations that frighten me. Somehow, by leaning on instinct or the tolerance of others or maybe by sheer dumb luck, I've managed to "fake it till you make it" time and again. But not this time. This time I should have said, "I don't know what I'm doing. I can't handle this." Why I've viewed that admission as a weakness most of my life is a mystery to me. I know now that it is a sign of strength. Only strong people can be vulnerable. Only strong people aren't afraid of others thinking they are weak. Strong people know that a weakness doesn't define them, it makes them stronger because they can get help when they need it.

I don't know what the purpose of Gala's year with us was, but I hoped one day it would be clear. She'd made me laugh and made me cry and driven me to the edge. "I'm done. This is my last dog," I would tell Nick, again and again. And then I'd be distracted by puppies or read more about the dogs dying in shelters and decide I couldn't give up on Gala.

I was hopeful for Gala now. As I prepared to say good-bye to her, I felt certain it was the right move. Yes, I wished it had happened ten months earlier, but I was going on faith that this year had been necessary, if not for Gala, then perhaps for me.

12

She's Really Gone

Without Gala, our house was very quiet. Not that Gala was a noisy dog. Without her, though, the energy level dropped. It didn't help that we'd had a string of unrelenting gray, rainy days.

I missed Gala. Until she was truly gone, I didn't realize how much of my day revolved around her. Now there was no need to close the baby gates or lock the kitchen door. I didn't have to set timers for crate time or wonder where Gracie was before opening a door. My mind no longer needed to manage dogs 24/7. Like the frog in the kettle analogy, we'd spent our year with Gala slowly adapting our lives to hers.

And now she was gone.

I was sadder than I expected to be. I wondered if I would ever see her again. I wanted her to be successful in her new foster home and, hopefully soon, with her new forever family. I understood that meant I had to stay out of the way. That whole first week I heard nothing from Susan. I was trying to be respectful; Gala was her charge now, not mine. I didn't want to badger

Susan, but she and Gala were never far from my mind, and I checked my phone incessantly for word.

I got many messages, and everyone I ran into asked, "How is Gala doing?"

I had no idea. Susan hadn't e-mailed, texted, or called me to say how things were going. I told everyone, "I don't know. I haven't heard."

I understood Susan's radio silence. I did. She was focused on Gala, and she knew lots of people in OPH and my blog readers were watching what she did. It was a lot of pressure to succeed. Taking Gala on as your first foster dog was like starting out at the Olympics instead of the baby pool. I got it. I did. But Gala was my dog. Or at least it felt that way. I wanted to know how she was. Was she listening? Was she sad? Was she chasing the cat? Did that damn trainer suggest again that she be euthanized when he met her in person?

Finally, I texted casually. How's it going with Gala?

She's fine. Just got home. Going for a walk.

And that was it. Nothing more.

"See? She's fine," said Nick when I told him. "Isn't that what you wanted to know?"

"Fine, but how fine? Like, fine, she's eating and sleeping or fine, she's doing great with training, or fine, but she misses you?"

"She's fine," he said and refused to indulge my ridiculousness.

That weekend, Susan posted more details on the OPH family Facebook page. That was how I would get the news of Gala. Like everybody else. Not like the person who had spent a year agonizing and likely gained wrinkles and more than a few gray hairs worrying over that dog. Not like the person who felt like she'd lost a dear friend. Not like a person who was still trying to come to terms with having tried so very hard and failed, who was still wondering if she'd done more harm than good to this beautiful dog that she dearly missed and wondering if abandoning her now was the ultimate harm. Nope, as far as Gala was concerned now, I was nobody special.

As the next few weeks went by, Susan would share little tidbits and a few pictures via text with me, but always in response to my nagging. To be fair, she worked full-time and then came home and had to take care of her house and life and put in time training Gala. She didn't have time to hold the hand of a hovering ex–foster mom full of regrets. And Gala was fine. Bottom line.

I needed a distraction. How about my one-hundredth dog? According to my kennel records, the next dog to arrive at our house would be my one-hundredth dog. An OPH volunteer created a graphic celebrating that fact using the faces of most of the dogs I'd fostered. It was a big deal. So why wasn't I excited?

Until I knew for certain that Gala wasn't coming back, I didn't want to take in another foster dog, even if it was my one-hundredth dog. When the e-mail came with the list of available fosters, I deleted it. Running all alone, I imagined all kinds of scenarios in which I stepped back in and saved the day for Gala. I imagined her missing me, depressed. Maybe she was behaving not because she was happy and smart and responding to Susan, but because she knew if she was good, she could come home. It was insane. I know that now, but at the time, it made complete sense.

We'd been through so much, suffered so much, that I needed validation that it had all been worth it, that I hadn't wasted eleven months, stressed my marriage, compromised our happiness, become a recluse, and traumatized my own dog all for nothing. I couldn't fathom that after two weeks with Susan, Gala was doing everything I hadn't been able to do with her in eleven months. It couldn't be true. I knew that. I knew that any day now, something would happen. This was Gala, after all; it could never be smooth sailing. I waited for the call, for Susan to say, "I can't do this, come get her."

"Wait? She might come back?" asked Nick, when I told him why there'd been no new foster dog.

"If something goes wrong at Susan's, I need to be able to take her."

"But I thought it was going fine with Susan."

"Maybe."

It was going fine. Gala was not coming back. In fact, Gala was doing so great in training, Susan had actually been taking her out off-leash. I commented on Facebook, "Amazing! So happy for her."

And I was. I just wasn't happy for me or proud of the fact that I was hurt and angry at being cut out of Gala's life. How easily and quickly Susan had been able to turn Gala around stung. It just underscored how horrible I had been with Gala. We'd had her eleven months, and she was a train wreck. Susan had her three weeks, and she was already happy and stabilized and "an excellent recall dog," whatever that meant.

And then there was Gracie. With Gala gone, Gracie transformed. She smiled and played and for the first time maybe ever, she jumped in my lap as I sat down to journal.* I held her and talked to her for a few minutes, but eventually I gently scooted her off my lap because I couldn't take the smell. Gracie almost always stinks. She has a horrible habit of rolling in dead things or horse manure. When the weather was warmer, she got hosed off on a regular basis, but this time of year, we just suffered her stench. I'd tried to explain to her that people would be more inclined to pet her if she'd didn't stink, but for eight years now, she was undeterred.

With Gala gone, Gracie was free to roam the house and taunt the cat and roll on the floor with abandon. It made me both happy and sad to see it. Happy to see Gracie so joyful, and sad that she'd spent this past year afraid. Her happiness was more confirmation that letting Gala go was the right thing, but it also added to the guilt and sadness I felt over Gala. How could I have been so stupid or stubborn or whatever it was that I let a foster dog reduce Gracie's life to such misery. For nearly a year?

Gracie was lying in the center of the living room, completely relaxed. I lay down beside her and looked into her big, liquid calf eyes. "I promise I won't let that happen again. This is your home. I know you aren't always happy to share it, but I promise I'll keep you safe when you do."

Gracie got up and trotted to the door. She seemed unmoved by my pledge. I needed to get up and get moving anyway. Addie would be home soon.

A year ago, she'd competed in Yor-Voice,† a local singing competition modeled after the national show *The Voice* and held at The Strand, the beautiful

---

* Just for the record, Gracie does not fit in my lap, and she's never been a snuggler.

† It was held in York, so you get the clever play on words, right? *The Voice* becomes Your Voice becomes York Voice becomes Yor-Voice.

historic downtown theater, to raise money for the Cultural Alliance for the Arts. I'd talked her into entering the competition last year in an attempt to bolster her confidence.

At the time, she'd been in the midst of auditioning for musical theater programs at renowned schools that only accepted fifteen to twenty musical theater students a year. Nearly two thousand wannabe musical theater majors auditioned for these spots, making the odds pretty much impossible. Still, my determined girl was undeterred.

That winter, she'd bravely traveled to Pittsburgh and Boston and Virginia and done her best, but seeing her competition made the reality clear. So many Barbie dolls and bunheads. Addie was neither. She'd always been her own person and created her own path.

As she awaited the results of her applications, she was excited about her final show with the high school. They were doing *Shrek*, and she'd always wanted to play Fiona; it was perfect for her. She auditioned, confident that as a senior, the role was hers (as was pretty much everyone else), but instead it went to a junior. The combination of her broken heart over being sidelined for her final show at school and the stress of auditioning again and again fruitlessly just about broke her. When I spotted the announcement for Yor-Voice in the paper, I insisted she had to go for it.

"I'll never win," she said. "This will be against adults."

"Worst case, you get to perform on the stage of The Strand," I said, and a little glimmer returned to her eye. She filled out the application.

A month later, she stood on that renowned stage and sang her heart out to Jason Robert Brown's "I'm Not Afraid of Anything." It was the perfect message not just for the world, but for her and for me. Whatever happened in the coming months, she would face it head-on. And she would be okay.

Suffice it to say, she brought down the house. Her powerful voice soared through that historic building, but more than that, the honest emotion she let loose won everyone over. There was thunderous applause, and I wasn't the only person in tears. At the end, after all the voting, Addie won both the People's Choice and Judge's Choice and carried home two enormous trophies, plus flowers and baskets of local goodies and gift certificates. Winning also meant that she got to come back the next year and perform once again on The Strand's stage as the returning champion.

I was excited to see her perform without all that pressure. We'd spent a few days combing the resale shops for the perfect dress when she was home on spring break and had found an antebellum dress that laced up the back and was covered with glittery stones. It nearly doubled her weight. For her return performance she sang, "Gimme, Gimme That Thing Called Love" from *Thoroughly Modern Millie*. She was so at home on that stage; it was a magical performance with cheers breaking out even while she was singing. Afterward, I met her backstage to help her with the dress. We'd loosened the lace-up back so she had room to sing, but now she needed it tightened, as she would be sitting through the rest of the show, serving as one of the judges.

She was literally glowing when I found her, high as a kite. Her heart was happiest on stage singing. I told her, "Remember this moment, this stage—you belong here." She hugged me and then hurried out to continue her performance as a judge. The rest of the evening, she offered kind and encouraging critiques of the other performers, always lifting them up. It was an incredibly proud moment for me. No matter what happens—whether she makes it on Broadway or not—one thing is for sure, my daughter is a star.

13

One-Hundredth Dog

Gala continued to thrive at Susan's. I was thrilled for Gala, but the more Susan succeeded with Gala, the more I felt like I had failed. Every "thank you for helping her" comment Susan got when she posted Gala's victories on Facebook sounded more to me like "thank goodness someone other than Cara took over." I kept these feelings to myself as I recognized them for what they were—childish and unflattering and so, so, shallow. This was about the dog, not me. But maybe it was about me, too. Maybe I needed to save these dogs as much for me as for them.

Whenever anyone said, "Thank you for saving [X dog]," I always felt awkward and unsure how to respond. "It's my privilege," was what I usually said, but that made it sound like the fact that the dog needed saving was acceptable or fun, which it wasn't. But I did feel like it was a privilege. There was so much in this world that was wrong and backward and desperate that I couldn't do anything about, but saving a dog? That was easy. Much easier than saving a person. So, it seemed like it shouldn't be a big deal; it was just a dog.

And yet, it was never just a dog; it was a big deal. Saving Gala would have been the biggest deal, but in the end, I couldn't save her, and I still wasn't convinced that we hadn't actually made her life worse, not better. I was as hopeful as anyone that her latest potential adopter would be the one. I wanted Gala to have her home, but I also wasn't sure I would be able to move past the pain of failing her until she had one.

Unable to put it off any longer, I decided to foster my one-hundredth dog. Maybe that excitement was just what I needed.

My one-hundredth dog turned out to be seven dogs. Willow Wonka was a black mouth cur (or so they said) with six gorgeous puppies slathered in wrinkles and rolls topped with long floppy ears. The pictures of Willow in a baby pool crammed inside a small concrete shelter pen made me draw a breath. Her eyes pleaded for rescue, and the butterballs around her feet looked scrumptious enough to eat. Yes! Send them my way!

A new volunteer pilot had agreed to fly the little family to Baltimore from Clemson, South Carolina, that Saturday morning. I'd recruited Deb, another OPH foster, to ride along to help bring mom and pups home. We planned to leave my house mid-morning to meet the plane that was expected in by lunchtime. The first hiccup came when I got a message at dawn that the plane was having mechanical problems. The flight was in question and the rescue coordinator on the ground in South Carolina was scrambling to find another rescue for the mama and pups who desperately needed to be moved from the overcrowded shelter.

So much for my one-hundredth dog. I messaged Deb and she replied right back that she was flexible and could go later if necessary.

An hour later, the plan was back on. The plane was fixable; Willow would be coming north that day. The foster coordinator sent me a link to the flight plan for our pilot so I could track the plane in real time. This was a good and a bad thing. It would have been a great thing if someone had explained to me how to properly read the monitor. I refreshed and refreshed, yet nothing changed, just the original plan as it stood the night before.

Nick was out of town and Ian was holed up in his room playing video games with his friends. I was distract-myself cleaning, scrubbing the kitchen counter when I got a text that said, The plane is in the air!

I texted Deb, Time to go! and packed up the lunch I had prepared to give the pilots. Because they fly between tiny airports with no restaurant services, it's OPH tradition to provide the pilots with a meal for their return flight.

What everyone neglected to tell me was that the plane was leaving from Baltimore for Clemson, not the other way around. All of the previous pilots OPH had commandeered to fly rescue were from the South and brought the dogs north before returning home. This new pilot, Michael, with help from another pilot, Jerry, was from Baltimore and heading down to Clemson to get the dogs and then bringing them back. You are probably already ahead of me here, so you know that when Deb and I rushed to the airport, just over an hour from my house, we would discover that the plane had left Baltimore and was on its way down to Clemson.

The tiny airport was run by one guy. He directed the planes in by radio and he also went outside and waved the planes in with his flags. He only chuckled a little as he explained my mistake and then he offered to let us hang out in a spare conference room that had more comfortable seating than the tiny airport lounge with its cracked vinyl loveseat and sticky table.

Now what? We considered our options. It didn't make sense to go home and come back, but sitting in the sterile, cold, boring airport waiting area was not the way either of us wanted to spend our Saturday. We decided to go exploring.

We made two discoveries on our exploration—the first was that there was nothing at all interesting to do in the marshy no-man's-land between Baltimore and Washington, which was dotted with warehouses, depressed strip malls that haven't been updated since the eighties, and many, many small houses and nondescript apartment buildings.

We made the second discovery when we stopped for gas. In my hurry to get out the door, load up the crate and towels and lunch for the pilots, I'd forgotten my purse. So, here's the kind of friend Deb is. Not only did she lend me the money for gas, she then bought me lunch. The only place we could find to grab a snack and a drink was a bar attached to a huge liquor store. It was

St. Paddy's Day, so it was a busy, busy place. We found seats at the bar and tried to distract ourselves with the basketball on television as I refreshed my flight tracker app again and again.

We'd been there almost an hour when a young woman approached us.

"I noticed your shirts . . ." she began. Deb and I were both wearing our rescue shirts with the OPH logo on the back. "I just want to thank you for all you do for the dogs. We adopted a rescue dog," she said and then told us a little about him.

It was probably the perfect reminder we both needed at that moment. This was why we'd gotten up early and given up an entire day and had waited hours—to save a dog (and her puppies). We thanked the woman for choosing to rescue.

A few moments later, the flight tracker showed that the plane had finally left Clemson for Baltimore, so we decided we should return to the airport to wait.

While sitting on the squeaky vinyl loveseat watching out the window for our plane, I got a text message from Susan: Gala has been adopted.

A chill ran through me. How perfect was it that at the moment, when I was about to meet Willow, Gala had finally found her family? Now I could move forward. Now I could save another dog.

I was so happy for Gala. This was what we wanted, right? The training, the quiet atmosphere, the focused attention paid off and now Gala was headed for her forever home. Finally. Happy ending.

And yet my tears came. I recognized that my tears were selfish tears. When you foster, the one thing that makes letting your dogs go easier was seeing your dog find her family. That was the payoff for ruined carpets and chewed-up chair rungs, endless potty walks and brokering the peace in your household. Seeing how happy and excited the new family was to have this dog that you have saved and you have loved made the letting go easier. After all we had been through together, missing out on that piece with Gala hurt ferociously, even as I knew that was the way it had to be.

"This is good," said Nick later that night as I cried. "Gala has a family."

"I know," I agreed. "But I'll never know them. I'll never see her again."

"Sure you can. I'm sure they would let you see Gala."

I felt so childish in that moment. I knew it wasn't about me. It was about the dog.

As if reading my mind, Nick said, "You have to focus on Gala. This is what you wanted for Gala. She deserves this."

I nodded and babbled on about how I was sure that Gala's new family would stay in touch with Susan, and that she would surely let me know what she heard, but I knew he was right—I needed to focus on the dog and the outcome. I needed to push myself and my selfish need to be the one to save her aside and focus on the dog.

It was all about the dogs. I told myself that again and again when I was inconvenienced or annoyed or exhausted—all things I'd been that day. It was about the dogs, not me. That shared belief is what makes it possible for so many different people with vastly different backgrounds and ideals to work together to save so many dogs. It was not about us; it was about the dogs. It took not just me, but my rescue family to save Gala. There's a reason why one of our mottos is "Together we rescue." It was time to really let Gala go and focus on the dogs to come.

It didn't help that Willow looked so very much like Gala. She even weighed the exact same amount (forty-nine pounds) and came from the same state. She was the same age Gala was when she arrived (two), and she recently had puppies (which Gala had also, although she arrived sans pups).

When I was asked to take a mom and pups, I didn't hesitate to say YES! But when I saw the pictures and the unmistakable Gala-likeness, I admit it wigged me out. Like lay-in-bed-and-wonder and miss-your-exit-because-you're-preoccupied wigged me out. I didn't know if it was a sign or a test or some kind of *Groundhog Day* scene—the universe here to teach me a lesson or offer me a do-over. It made me wonder why there was an endless stream of Galas coming from the South. All along I'd been focused on my end of things—the foster dogs and the adopters—but it occurred to me as I loaded up yet another litter of pups to bring home that there never seemed to be an end or even a slow-down. When would all the dogs be safe? With all the efforts to spay and neuter, the rescues working nonstop, the transport vans running north, at what point would this problem be solved? Would I still be fostering dogs when my grandchildren came to visit?

I tucked those thoughts away in the back of my mind. The problem seemed so much bigger than me. Surely someone somewhere had a plan. What I needed to do was keep doing my part. And my part meant caring for the dog in front of me.

I named the new dog Willow Wonka because she had six solid brown pups. So they were Willow Wonka and her Chocolate Factory (Augustus Gloop, Mike Teavee, Charlie Bucket, Veruca Salt, Violet Beauregard, and Oompa Loompa).

I was cautious around Willow at first, worried that she would be protective of her pups or cautious about new people. I looked for the fear that creased Gala's brow but saw none of it in Willow. She thumped her tail at the sight of me and would nudge my arm when I picked up one of her puppies as if to say, "See? Isn't he gorgeous?"

Willow herself was quite a personality. She was clearly a teenage mom—much more interested in me and the noises outside and the cat and FOOD than she was in those babies. In fact, I was rarely able to see her nurse them because whenever I checked on her, she would leap to her feet to greet me excitedly at the gate, leaving the puppies squalling in her wake. Their chunkeroo-ness testified to the fact that she was, in fact, feeding them when I wasn't watching.

Willow bounded around the yard like a puppy herself, nearly pulling me off my feet. Inside, she was a climber and explorer. She was restricted to the puppy room and the hall outside the puppy room, but that hadn't limited her capacity for trouble. She managed to reach my plant bench (beyond a fence and a barricade) and toppled a tray of seedlings. She climbed on the worktable in the hall where I mixed up the magical concoctions of puppy mush (but thankfully she wasn't aggressive enough to open treat bags or coconut oil containers or the food vaults). Her favorite perch was on top of the crate that brought her here, which still sat in the hall outside the puppy room waiting for me to carry it out to the garage. No lounging about on the comfy bed I provided her. I could tell we would have lots of fun with this silly dog in the weeks to come. I could also tell that weaning the pups would not be a long and drawn-out process.

The puppies were beyond adorable. I wasted hours just staring. Or trying to stare, because when I sat down beside the box, Willow wanted my attention. If I leaned into the box to look, she would jump in the box, trampling puppies in the process to be sure I was looking at her. If I ignored her, she'd lick my face, nudge my arms, insist I pay attention to her. She seemed to be love-deprived and was stocking up as fast as possible.

The fact that Gala found a home at the exact moment that Willow was winging her way to me seemed like more than coincidence. I wondered if Gala had sent me Willow. Willow's gorgeous, happy presence and her immediate bonding with me was so very much like Gala's arrival in my life. Maybe Gala knew I would need a distraction as big as this little brood to help me through losing her. I didn't get to meet Gala's family, but I had Willow.

Most of the time, I'm able to be stoic about the fostering business. Save one, let it go, then you can save another. That's how it works. There isn't time for tears—this is about the dogs. But this past year that began with the loss of Darlin's babies and was consumed by Gala's odyssey had not been an easy one. There had been plenty of tears and more than a few curse words. So maybe, just maybe, Willow's presence was a sign—from Gala or one big it's-going-to-be-all-right from the universe.

At least that's how I decided to take it.

14

Hatching a Plan

For the first ten days, I held my breath. I wanted to be absolutely sure there was no chance the new puppies had parvo or some other contagion. These pups had been in a shelter, supposedly protected by the fact that they were nursing, but what had they carried out with them? I'd only seen parvo from a distance, but anyone in rescue knows the danger. Unvaccinated puppies are at great risk because parvo is often lethal, and I'd watched from the sidelines as other foster homes had struggled to save parvo pups. We were ten days out and the Chocolate Factory pups were fat and healthy, sporting little pink bellies and skunky puppy breath, so we'd made it.

For a while, life was good in our puppy house, but how could any house filled with puppies not be good?

As days passed and I watched the pictures on Facebook posted by Gala's new adopter, I began to relax. Gala was safe. It didn't matter how she'd finally found her way to a forever home; she was there. And I needed to squish the prickly, clinging ego of mine that wanted credit. In the end, my months and months of struggles with Gala were not important, and I certainly didn't need or deserve a shiny medal for my efforts.

And yet, every picture that appeared on Facebook thickened the lump in my throat. I missed her, and I missed that her new family didn't know about us—her old family. All her new family knew was that they had a gorgeous, energetic, extremely popular* new dog. They had no idea what Gala's last year had done to my heart and my commitment to dog rescue.

For the first time since we began this journey, I questioned whether we were making any kind of difference. Dog after dog was still dying in shelters no matter how many foster dogs I took or didn't take.

Busy as I was with the puppies, the spring garden, and the upcoming book, most days didn't leave a lot of spare time to think about the larger issue of dog rescue because I was too busy rescuing dogs. But as I mourned Gala and prepared to launch my book, I read further and wider about what could be done about the situation beyond the Band-Aid that was my puppy room and so many others like it.

OPH and other rescues did amazing work, and yet there remained an end-less stream of unwanted dogs whose lives were in danger of being extinguished if not for rescue. Instead of simply selecting the next adorable dog or litter of puppies to foster, I began to look beyond that list. The term "economic euthanasia" popped up in my reading and I wondered, was it possible dogs were dying because of a simple lack of funds?

Shelters in some of the rural areas of this country, particularly in the South, did not have budgets or facilities that could care for the number of dogs entrusted to their care. They needed money for food, staff, equipment, buildings, medical care. When there was not enough money to feed, house, or provide medical care for the dogs, the dogs were euthanized, regardless of how adoptable or healthy they were.

We all wanted to believe that didn't happen, especially in a country as rich as ours, but I was learning that it did. By calling it "euthanasia," it sounded

---

* Every post about Gala on Facebook triggered an avalanche of comments and likes from OPHers and blog readers.

like it was a merciful action, but having met over a hundred dogs now whose lives could have easily been snuffed out because of this brand of euthanasia, I realized it was not euthanasia at all; it was killing, plain and simple. Maybe calling it euthanasia made it more palatable for the general public, but the idea was becoming a growing knot in my gut. It was wrong. It was preventable. So why the hell wasn't anything being done to stop it?

As I contemplated this situation and my role in it, a message from a rescue coordinator in one of the OPH partner shelters in South Carolina came across the rescue's Facebook page. It was in response to the news that we would be unable to pull dogs from their shelter because our foster homes were full:

> Over the holiday weekend, the shelter took in 44 dogs—and the inflow continues every day as always. There was minimal space available for intake last Friday and it was quickly filled. On Monday the euthanizations began. The first to go were dogs surrendered on Friday because their people were going away for the weekend and didn't want to be bothered with finding someone to care for their pet. Court cases and strays take precious space because they must be held for specific periods of time.
>
> The sight of beautiful dogs lying dead on the floor, to never have another chance at life, is beyond heartbreaking. We were counting on next week's transport to save precious lives, so this news is devastating. We are so very grateful for the many dogs saved thus far by OPH.
>
> Today, I'm praying for a miracle.

As I read this message, Willow sat beside me, her head on my thigh. OPH had pulled Willow and the Chocolate Factory pups from that very shelter. Money could make a difference at that shelter, not just in terms of much-needed food, medical supplies, and space, but to help them increase staff so that more could be done to advertise their dogs, educate their community, and provide resources to the families that adopt from their shelter so there were fewer owner surrenders. Money was what made it possible for Willow and her pups to be flown out of there before their time was up.

So, yeah, money was good. But money alone would not solve the problem of killing dogs because there wasn't enough space/time to save them. Foster homes could make a difference. If we had more foster homes, we could save more dogs. The message of my book—that fostering is one way anyone can help save dogs—was needed now more than ever.

If there were more foster homes, it would lessen the stress on shelters to stretch strained budgets, and maybe they wouldn't be forced to make decisions about which dogs they could afford to save and which would have to die. But how could there ever be enough foster homes? Foster homes wouldn't stem the tide of dogs arriving at the shelter. Fostering could give them breathing room, but, clearly, it wasn't the only answer.

I needed to do more than write a book. I needed to go down there. I needed to see this for myself. Sitting there with Willow, I began to hatch a plan. I would use my book advance money not just to tour with my book, but to rent a van, fill it with donated food and meds and supplies, and take them to the shelters. Along the way, I would write about it, using my words to shine a light on the situation.

For Christmas, Addie had given me a sign that said: "Saving one dog will not change the world, but surely for that one dog the world will change forever."

I think she gave me that sign in response to my struggles with Gala. She knew how frustrated I was that for so many months, I was only focused on saving one dog while I knew there were so many that needed saving. But if lots of people stepped up to foster and focused on just one dog, eventually maybe we could change the world, at least the world for homeless dogs in struggling shelters.

15

Post-Traumatic
Gala Disorder

began to make plans, but the book was still four months away from publication, and the mess in my puppy room required all my attention. In fact, if this was what all puppy litters were like, I'd have quit fostering puppies long ago. It wasn't that these pups pooped any more than other puppies. It had more to do with what they did after they pooped.

After they pooped (occasionally, but rarely, on the puppy pads), they ran and wrestled over and through their poop, sometimes even sleeping in it. They tracked it everywhere. I found myself scrubbing it off the walls. Toys, water bowls, and bedding had to be changed almost every hour, and just that week they'd upped the ante when they discovered that they could shred their puppy pads to create unending fun.

By default, I was becoming a bit of a puppy expert. Hounds, in particular, seem to take special joy in making messes. They also had an all-in attitude when it came to food. Mealtimes were a free-for-all. No matter how carefully I set out their bowls and made sure to put equal portions in every compartment, even adding an extra spare feeding space, kind of like a reverse musical chairs, nothing could stop the bedlam. Food and ears began flying the moment I released the puppies to eat. Start to finish they demolished every speck of food in less than a minute.

"No more hounds," I pledged, but knew I'd never stick by that. It always seemed to be the hounds that got to me. I'd sworn them off two years ago after we'd fostered a redneck hound dog who had nearly ended my marriage with her endless howling and her penchant for pooping anywhere, anytime, including on the beautiful cedar porch that Nick built. And yet, I eventually found their tricolor, olfactory-driven, happy-go-lucky enthusiasm irresistible. All the same, when Willow's puppies were adopted, I breathed a sigh of relief.

Unlike her puppies, Willow was a perfectly mannered guest. Housebroken, crate-trained, quiet, and friendly, Willow even got along with Gracie. She had destuffed more than her share of toys, but she had yet to chew anything inappropriate. She followed me like my shadow all around the house.

Willow was what we called a "turnkey" dog, quite the opposite of Gala, despite their eerily similar appearance. And yet, when I introduced Willow to new people I found my heart racing as my mind envisioned her leaping at the new person, snarling and threatening. Rationally, I knew she was not Gala, not at all, and yet my sweaty palms and short breath made it clear that some traumatized section of my brain couldn't accept that.

"It feels like I have post-traumatic Gala disorder," I told Nick.

He laughed, but then softened and said, "That kinda makes sense."

Prior to Gala, I never assumed the worst of any dog. I never worried that a dog might snap or snarl suddenly with no warning, but now I carried an irrational fear with me everywhere. I'd changed my running routes to avoid the loose dog that had fought with Gala and rerouted again when another neighbor began allowing their 180-pound Great Pyrenees to run loose. On more than one occasion, he had charged at me, stopping short of actually doing anything but warning me. But now I was too frightened to pass that house. I loved dogs. I was a dog person. But something had changed; now I saw every dog as a potential threat.

And none of it made sense because never, not once, had I ever felt threatened by Gala. She'd loved me beyond reason. It was as if I couldn't reconcile the loving, gentle, adoring Gala who snuggled at my side while I read or licked my hand for attention with the dangerous dog who threatened strangers and attacked Gracie. She couldn't be the same dog. But she was, so did that mean that every dog had a dark side?

"Maybe I should stick to puppies for a while," I told Nick.

And so we welcomed a string of new puppies that summer as I prepared for my book launch and tour. Zander, a four-month-old lab puppy from Tennessee, was a gentle soul who collapsed in an adoring heap whenever you touched him. He was one of the easiest foster puppies we'd ever had—housebroken and mild-mannered, his worst habit was chewing shoes left available to him.*

Willow indulged Zander, loved our visitors, and listened in an I-will-do-anything-you-ask-especially-if-you-have-a-treat kind of way. So, it didn't seem unreasonable to leave Ian in charge of the foster dogs and Gracie overnight one Friday so Nick and I could drive to New Jersey to see Addie perform in a benefit showcase. We would stay over and, since she had finished her first year, pack her up the next day and bring her home from college.

I left Ian a list of instructions and even measured out the dogs' meals and labeled them so he wouldn't be confused. He wouldn't even have to do much walking of dogs since Willow was spayed the day before and would still be on crate rest and Zander could play in the puppy yard. What could go wrong?

It was a beautiful night and Addie's performance was flawless, but the cell phone in my pocket kept vibrating. Finally, I glanced at it. Ian. What could have gone wrong? Easiest foster dogs ever. At intermission, I finally talked to my tired and angry son who had just gotten home from an invitational track meet that hadn't gone well. Willow was having intestinal issues, probably a reaction to the meds she was on, and had been in her crate longer than usual because the meet ran late. My usually helpful, but momentarily furious, child did not want to deal with a s%#t storm in a dog crate. He assured me that

---

* Zander was confined to the kitchen, whereas shoes belong in a shoe cubby or your room, so in a perfect world he was never granted access to them. Alas, ours was not a perfect world.

Willow was acting normal otherwise, begging for her dinner and jumping all over him in her excitement at his return home.

I gave him the most long-distance sympathy I could muster and then said, "Just put the crate on the porch and let her sleep in the kitchen."

I figured I could clean the crate when we got home the next morning. I understood his anger, but I also worried about my best girl, who I was certain was not only uncomfortable physically but felt awful about the mess she had made. Willow only wanted to please, and she cowered at a raised voice, so it was likely she was having a pretty tough night.

At breakfast the next morning, it seemed odd that we hadn't heard from Ian. The dogs were used to getting up at six. It was after eight when he called. Willow was still having intestinal issues. Only now they weren't confined to the crate. They were all over the kitchen. I gave him a quick this-is-how-you-mop-the-floor lesson and reminded him of how deep he was in debt to us since we'd forked over serious funds for his latest computer. I promised him we'd be home soon after we squished Addie's dorm room into our little Subaru.

On Sunday, I took Zander and met up with my former foster dog Edith for our first K9&Kds Event. K9&Kds was a program I'd helped create with a group of other OPH volunteers. It was a program to educate kids on how to safely care for and interact with dogs,* but it also shone a light on dog rescue and the good dogs that we'd saved. Doing the research to write the program was somewhat self-serving in that I was desperate to know how to protect myself from being bitten. I was grappling with my newfound fear of dogs, and working on this program was one way to whittle away at it.

Much of what I learned was new to me—dogs can be frightened by people wearing sunglasses or hoodies or baseball hats. Looking them in the eye was a threat, as was approaching them head-on. If I didn't know these things after

---

* One of the most common reasons an adopted dog is returned is because it bit a child, and most of those bites could have been prevented.

more than fifty years of living with dogs, how many other people didn't know them either? It occurred to me that while K9&Kds was designed for children, we would likely be teaching a lot of adults at the same time.

After Zander, we welcomed another new puppy. Hops was ten pounds bigger and at least ten times more trouble than little Zander, who had been adopted by an excited young couple who named him Enzo.* Hops was a gangly, sweet, goofy boy who seemed to grow larger every day. He was forty pounds, but his feet were so big he looked like he was wearing galoshes, so even though he was six months old, he was far from finished growing.

Like a gangly kid in a growth spurt, he routinely ran into doorways and walls and coffee tables, unable to get his long legs out of his own way. He was labeled a lab mix but looked like he was put together with spare parts from a handful of breeds, possibly including shepherd. He had a loose discombobulated swagger that made me smile and think of teenagers trying (and failing) to look cool.

Nothing on the counters was safe. In his first few days with us, he polished off a bar of cream cheese, sampled the newspaper, and [insert frustrated shriek and several curse words] broke my favorite tea mug.†

While Zander had simply stockpiled shoes in his crate, Hops had the ability to do permanent damage if he could just stay focused long enough. Thankfully, some other treasure usually caught his eye and like a severely ADHD youngster he was on to the next adventure in moments. Everyone was learning to put their things away!‡

---

* They created an Instagram account for him—@Enzothelabdog—so I am able to track all his exploits even now.

† The huge handmade pottery tea mug (really a beer stein) held enough tea to get me through a morning of writing.

‡ Somehow even after 107 foster dogs my kids had not learned the importance of securing their belongings.

Hops was very people-oriented and followed me like my big loping sidekick. I quickly dispensed with the leash, as he never left my side and the leash only raised the possibility of him tripping me a hundredfold. He liked to keep one part of his body in contact with me when we were outside for a walk. Even the cat, while interesting, couldn't pull him from my side.

We took Hops to our first adoption event held at Gunpowder Falls, the local brewery just over the hill from us in a small industrial park that also housed a cheerleading and gymnastics studio. Maybe it was time Gunpowder had its own brewery dog, I told Kristin, the taproom manager, as I introduced Hops. This one was meant for them. Conveniently, the owner was away for his daughter's graduation.

As it turned out, Gunpowder was the perfect location for an adoption event. Not only were beer drinkers friendly and generous and not averse to considering adopting a dog, but the families coming in and out of the gymnastics studio had no choice but to follow the siren call of friendly dogs. Hops and the other dogs lapped up the attention.

As summer marched along, I was busy planning my trip south. I mapped out nine shelters and rescues that partnered with OPH scattered throughout North Carolina, South Carolina, Tennessee, and Virginia. Then I looked for nearby metropolitan areas and asked my publisher to set up signings at bookstores in those areas. None of the shelters were very close to the cities. Obviously, the need was greatest in rural areas. As the route began to take shape, I plotted it over and over on Google Maps, writing down distances and times, and searching for friends within reach who might provide housing.

In a different time, book tours were arranged and funded by publishers, but these days that is a rare occurrence for any author not on the *New York Times* best-seller list. These days, the majority of authors have to pitch in on their own promotions. Bookselling is mostly done online, so blogs and websites and social media sites are where the biggest efforts and dollars are spent. If you want to go out and meet the public, you'll likely have to do it on your own dime. To keep costs down, I found friends with guest rooms and planned to pack my lunches. It was exciting and maybe a little bit scary. I'd pledged 10 percent of my proceeds to OPH, but beyond that, I was prepared to spend every last cent of my advance not just promoting my book, but spreading the word about dog rescue, fostering, and the shelters in my path.

16

Unicorns and a Beauty Queen

I t was time to focus on setting up my book launch and book signings, including setting up a new website for the book that included pictures of my former foster dogs and their stories. This meant contacting the adopters, and it was great fun hearing how "my" dogs were doing. I even arranged for some of the dogs to join me at book signings so that they could sign books along with me using an ink pad.

Hops was adopted by a smart young couple with many, many questions. He would be their first dog, and what a good one, I assured them. It was time for another foster dog, which turned out to be two puppies, unicorns actually. What? You don't believe in unicorns? In rescue work, we have them, and they were headed to my house!

It is rare to see hypoallergenic dogs in rescue, rarer still to see hypoallergenic puppies. But my puppy room became home to two miniature poodley pups who reminded me of the shih tzu we had when I was a kid, minus the bulging eyes. They were tiny and precious, and without all that fluff, they'd be no bigger than large rats (but much cuter).

They were smaller than they'd appeared in their pictures—the camera and the fluff added serious bulk. I named them Thing One and Thing Two, the Seuss Boys, because of their wild hair made wilder by their whirling dervish nature. They weighed just three pounds of precious and were only thirteen weeks old.

I was away all day at the PA BookFest on the day of their arrival, so Nick picked them up from a transport arriving from South Carolina. He texted me when they were safely home. Addie (who was once again working for the summer as a Starbucks barista) said they looked like the dogs that fancy women brought into Starbucks in their purses. Ian said they were cute. Nick said they were noisy. I couldn't wait to get home to meet them!

The Seuss boys were more like puppy dolls than dogs. They had bright button eyes and pranced when they moved. Their little tails never stopped wagging, and they spent their days crouched at the doorway to the puppy room, every nerve of their being poised for flight the moment anyone happened by. Getting a picture of them was nearly impossible—every shot I took was a blur. I loved their smallness. The "ferocious" barks were comical instead of annoying. Their poops were so tiny, it was like cleaning up after guinea pigs.

Gracie wasn't sure what to make of them. She watched them and gave her customary snarl greeting, but you could see the confusion in her face. Are they dogs or rodents?

Of course, they already had adopters. In fact, one of them had an approved adopter before he was even loaded on the van in South Carolina. No one in OPH was surprised by this. We knew how rare it was to find a possibly hypoallergenic, miniature dog in rescue, but to find two puppies?! In only a few days, the Seuss Boys had over forty adoption applications!

"We just have the two gerbils . . . Certainly, we can handle another dog . . .," I suggested to Nick over a beer one night.

"Is that a question?" asked Nick, but he knew better than to protest, and he didn't. Especially after he saw Billie Jean. She really was a beauty queen.

Two days after the Seuss Boys arrived, I picked up Billie Jean, a dog who had been in OPH care for over a month. Most of that time was spent in a boarding facility in Virginia because there weren't any foster homes available. I'd seen the pictures posted by other volunteers who had taken her to events or for a sleepover. A boarding facility was no place for this busy heeler mix.

Billie Jean was housebroken and crate-trained and got along with everyone in the house except the cat. Our cat, Hermione, had survived 113 foster dogs to date, but number 114 was almost her undoing. Billie Jean was relentless. She. Must. Chase. Cat. Poor Hermoine began spending more time outside than in, despite the rainy week.

Billie Jean was an Australian cattle dog mix, which meant that she was busy. The dog had things to do and places to go. Her bright, clever mind was always up to something. She loved her toys and, in the absence of a human to engage with her, would play with them by herself—tossing and pouncing and shaking and chasing.

Billie Jean became my devotee, shadowing me everywhere, even waiting outside the bathroom door. Maybe the quality I appreciated most about her, though, was that she was quiet. When the dogs watched out the window as the barn cat streaked across the yard, Gracie would bark for twenty minutes even after the cat was long gone, but Billie Jean just watched the spot where the cat disappeared into the woods, silently. She knew better than to waste her voice.

Ian quickly fell in love with Billie Jean, giving her lots of extra attention. He even let her hang out in his room. I couldn't remember the last time a foster dog was invited into that space.

The unicorns' time with us went quickly. Puppy fostering protocol dictated that they stay with us for two weeks to ensure they were healthy, happy, and ready to go to their forever homes. But their continued presence was tough on the rescue. It was finally decided that they be taken off the website since the influx of applications was clogging the system. Applications were processed in the order in which they're received, so their applications were delaying the adoption of plenty of other dogs.

I think having these rare little guys was good and bad for the rescue. They certainly garnered a lot of attention and an unprecedented number of applications. This was good because it introduced OPH to a lot of new potential adopters which would hopefully translate to saving more dogs. The bad part was that inevitably many of the applicants for these precious pups would be disappointed. It couldn't be helped, but it didn't take away the sting for people who had their hearts set on those Muppet lookalikes.

For that I was sorry, but I hoped the people who were ready to open their hearts and homes to a new puppy would keep looking and be open to the many hornless unicorns we had available. Because while I said these puppies were unicorns because they were rare and special, by definition that meant we had an entire website full of unicorns, because every dog was rare and special. They were all good dogs for the right person.

17

Fame

I'm pretty sure there is truth in this equation: Book success = more dogs.

One Tuesday night, one week before the book was released, Nick and I had a date to see a show at the same summer theater where Addie had performed for so many years. Nick had just arrived home from work, and as I waited for him to change, I checked my e-mail one last time. The book was less than a week from publication and reviews were starting to come in. I was also surreally in a back-and-forth with the arts editor at the *New York Post* for the piece she was writing about my book and foster dogs.

Then a text popped up from my friend Mer: I am sitting in the waiting area at my mom's hairdresser and look what I found!

What followed was a picture of the People's Picks section in *People* magazine, and one of the books featured was mine! Right there. In *People* magazine. I wanted to run out and buy a copy of the magazine, but we were already late for the show, so I turned my phone off and we headed to the theater. The show was wonderful, but as I watched, little internal text messages kept going off inside my head: *People* magazine! My book! OMG!

After the show, Nick and I raced to the local Rutter's to buy a copy of the magazine and went home to open champagne. That night was the first inkling I had that this book was going to take me places I'd never been before.

With the unicorns finally launched and the stress of the book piling up, what I needed was more puppies! And after I learned that a photographer for the *New York Post* would be coming to our house for a photo shoot, I decided to foster another dog too. Maybe I could hide behind the chaos of too many dogs.

"You really are becoming that crazy dog lady," said Nick.

"They will keep me sane," I reassured him.

On Friday night, we picked up three darling pups who were one half of the Breakfast Pups. Adding to the carb theme (the other pups in the litter who had gone to a different foster home were Waffles and Pancake), we named them Biscuit, Muffin, and Grits. They were chocolate-colored houndish lab-looking dogs—basically, dogs with long tails and long ears and plenty of happy energy who had seriously powerful noses.

Their supershort, sleek coats glistened. They arrived smelly, so before we'd even been properly introduced they landed in the mudroom sink. Thankfully, they liked water and didn't mind the baths at all. This was especially good as I was bathing them at 11:30 at night. They were joyful, sweet pups who loved toys and romped, wrestled, and sometimes argued, but snuggled together in a little spoon line when they slept. They were gangly with big feet and weighed nearly fourteen pounds each. If they truly were only seven weeks old, then they were going to be seriously big dogs.

This time of year, shelters are full to bursting and have to make hard decisions, so we'd also picked up an extra dog to add to our pack. And in a cosmic karma payback, the extra dog turned out to be one of the nicest we'd ever fostered. Snoopy was a dream—gorgeous, sweet, mostly housebroken, crate-trained, not a barker, loved people, loved other dogs, and (so far) was only mildly interested in the cat. His rescue name was Barkalona, but since that was a mouthful and I couldn't seem to remember it, we tried out other names like Baloney and Barko, and Ian called him Long Nose because of his rather elongated pointy nose, but he looked like a Snoopy, so that was what stuck.

Snoopy was listed as a border collie, but I was doubtful about that heritage. He had hound ears and a hound's sniffing habits, and he swaggered with loose hips on long, long legs. When he ran he pranced a bit, as if he knew just how gorgeous he was.* Really, though, it didn't matter—he was one fabulous dog.

As I headed into the launch week for *Another Good Dog*, our house was full of dogs. And this was good. Dogs calmed me, and with the hype level starting to crank on the book, spending all my free moments walking dogs or playing with puppies or doing all the tasks necessary to help these precious souls find their families was just what I needed. It was a daily reminder of why I wrote the book—to help another good dog find its home.

Having a photographer who is regularly paid $10,000 per shoot come to my messy, dog-filled house on a scorching hot day to take my picture was not something I ever imagined happening in my lifetime, and yet it did. Sean was incredibly nice and easy to work with and treated me like I was a Disney princess (who he actually photographed regularly). He handled dogs leaping on him well for someone who admitted he wasn't necessarily a dog person.

For two hours, he posed me with dogs, without dogs, on the porch, on the deck, by the barn, with Nick, with my kids, and then sitting in a hammock with a lapful of puppies. That hammock shot, one of the last of the day when my shirt was sticking to me with sweat and my hair was fuzzy, of course, that was the shot that landed in the Arts section of the *New York Post*.

My friend Nancy, who adopted my fiftieth foster dog, Edith, and is a professional photographer herself, was here to act as an assistant holding lights and moving stuff out of the way. When it was all said and done, the two of us relaxed in the puppy yard with a beer and our herd of dogs.

---

* So gorgeous he landed on the cover of this book!

"That was cool," she said. "He was really good."

Cool was probably not my word for it, but I was happy it was over. I was, perhaps, irrationally self-consciousness about my appearance. At fifty-two I avoided looking at or having pictures taken of myself. It was hard to reconcile the image I had in my brain with the woman whose freckles were finally being upstaged by wrinkles, whose hair was straight as a board one day and fuzzy as a Muppet's the next, and who weighed twenty pounds more than she had before the baby (who was now sixteen!).

Promoting my new book and the message I felt so passionately about—how fostering dogs would save lives—was going to require I have my picture taken again and again. Little did I know at that point it would also mean I'd be on television multiple times, too. I needed to accept that this was me at fifty-two, and no, it wasn't how I wished I looked, but there was no fighting time and, really, did I want to let my vanity stand in the way of getting this message out or enjoying the opportunities that would come with the publication of the book? It was a battle I would fight daily in the coming months.

Puppies are easy to place, so our house would soon empty out and give me plenty of space to stress about the book tour. Snoopy would be adopted the next weekend, and as soon as we got their tummies right, the Breakfast Pups would be right behind him.* Among all the puppy-ness, I worried that Billie Jean was being overlooked. With a heart of gold and whip-smart, that dog was a keeper, but maybe a bit too intense for many.

The book officially launched with a party at the little brewery just over our hill and included adoptable dogs, dogs featured in the book, and even the cover girl—one of Edith's puppies, Harriet Beecher Stowe, all grown up! I'd brought an ink pad along, and the dogs signed copies of the book while guests enjoyed beer and scrumptious food prepared by my ever-supportive-even-if-we-aren't-dog-people book club.†

---

* Like many shelter dogs, they arrived harboring plenty of worms, and the battle to rid them had created some pretty horrendous diarrhea. Yes, even when you're an almost-famous writer who has graced the likes of *People* magazine and the *New York Post*, you still have to scrape puppy poop off the floors and walls.

† Although many of them were and the ones who weren't were leaning in that direction.

The party went off without a hitch except for one passing thunderstorm that drenched everyone who couldn't squeeze under the tent. Distracted by the storm, I forgot all about the cake I'd spent days agonizing over, which featured the cover of the book emblazoned across the top. Still, it was a beautiful evening and an appropriate launch for the book tour that would begin in earnest the very next day and continue for two months.

18

And . . . Go!

Many of my book signings were within driving distance, so being "on tour" didn't generally necessitate I spend nights away, just that I spend the days driving so many miles that I eventually drove our poor little Subaru right into the ground.

I had so much help and support that most days I couldn't say thank you enough, and truth be told, I felt a bit guilty. I was being praised for all my work as a foster and for how many dogs I'd saved, but I knew of so many amazing people at OPH and its partner shelters who were doing so much more than me and my little foster home. I was grateful I could do what I could, but I knew it was only because of so many other people, not the least of whom were Nick and my kids, who had suffered through the poop and the plunder that the book made out to be funny.

At event after event, adopters and some of my previous foster dogs joined me, making each signing feel like a reunion. My very first foster dog ever showed up at a signing at a brewery in Baltimore, along with several of the Hamilton puppies, a litter named after the characters from the show who still got together annually for a birthday party. That event was extra special because Snoopy's new family met us there to officially adopt him.

The event was so much fun it ran a few minutes over, so I was pressed for time as I headed into beltway traffic. I was scheduled to do a live phone interview with *Talkin' Pets*, a nationally syndicated radio talk show, at 5:10 P.M.

At 5:03, I'd just crossed the state line into Pennsylvania and had a serious dilemma. I had to pee. There was not enough time to make it home before the interview, so I swung into the Pennsylvania Welcome Center and prayed my phone wouldn't ring while I was in the crowded bathroom. I'd just returned to my car when the host's assistant called, so I sat in the rest area watching parents wrestle with children, truckers smoke cigarettes, and dogs do their business as I was interviewed for the first time live on national radio.

Being the queen of best-laid plans, I generally choose to assume the best. The way I see it is why waste all that negative emotion dreading and worrying and stressing something when you can instead bask in the view from your rose-colored glasses?

We were now four days away from the start of my southern book/shelter tour, the one in which I would drive an enormous cargo van stuffed with donations south, crisscrossing six states for ten days visiting bookstores and shelters. Billie Jean and Grits were still at our house. I had promised Nick that all of the foster dogs would be gone when I left for the big tour. I expected that the puppies would be adopted and long gone, and I never expected Billie Jean to be here all summer. She was so adoptable.

The girl pups had been snapped up, as I'd predicted, but their little brother lingered, stealing my heart on a daily basis. He was funny and happy and sweet, sweet, sweet. His long, silky ears were just so petable—like a stress ball, only better, and I fingered them while worrying through the list in my head of tour preparations. I couldn't keep Grits; I needed to leave room in my heart for all the dogs to come. As luck or fate would have it, an adopter material-ized on the eve of my trip and I said a quick good-bye while packing the van.

I almost succeeded in fulfilling my promise. Billie Jean's potential adopters were scheduled to meet her the day after I left on tour. I assured Nick there was no way they would pass and sent up a silent prayer for some adoption magic.*

My heart was Christmas-Eve-excited as I lay in bed the night before we left on tour. I couldn't wait to see the places where my dogs had come from and meet the people who had first saved them.

I'd be traveling for most of the tour with my dear friend Lisa, who had volunteered to keep me company on the road. We packed a cooler of cheeses and fruit and peanut butter and even a few bottles of wine for our adventure and hit the road early on a Saturday morning headed for Arlington, Virginia, with high hopes and a van full of donations for the shelters.

Lisa and I have been friends ever since our boys connected over identical Halloween costumes when they were preschoolers. Thirteen years later, both those boys now tower over us. We've been PTA copresidents and briefly ran a business together making and selling beaded jewelry. She'd helped me through Ian's initial diagnosis with alopecia, a rocky time in my life, and had been my indomitable cheerleader as I launched my writing career.

Lisa is a powerfully positive person whose company and counsel I have sought time and again. We've shared books, recipes, parenting advice, and plenty of wine and laughter, plus book club, bootcamp at the Y, girls' weekends, and even several rainy camping trips. As a teen, she was Ms. Federalsburg and a cheerleader, and she still radiated that beauty pageant queen aura. Lisa was a positive force in the lives of everyone around her and brightened any room with her presence. She had a knack for finding the silver lining in a situation, but she also had a soft heart that produced tears at a moment's notice when she encountered any kind of cruelty or injustice.

What Lisa was not, was a dog person. Over the years, she'd accepted my animal habit. Tentatively petting my foster dogs, happily cuddling puppies, and tacitly avoiding my cats. She listened to my dog stories and nodded, but I always knew that she was just humoring me, more or less astounded at the

---

* I've always believed in adoption magic—that sometimes dogs hang around longer than necessary because the right people aren't ready for them yet. Billie Jean was so special, and she deserved the right people.

detail of my observations concerning the latest foster dog. Still, she supported my dog habit and even carried my book in her shop, Soul Shine, an adorable boutique that sold unique clothing and handcrafted jewelry with a positive message.

Our van was crammed to the ceiling with over a thousand pounds of dog kibble and over a thousand cans of dog food, plus cat food, cat litter, bleach, sheets, towels, blankets, cleaning supplies, collars, leashes, toys, and treats. The generosity of my dog-hearted community overwhelmed me.

Driving the nearly overloaded van* felt more like steering a ship. Its weight and height demanded that I not make any sudden moves, so we cruised in the slow lane all the way to Virginia. As we crept up the streets of Arlington, I pondered whether I would be able to parallel park our behemoth and was relieved when we spied the Humane Society of Arlington with its large, mostly empty parking lot. I waded into a shady spot and then knocked on the door to ask permission to leave the van there for the day.

The Wags n' Whiskers Festival was in full swing when we arrived. Colorful tents lined the center of the cobblestone outdoor mall full of upscale shops and restaurants. Vendors offered gourmet dog treats, custom collars, handmade dog clothes, and unique toys. Others offered services like grooming, walking, doggie day care, training, and even pet funerals. OPH and many other rescues had brought out adoptable dogs and educational information.

We found the OPH booth, and I introduced Lisa to the volunteers in our booth, as well as Jen, the founder of the rescue. Two large dogs, still essentially puppies, began wrestling in the booth, eventually upending the water bowl and knocking into the book table we were setting up. One nearly slipped his collar as volunteers scrambled to separate them.

"Should I be wearing an OPH T-shirt?" Lisa asked.

"It's okay," I told her. "You're fine."

"Well, I'm just gonna take a look around," she said and disappeared to explore the festival.

---

* Nick had calculated our load before we left to be sure the van wouldn't collapse under its weight, and we were under the limit, but not by much.

As the day wore on, we chatted with the dog-loving public as they passed by with pampered pets in strollers and backpacks, on leather leashes, wearing hair bows, glittery collars, and cushioned harnesses. I signed books and OPH collected donations. Local US military servicemen and -women had volunteered to help at our booth, holding the leashes of some of our adoptable dogs. It was a fun day.

That night we stayed with a college friend of Lisa's just outside of Richmond. We enjoyed delicious food, excellent wine, and great company, relaxing on their outdoor patio. It was the perfect start to our adventure. I thought, This is gonna be great.

19

Warning Signs

The next day was National Dog Day,* and we would appropriately be signing books at the Barnes & Noble in Richmond in the company of adoptable dogs brought out by OPH volunteers. Before the event, Lisa and I met with Laurie, the director of OPH, to talk about our upcoming shelter visits. We'd scheduled about two shelter visits per day between signings. I was excited to meet the people I'd only heard about and to see the dogs and the shelters.

Laurie warned us that it might be hard to see some of the situations. "Call me," she said, "if you need to talk about it."

She was so serious, so concerned. I nodded and assured her we'd be fine, but inside, a tiny warning bell went off. Remarkable, I know, but I was oblivious and so distracted by my book's launch, my good friend's presence, and the

---

* Who decides these things? I've always wondered that. There is also National Puppy Day, National Black Dog Day, and National Pet Day. Odds are there is also National Retriever Day and National Weiner Dog Day, and maybe even National Dog That Rolls in Horse Poop Day (that's Gracie's day).

fun we'd been having so far. Yes, yes, the shelters would be sad, I thought, but we have a van stuffed with donations. That should brighten their day!

"I'm sure you'll want to bring them all home," she said.

I nodded. "We're picking up six dogs at Scott County. I don't think we can fit anymore."

Scott County, Virginia, along the Tennessee border, would be our last shelter visit. I'd already worked with Mindy, the OPH staffer who pulled* from Scott, to select six dogs for the fosters who were available. We'd have an empty van by the time we reached Scott and had brought along crates to pick up our six dogs. It would be my first transport and one of the parts of the trip I was most looking forward to. Though at that point, it was nine days away, so it was hard to imagine.

Laurie asked me to be on the lookout for a "wiggly-butt" pit bull. A dog that could be a good representative of the breed. Yes, she knew it would need special approval from OPH's board, but if I found one (or two), I should let her know and she'd see what she could do. OPH, like many rescues, struggled to find adopters for dogs who looked like pit bulls, which meant they didn't pull very many because it usually meant a long time in a foster home, preventing us from pulling other dogs. Laurie, like me, has a heart for pit bulls, so she was always looking for opportunities to move the needle on attitudes about the "breed."

"It's going to be hard," she said again. "Call me if you need to talk about any of it."

Her words made me hesitate, but only for a moment, and then we were back on the Thelma & Louise adventure, signing books and meeting people and cuddling adoptable dogs.

Just before the event at Barnes & Noble started, Nick called. In my absence, he'd had to handle the meet and greet for Billie Jean. The family looked good on paper and had asked lots of great questions and now they were at my house in Pennsylvania. We'd been driving through Richmond in search of the tiny

---

* When rescues arrange with a shelter to take one of their dogs, it's called "pulling" that dog, so the people responsible for working with the shelters and making those decisions are called "shelter pullers."

vegan-friendly restaurant where we were to meet Laurie when the meet and greet started. Nick had texted during the process to let me know how it was going and Lisa read the texts out loud to me, essentially a play-by-play.

Billie loves them, especially the kid.

Nice family. Would be great home.

Husband seems hesitant.

They're having a conference.

Billie's being really good.

Might be a no-go. Can't tell.

Then radio silence until just before the signing, when my phone rang with the good news that Billie Jean had been adopted. I didn't have time to dwell on it, but I was a little sad that I didn't get to tell her good-bye or meet her new family.

I mugged for a few pictures with the sign announcing my visit outside the store and then spied Homeboy, who'd come to sign books with me. It was such a treat to see her,* and she spent the entire event sleeping at my feet between signings. Her wonderful mama, Jennifer, had driven several hours to Richmond and even coached her on having her paw handled so that Homeboy (now Nahla) could sign books with me.†

As I was signing books, a woman about my age turned up in front of my table and stood there smiling knowingly. It took me a moment and then her name came back quickly: Allison, the friend I had spent hours sharing dreams with in high school—she was going to be a dancer, and I think at that point in my life, I was going to be a horse trainer. My fondest memory of her was creating an elaborate scheme to invite the boys we had crushes on to go with us to the Sadie Hawkins dance. We'd made formal requests on parchment scrolls and enlisted our younger brothers to act as messengers, presenting them

---

* No, that's not a typo. Homeboy is a girl—and the star of one of the more embarrassing stories you can find in my book *Another Good Dog: One Family and Fifty Foster Dogs*.

† This was my first Barnes & Noble signing, and I was happy to discover that the universal carpet in nearly every B&N I encountered from then on was a wonderful inked-pawprint-hiding pattern that would conceal the fact that getting the washable ink off paws is nearly impossible with a squirming dog and a wet wipe.

to our potential dates one evening on their doorsteps complete with trumpet announcement, while we giggled from our car, parked around the corner. Both guys said yes, and neither turned out to be more than a one-dance date, but it wasn't about the dance anyway, it was the fun we had creating the ask. These days elaborate "asks" seem to be all the rage for proms, but thirty-five years ago, we were charting new waters. There was barely time for a hug and a quick exchange of life stats, but Allison was the first of many people who would emerge from my past when I signed books in towns all over the country.

After the signing, we made a quick exit, since we still had a long drive ahead. The good luck wishes and hugs had to be brief, but I was touched by how many of my OPH family had come all the way to Richmond to see us off and celebrate the book.

Back in the van, Lisa and I headed to Virginia Beach to visit one of my oldest friends from childhood. It promised to be a night of decadent food and plenty of wine. The trip was starting out just as I imagined it, but the next day all that would change.

20

Rescue Gets Real

O n Monday morning we woke to regret the feast and the wine we'd
had the night before with Lisbeth and Paul. Admirably and despite
the late evening and festivities, both of them had already headed out
to work. I made a cup of tea and sat in their sunroom thinking about the
coming week. I was so glad to have Lisa's company. Originally, I'd planned
to make the trip alone, or bring along a dog, but the logistics of that plan
proved unwise. When I'd casually mentioned the idea of joining me on
the trip, I was certain Lisa would say no, but gosh I was glad to have her
along, and in the days ahead her presence would make what we saw and
learned bearable.

We set off for Lenoir County SPCA in Kinston, North Carolina. The
drive from Virginia Beach to Kinston took us past the Great Dismal Swamp
to a town of strip malls and scattered houses. Stubby pine trees, rusted out
cars, and the obvious relics of more prosperous times were littered alongside
the narrow, flat roads. After a few wrong turns, we finally located the SPCA,
just past the highway and the railroad tracks, beside a water tower on a tiny

lot surrounded by scrub trees and swampland. It was a small brick building with a storage pod in the parking lot.

After a quick introduction to Helen, the rescue coordinator, I raced for the bathroom, as there hadn't been an appropriate place to stop to pee on our way into town. The tiny staff bathroom was dimly lit and lined with shoes and boots. A large roach scrambled across the floor and I squished it with my foot. Starring at its mashed body, listening to the cacophony of barking on the other side of the door, overwhelmed by the smell of cat urine and disinfectant, the reality of what we were doing finally hit. This wasn't another fun stop on a girls' road trip. This was serious. This was real. What did I think I could accomplish showing up with a few cases of dog food and some cat litter? I took a deep breath and tried to make out my reflection in the chipped mirror. I was no reporter, no activist, what was I doing here? It was much easier to be a "rescuer" in my happy house tucked into the hillside in Pennsylvania. What could I possibly do here besides interrupt their busy day and gawk at the situation?

I caught up with Helen and Lisa and was introduced to Sherry, the young apple-cheeked blonde who ran Lenoir. She smiled and waved from where she was supervising work in the medical area. Helen promised we'd have time to talk with Sherry after our tour.

We followed Helen through a narrow hallway made narrower by the stacks of crates filled with kittens. When I pulled out my phone to take a picture, Helen said, "Oh, don't take pictures of those crates, it's against regulations for them to be here, but we don't have anywhere else to put them." The kennels were beyond capacity. The puppy room was crammed with puppies and small dogs and one dog who had given birth the night before. The cat room was overflowing, hence the kittens in the hallway.

Helen led us through the noisy row of indoor kennels and then outside to see the rest of the adult dog population. They lived in chain-link fence kennels attached to the side of the building and another row freestanding across from them under a line of trees. The kennels had concrete floors; some had small igloo doghouses for shelter, others relied on the tarps that covered the tops of the kennels or the tin roof attached to the side of the building. It was sweltering that day, but I considered what a North Carolina winter was like living outside in these kennels. Was it legal to keep dogs outdoors all the time? I naively wondered. Clearly, the rules were different down here.

There was another set of tall kennels in the center of the dirt yard filled with dogs, and Helen said, "Those are the emergency kennels for Animal Control to use when they drop off dogs after hours. There shouldn't be dogs in there." And yet there were.

As if on cue, an Animal Control officer pulled in with two more dogs. Sherry hurried out to meet them with her microchip gun to scan in vain, as it was rare to find a chipped dog, Helen told us. I watched as Sherry shook her head and lifted one of the dogs out of the back of the truck.

"Where will she put those?" I asked Helen.

"I have no idea," she said, knowingly. Sherry was a magician when it came to making room, that much was clear. When the choice came down to violating a fire code or destroying a dog, it was easy.

Helen and Sherry were the first heroes we would meet on our trip. Helen was a volunteer who worked full-time as a court reporter and spent every other hour at Lenoir evaluating dogs and locating rescues all over the country to take them. As she introduced us to dog after dog, the twinkle in her eye gave away the love she had for every one of them, but her practical, knowledgeable words made it clear she knew exactly how hard her job was. Still, she was hopeful and proud of how far they had come at Lenoir.

Lenoir takes in about one hundred dogs a month. It was nearly the end of August that morning and I asked how many they'd adopted out.

"We've adopted out three so far this month," she said.

That was the norm in this impoverished community. Most of the dogs' only chance was to be pulled by a rescue, so Helen worked her contacts, logging hours through e-mail, Facebook, and phone calls finding rescues who were willing to take dogs. She spent as much time as she could with all the dogs, evaluating them for behavior and personality so that she could tell rescues as much as she could about each dog.

I asked Helen if they had any "wiggly-butt" pit bulls. She knew exactly what I meant and led me to a kennel where a black-and-white pit bull was leaping frantically to get our attention. She lunged at the fence, again and again, barking hysterically.

"That's not who she is," said Helen, by way of explanation. "If I brought her out, you'd see."

"Can we do that?" I asked.

She nodded. "Yes. I've got another I want you to meet also."

She introduced me to Zilla, a big, sweet boy who was heartworm positive and had been at Lenoir since March. A male dog as big and burly as he was who was also heartworm positive would be challenging to adopt out or find rescue; it was a miracle that he was still alive, or maybe a testimony to the will of Helen.

We headed back inside to talk to Sherry, who was busy accepting a cat and her litter of kittens from a woman who'd found them by the side of the road. Sherry cuddled one kitten under her chin and directed another shelter employee to go back out to the woman's car. "There's one in the cup holder and another behind the seat."

After the little family was settled in, Sherry sat down with us in the sliver of shade along the side of the building that faced the woods. It was late morning and already brutally hot. As we talked, it was clear that Sherry was smart and dedicated to her impossible job. She had an enormous heart and an easy smile. The stream of need was endless at Lenoir.

I told Sherry about our van loaded with donations and asked, "What can we do for you? What do you need?"

She shook her curly head, overcome with emotion, glancing up at the blue sky trying to blink back tears. "Everything?"

I prompted her and Helen for specifics and they said, "Something for the fleas would be amazing. Maybe Capstar?"

Lisa scribbled down everything they said, and I swallowed my shock to learn that the county doesn't provide flea or tick treatment or heartworm preventatives for these dogs living outdoors under the trees, alongside a mosquito-infested swampland. They also didn't provide dewormers, which meant the shelter staff was fighting a losing battle and likely feeding twice as much food as they needed to worm-riddled dogs and cats.

"Milk replacer is another thing we don't have. I'm always running to the store for it."

Milk replacer, like treats and toys and bedding, was not included in the shelter budget, so the staff bought it out of their own pockets unless it came in through donations.

One of the shelter staff came around the back of the building with Vanna, the black-and-white pit bull, on a leash. She wagged her tail and just as Helen promised, wiggled her butt, rolling in the grass with joy as I petted her. She licked my hand and smiled at all of us.

"I'd love to take you home," I told Vanna. I snapped pictures and took a short video. "I'll do what I can to get OPH to pull her," I promised Helen.

"I've got one more I want you to meet," Helen said. I imagined she always had one more.

I said good-bye to Vanna and the shelter employee brought out another pit bull. This one was brindle—chocolate and black. She was terrified to be out of her kennel. The employee had to carry her out, she was too afraid to walk. When he set her down, she pressed herself to the ground, pulling all her limbs beneath her. I stroked her back and she licked my hand and wagged her tail, but she wouldn't stand.

"She's such a sweetie. She needs to get out of here," said Helen.

Clearly, she did. Whether she was a timid dog when she came in or the stress of shelter life was breaking her down, I didn't know. As much as my heart wanted to pull this dog, I remembered Laurie's words. Like Zilla and Vanna and so many of the others we'd just seen, she was too big, too bully, too hard to find a foster home for, let alone an adopter. It wouldn't be easy to get OPH to pull any of those dogs based simply on their stats. Would any rescue step up?

I didn't blame OPH. I understood that they were different from many rescues because they didn't have a building and they relied on volunteers, like me, untrained for the most part, learning as we go. They could only save dogs they had foster homes for, and most of our fosters had children and pets of their own; some lived in apartments or townhomes. Many couldn't take large dogs or bully breeds. Even when there was an available home, they were hard to adopt out, and saving one meant not saving dozens of animals that could be fostered and adopted in the time that one large bully breed dog spent languishing in a foster home. I thought of Gala; she was part pit bull and pretty big. How did she make it north? Yes, the guidelines made sense, but it didn't change the reality of what we were seeing—sweet, deserving dogs in kennel after kennel.

I couldn't save the pretty brindle girl or Zilla, but maybe I could save Vanna. I began sending photos and videos of my encounter with Vanna to Laurie and the shelter pullers at OPH. "We can't take her without a committed foster," was the reaction. So, I wrote about her on my blog and posted her on Facebook. Who can foster this sweet pup? Who will save her life? Words were my only weapon in this war to save dogs, and what I saw each day of the tour only sharpened my sword.

Visiting this clearly overwhelmed shelter, meeting so many dogs in desperate need of rescue and leaving them with nothing but our sympathy and a few supplies was maddening. Helen and Sherry were working so very hard at a problem that only seemed to grow. They were shoveling sand as fast as they could, trying to move an endless beach being constantly replenished by a vast ocean. They seemed like the only thing standing between so many good dogs and certain death. But they were only two people, and one of them was a volunteer. How had it come to this and why did the community, the government, any of us, allow it? I would do everything I could to support them and to spread the word, but it was going to take MUCH more than my little shelter/book tour.

Driving from Lenoir to our next stop, A Shelter Friend rescue, Lisa and I didn't listen to a podcast or turn on music. We both sat with our own thoughts and watched the monotonous flat landscape of the rural South. I don't know what Lisa was thinking, but I was trying to grasp the enormity of the problem. I don't remember the roads we traveled or the hours that passed. I was lost in the vast sadness etched on the large, wide, scarred face of a gray pit bull I'd met. Face after face paraded through my mind. So many dogs, some racing around their kennels, but many shut down, quiet, confused. Would they still be alive in a week? In a month? Who would give them their chance? And who abandoned them to this fate?

Searching for our next stop, we crept up a narrow road lined by cornfields. We were in Bladen County, North Carolina, an impoverished county filled with tobacco fields and chicken farms. This was where I would finally meet a woman I'd been hearing about since my first days in rescue—Silvia Kim. Not only was she a rescue legend within OPH circles, but I'd also read about her in Kim Kavin's book *Little Boy Blue*. Kim is a talented journalist who adopted a rescue puppy and, intrigued by his story, followed the trail of his rescue south to Silvia. Silvia has single-handedly saved thousands of dogs and cats in Bladen County, a forgotten place just past the swamps of North Carolina.

Silvia was a tiny, energetic woman who hugged us upon introduction. She told us not to mind Tom, the turkey that squawked at us as we climbed out of the van. She walked us around the property and introduced us to dozens of dogs and cats. She knew every name, every story. We were tailed by a flock of ducks and geese—and Tom—all following Silvia like the poultry Pied Piper. Occasionally, an employee or volunteer would appear with a question or a kitten; Silvia's knowledge and energy were impressive. Her directions were quick and decisive, and more than once she rolled her eyes and sighed before patiently explaining how to deworm the new cat or which kennel needed the repair. Clearly, her heart had seen every awful thing people were capable of doing to an animal. She'd been in this business since before OPH existed and told me that the first time Laurie (one of the original founders of OPH) came to A Shelter Friend, she cleaned out their shelter, taking every dog.

The dogs lived outside in kennels set up in a concrete pavilion, the sides open to the weather. Silvia paused to exchange kisses with some, ran her hand along the fence offering a touch to others, stopped to refill a water bowl. She took me inside one kennel with a friendly little hound to show me the chew-proof doghouses that she desperately needed. They were metal and cost about $250 each—the dogs' only protection against the weather. If she used cheaper kennels, the dogs chewed them, and if the county inspectors saw chew marks on a doghouse, Silvia would be cited. I wondered but didn't ask, why chew marks on a doghouse were a danger to the health of dogs who'd been rescued from the kill list at the county shelter.

Silvia pulled most of her animals from the county shelter in Bladenboro on Mondays because they euthanize on Tuesdays. We met an elderly dog with sores and growths all over his body, his bones protruding, much of his hair gone. He smiled at us and was clearly thrilled to see Silvia. When his owners surrendered him to the shelter in Bladenboro, they adopted a kitten to take home instead. Silvia shook her head and muttered, "People." She led us down the row of kennels, ticking off the sad, sad stories, and then around to the back of the property to see two parvo puppies she'd impossibly saved. We walked through the cat trailer, full to bursting with cats and kittens, and apparently, ringworm, an endless battle in many shelters.

This was only our first day. My heart ached already, and there were seven more shelters to visit. It was hard and sad and deeply frustrating that all we could do again was offer a few bags of food and some supplies, which would likely be used up before we even finished our tour. What I wished I had more of was hope. Hope that this situation would change. Hope that the message of spay and neuter would begin to gain traction. That people would stop giving up on dogs who never gave up on us—even though we let them down again and again.

I didn't have answers, only words. Writing from the Comfort Inn in Lumberton, North Carolina, I struggled to find those words. I wanted to share what we were seeing and feeling, but my head and my heart were overwhelmed, my soul completely worn through with images of dog after dog and the desperate need. How was it that I didn't know this was happening? Or maybe I did know, but I didn't understand. It was one thing to say that I foster dogs that come from shelters where dogs are dying; it was another entirely to meet those dogs.

I posted the addresses of Lenoir and A Shelter Friend on Facebook and listed their needs, but what we really needed were more foster homes, more rescues. Helen said again and again, "What many of these dogs need is just more time, but without rescues to take them, we can't give that to them." She and Sherry and Silvia were working so very hard to save every dog, but if we gave them more resources, more support, more time, would it ever be enough? Or would the endless stream of unwanted dogs dumped at shelters for reasons as shallow as not paying someone to care for it while on vacation or we just got new carpeting or he's too old/big/noisy/in the way only eat up those resources and keep on coming?

That whole day, and even when I lay down to sleep, in my mind, and sometimes out loud, I kept asking, What is wrong with people? I didn't know the answer to that question. I wanted to believe that the people who had filled our van to the ceiling with donations, the women like Silvia, Helen, and Sherry, who gave everything they had to the dogs in their care, and the efforts of rescues like OPH full of foster families who blindly took in animals they had never met, could one day outnumber the others. I believed we were keeping the tide from rising any higher, but would we ever turn that tide?

That night, after writing out all my thoughts and having a long hot shower to wash off the dog hair of the hundreds of dogs I had met and a cold beer at the Mexican restaurant across the highway from our hotel, all I wanted to do was sleep. But Lisa insisted, "You have to tell them." She was intent on doing a Facebook Live video to share how we were feeling right then. It was so much bigger than the two of us, and all I wanted to do was wake up and start over, but my dear friend, who has one of the givingest hearts I know, wouldn't rest.

"I look horrible," I pleaded. My hair was wet; I was wearing my pajamas; I was done.

"That's not important," she insisted, not denying that truth, but not allowing me to hide behind vanity.

Finally, I relented, and she started the video, introducing it with her apple-pie-happy persona and then turning the camera on me. I hesitated, afraid to even look at the camera, but then I started talking, spilling out all we saw—the old, abandoned dog with the sores, the kennels at Lenoir open to the elements and filled with pit bull faces, Silvia's unrelenting energy, Sherry's tears, and Helen's superhuman resilience. I wanted them to know that this was happening. Right now. In North Carolina, not that far from where many were planning to vacation.

When it was over, we went to bed. In the morning there were hundreds of comments and thousands of views. But the problem remained the same, and so we drove on to another shelter, one that would break the pieces of my already broken heart.

21

The Difference
One Hour Makes

Tuesday morning we headed for Charlotte, North Carolina. I was excited to get to Charlotte, not because of the book event planned, but because I would see friends I hadn't seen in years. We were going to stay with my college friend Eli* and his husband, Greg. Eli was one of my favorite people in all the world. His humor and unabashedly honest heart were and still are a rarity. I've saved every letter he's written to me because his voice and his presence carry right through the paper. It had been over fifteen years since I'd seen him last.

In addition to catching up with Eli, I'd planned to meet with some other friends for dinner before my book signing event—adults who were kids the last time I saw them and now had spouses and children and jobs. When I

---

* Although when I met him, his name was Rod, so that's what I called him when I saw him, but for the book's purposes he is Eli (even if he's still Rod in my heart).

thought of them, they still had acne and teenage angst, and I wondered if I would recognize them. As we drove toward Charlotte, I got another text from Barb, a dear friend who had recently moved to the Winston-Salem area and planned to drive down to see us. The party just got bigger and bigger as Nick informed me that one of his coworkers who lived in Charlotte was also planning to come to the signing to meet me.

But first, we would stop to visit Anson County Animal Shelter. It was an hour outside of Charlotte, but it might as well have been on the moon. The bright paint couldn't mask the aura of despair. The kennels were overflowing, the dogs desperate for attention. Maureen, the director, told us she had no fosters, very few volunteers. She seemed defeated as she explained that no one came to walk the dogs or play with the kitties or take pictures or help Maureen with moving dogs out through rescue.

I would later learn that Anson, like too many shelters, had succumbed to personality conflicts, ignorance, and agendas, a problem much too common in a world where people are driven by their passion and not a paycheck. There had been a crisis, complicated and ultimately deadly for too many dogs. There was plenty of fault to pass around, but Maureen, as the paid staff, was the only one still at the shelter, effectively the last woman standing and ultimately, at that moment, a one-woman show.

There were too many dogs at Anson; they were at capacity. We knew what that meant. As Maureen led us through the buildings, the sound and the stench were overwhelming. The dogs began to blur together, but one dog, Oreo, a fifty-pound male boxer mix with black patches over his eyes, drew me back to his kennel again and again. When I put my hand against the fence, he would place his face against it and sigh, remaining there for as long as I did. He wanted so desperately to be touched; he didn't bark or whine or jump at the fence, he simply watched me, the sadness in his eyes bringing tears to my own. I wanted to save this dog, but I knew, like Vanna and all the others, he didn't fall within the parameters of what OPH would normally pull. There were at least a hundred dogs at the Anson shelter, and Oreo had been there too long already. "I'm gonna do all I can, buddy," I told him. "All I can." But I knew, even then, "all I can" would likely never be enough.

In the outdoor kennels, we met a fawn-colored Great Dane mix with white spots. He'd been surrendered because he bit a nine-year-old. No one knew why, and he'd been nothing but a lover since arriving at Anson. I thought of all the YouTube videos I'd seen of children riding dogs as large as this, and I could guess what had happened. Because of the bite history, no Great Dane rescue would touch him, and I knew he would likely die at Anson.

One small brown dog was curled in the back of her kennel, trembling and avoiding our eyes. We called to her, but she only shifted, growled, and turned her back to us. She had lingered at Anson so long it was likely she was no longer adoptable. She was depressed and not eating, but had also recently become dangerous to handle. Maureen said, "We're going to have to euthanize that one soon." She wouldn't die because of how crowded the kennels were; she would succumb to shelter stress.* Clearly, she was suffering. With no adopter and no rescue in sight, the humane thing to do would be to euthanize her. And that broke my heart. We did this to her. In our effort to care for her, we had killed her.

Like Lenoir County, the dogs at Anson's only hope was through a rescue. Local adoptions were few and far between and even if they did go home, the dogs would leave unneutered and unspayed because Anson didn't have the funds to spay/neuter and they didn't have access to a low-cost clinic. When they adopted out a cat, they knew that cat's kittens would very likely make their way back to the Anson shelter.

This surprised me since there was a veterinary practice literally next door. Maureen told us that she had to wait sometimes up to three weeks for an appointment, and most adopters wouldn't wait that long to pick up their pet, so they sent them home and hoped the adopter would take care of it. Oreo had been the rare dog at Anson adopted not just once, but twice. Both times the adopter never had him neutered, and both times he had run off† and been

---

* Some dogs cannot handle the stress of living in shelters. They develop stress-induced compulsive behaviors like spinning, chewing aggressively, and jumping. Some become defensive and growl or even bite. And some react to the stress of shelter life by becoming dangerously depressed, developing symptoms like self-mutilation, loss of appetite, and lethargy.

† Most likely in the hopes of producing Oreo Juniors.

returned to the shelter. I made a note to look into this and later learned that the lead vet at the clinic was the former director of the Anson shelter and presided over it when the shelter was killing easily 50 percent of the animals it took in. Likely, he had personally handled the killing of thousands of dogs over his years at the shelter. Another volunteer told me the vet didn't like to work on the Anson animals because they were just shipping them up to the "Yankees."*

A few days before our visit, a local woman came to the shelter in need of food for her cat. Anson, like most shelters, handed out food to nearly anyone who needed it with the hope that it would prevent the animals from ending up in their kennels. While the receptionist was fetching a bag of cat food, the woman stole their donation jar off the counter. "That container was worth $150 itself, but she wanted the $90 inside," Maureen said, grimacing and shaking her head. They captured it on their security camera and had shown it to the police, but Maureen doubted anything would come of it. "I'm gonna put her sorry face on Facebook, though," she promised.

The Anson shelter is just over an hour from Charlotte, North Carolina, a progressive city full of young people and professionals and fabulous restaurants and at least one awesome independent bookstore. After we unloaded donations for the Anson shelter, we headed to Charlotte and a respite from the hopelessly sad quandary that was the Anson Shelter.

I enjoyed seeing so many friends, but my heart was still back at Anson, standing outside Oreo's kennel, my hand pressed against the fence feeling his warm face. For the book event, we partnered with Greater Charlotte SPCA, a foster-based rescue. They brought some adoptable dogs to meet the dog-loving book public. I was happy to meet them and happy to help spread their message. They were saving many dogs. There was also an excellent no-kill Humane Society shelter in Charlotte. In fact, I saw dogs everywhere—it seemed to be a dog-loving city. Which was why it was hard to believe that Anson was so close.

Every chance I got as I talked with old friends and new, I said, "Go to Anson. Go help." I encouraged the young bookstore clerks who lived in

---

* Most rescues that pull from Anson are located in northern states, and they pay the veterinary bills of the dogs they pull—usually covering not just spay/neuter, but health certificates, heartworm testing, vaccines, and microchips, plus any other necessary procedures.

apartments and couldn't own dogs to go spend an afternoon walking the dogs or take one out for a doggie date or even for a sleepover. Getting those dogs out of that shelter, for even an hour, could make a difference. I thought of the little brown dog. I knew that difference could literally save lives. Many of our cities, at least the cities we were visiting, had shelters blessed with resources and a supportive public, but if you looked a little farther, past the interstate, out to where the poverty level rose, the houses were fewer and farther between, and the Dollar Generals were the local grocery store, that was where the dogs were dying.

In just the first few days of the tour, I was realizing that the situation was far worse than I imagined. I'd wanted to believe that things would be better. I'd heard some stories but had thought, not in this day and age, it can't possibly be that bad.

It was.

22

Too Late

"Crap!" I yelled Thursday morning when I woke and looked at the time.

After the book signing the night before, we'd come back to Eli and Greg's little house tucked away in a tree-lined neighborhood of hipsters and young families. Their snug bungalow was welcoming and crammed with amazing antiques and unique touches. Between their syrupy southern accents, their wicked sense of humor, and the emotional toll of the last few days, Eli and Greg kept us laughing until the wee hours, many times to the point of tears. It was wonderful to shed the heavy cloak of sadness we'd carried into Charlotte.

Eli told stories from our college days, and I remembered that intensely curious and independent, but far too naive, girl I had been. Gosh, I missed her. I sometimes wonder if I'd known back then about what was happening to the animals in our shelters if I might have applied some of that rampant idealism to the issue much earlier. I'd probably be living in a house with twenty-seven cats and sixteen dogs by now.

The stories also made me think of Addie, my curious, independent, and much less naive girl. I would miss her this year as she headed off for her second year of college. I wouldn't even be there to move her in; I'd be walking through a shelter in Tennessee somewhere. Perhaps this tour was opening my eyes to a second chance. My kids were nearly grown, already self-possessed and in charge of their lives. Maybe I had some available energy to apply to this problem. Maybe I could make a difference.

But first, we had to get our hungover butts out of bed and hustle to Oconee Humane Society, which was three hours away. We should have been on the road already. We scrambled to gather our stuff, said a hasty good-bye, and hit the road. We were about an hour away when I asked Lisa to call and let them know we were running late. I listened to Lisa's side of the brief conversation and watched as her eyes grew wide.

When she hung up, she said, "There's a TV crew setting up and a reporter from the paper waiting."

That's when I remembered the e-mail from Lynn, the rescue coordinator. She'd told me that their marketing director, Angel, had alerted the local media. She expected they would come out. But, somehow, that fact had been buried beneath all that we'd seen the last few days. Lisa scrambled to change into an OPH T-shirt and I found a baseball hat to cover my sleep-flattened hair. There wasn't much more we could do to improve our appearance beyond slapping on a little lipstick.

"It'll have to do," I said and pushed the van, loaded with thousands of pounds of dog food, faster over the bumpy, rural highways that were taking us to Oconee County.

At the shelter there was indeed press, plus Lynn, the hero who worked tirelessly to save dogs at Oconee; Angel, who was the sunny face handling marketing; and many, many other volunteers who came every day to walk dogs and take pictures and do everything they could to save as many dogs as they could—which sadly was not all of them.

Oconee is a large shelter that can take in up to five hundred dogs in a month. Like many of the county shelters, there were two sides to Oconee. One side, the Humane Society side, was where you found Lynn and Angel and lots of volunteers. It had a grooming room, a whiteboard listing which dogs had both their walks that day, at least eight fenced-in outdoor play areas, a bright, welcoming lobby, and, just off that, an indoor and outdoor cattery. The Humane Society side of the building was where dogs were available for the public to adopt.

The other side of the building had its own entrance, but was also connected inside by a large metal door labeled no admittance. It was run by Animal Control Officers (ACOs). The dogs in these kennels were brought in by ACOs for a plethora of reasons—arrests, domestic disputes, code violations, fire, death, or bite hold.* But some were simply dumped at the shelter, found as strays or dropped off by owners who had every excuse under the sun as to why they could not or would not care for their pet.

Dogs who were not claimed by their owners and had finished their stray hold† could be released to the Humane Society when they had available kennels. Dogs deemed unadoptable by the ACOs would be held until that status changed, a rescue stepped in, or until space was needed and they were destroyed.

As Lynn took us down the row of kennels on the Animal Control side, I noted the large hand-scrawled Xs that covered some of the kennel cards. I asked Lynn what they meant, and she shook her head and said, "That's never good."

These were the dogs who would be euthanized when the shelter ran out of room. Oconee was at capacity, which was why Lynn, Angel, and the others scrambled to get as many dogs adopted or out through a rescue as they could. The more dogs they moved, the more kennels would be opened up for dogs from the Animal Control side, thereby extending the lives of the condemned dogs and the possibility that a rescue might pull them.

One little pup, a pit bull named Ski, had a big red X and sat calmly in her kennel when I bent down to say hello. She looked terrified but wagged

---

* Most states require Animal Control to quarantine any dog reported to have bitten someone for about fourteen days. Then, depending on the state, the dog may be returned to the owner, who agrees to follow a protocol to keep the public safe, or it may be killed. The hold period is to be certain that the dog does not have rabies.

† Most states have "stray holds"—a prescribed number of business days that the shelter will hold a dog before releasing it for adoption or killing it.

her tail and licked my hand. Lynn didn't know her story but promised to find out. I sent pictures to our shelter puller and began my campaign to save Ski's life.

We walked silently down the rest of the row. There were so many dogs, so many Xs. Why save one and not the other? I didn't have time to decide, but it did make me think of that philosophical challenge we argued in one of my college classes: if the ship is sinking and there are only five spaces in the lifeboat, who do you save? Choose which of the possible survivors' lives are worth most. This was a real-life version of the same situation, and I wondered how the ACOs made their decisions and if they agonized over them as much as my college classmates did when we stayed up late drinking chai tea and arguing passionately.

When I pressed Lynn for a reason, she said it was likely "color, breed, or space." Ski was black and labeled a pit bull mix. Had her card said black Lab mix, I was certain a rescue would have pulled her. She was only a puppy.[*]

The more I thought about it, the more I realized that instead of being angry about the Xs, I should be grateful. Why should a shelter hide the fact that they planned to kill a dog? Maybe if more shelters were as transparent, the public would be outraged enough to stop the killing. There were Xs on plenty of the dogs I met at Anson; they were just kept on a list or a computer somewhere, far from the public eye.

Oconee's Xs at least increased the urgency of the situation and hopefully the likelihood that a dog would be pulled by a rescue. The ACOs were not the bad guys, not really. It wasn't their fault there were too many dogs turning up in their shelter. Their job description wasn't to market and adopt out the dogs; they were tasked with keeping the public safe by handling and housing animals that became a "nuisance" in one form or another. They had no control over how many kennels were available. They had to be professionals, trained in the lifeboat dilemma.

---

[*] On a subsequent visit, this very scenario would play out for another six-month-old black pit bull mix puppy named Sheba. Her card was marked with an X, while a lookalike puppy three kennels down was labeled lab mix and marked for rescue. I documented it on a Facebook video and angered plenty of people.

Would we have felt as convicted about trying to save Ski if she didn't have an X? Truthfully, I would have seen an adorable six-month-old puppy, figured she would easily get adopted, and walked right past. The fact that she was black and possibly a pit bull wouldn't have entered my mind. But I didn't know the numbers, only the stakes. Maybe the Xs gave a dog a better shot at being rescued. Maybe the ACOs here knew that. Maybe those Xs would make somebody do something.

Oconee had a good spay/neuter program and was able to offer spay/neuter operations to the public for free, and yet they told me that summer they'd taken in more dogs than any other summer in the past. Their building was welcoming and their people positive and friendly. They had utilized the local media to get attention for their dogs. They were doing so much right, and yet the dogs still came.

Much of this was a culture problem. I was learning that many people in rural, poor areas simply did not value their pets. Dogs were more like livestock. One shelter worker told me, "They'd just as soon bring a cow in their house as a dog." Many in the community didn't embrace spay and neuter. "It's just a dog/cat," was the common refrain. They didn't see the point of going to so much fuss over an animal; so even when it was available at low cost or free, they didn't take advantage of it. And when a dog became a burden—in terms of expense, time, space, or behavior, instead of solving their own problem, they dumped the dog. And open-intake, county-funded shelters made it easy.

There were changes that could be made through legislation, education, and innovation, but when a shelter was overloaded, job number one was simply caring for the dogs in front of you. There was precious little time to petition local government to create change. There was no time to get out to the places where the message was sorely needed. There was no time and, generally, little money to prioritize innovative programs.

Once again, I realized that foster homes could create the breathing room that shelters needed. If their kennels weren't loaded beyond capacity, there would be time for assessing and working with dogs that needed more training to be successful. There would be time to start up new programs, partner with other shelters, and offer community outreach and education.

There is so much to be angry about in dog rescue. At the event at Park Road Books in Charlotte the night before, a man who had been quietly listening to me talk about what we'd seen in the shelters so far asked, "Aren't you angry?"

I was angry, but anger wouldn't solve this problem, I told him. "If we focus on every aspect of this situation that calls for anger, we'd get nothing done and it would eat us alive. We have to focus on the dogs. This is about the dogs."

Anger could motivate—history proves this again and again—but it can't bring the change that needs to take place in people's hearts. That requires a different way of thinking. The people who needed to change to improve this situation weren't likely to respond to my angry rants or even the most elaborate guilt trip. What they just might respond to was example and experience. If they saw us driving south to save dogs within their midst or if they met one of those very dogs at an event like we'd hosted in Charlotte or at a neighbor's house, just maybe we could move the needle.

I was becoming more and more convinced that the real disconnect was between the public perception and the private reality. What we were seeing in the shelters wasn't public knowledge. To say that 30 percent or more of the animals that arrive at a shelter don't make it out alive may not seem significant until you meet one of those 30 percent or listen to the stories of the shelter workers who work so hard to lower that number while simultaneously being blamed for it.

Before we left Oconee, I signed a stack of books and then was miked up for an interview with the local Fox affiliate. Unlike other TV appearances in which I've frozen up like Elsa in the ice castle, this time I was fired up by the fresh sight of those Xs. I might have been running on fumes after the night before, but the words I spoke bypassed my head and came right from my heart.

"This is a fixable problem," I said. "This can be done. If more people open their hearts and their eyes, we can save these dogs."

We left Oconee to head just over the state line to Georgia, where we planned to spend the night at Proud Spirit Horse Sanctuary. Proud Spirit is run by Melanie, a woman I knew only through her books and a few Facebook messages. Lisa and I stopped for gas and while the giant tank filled, I called Laurie, the director of OPH. She was quiet while I told her about Ski and about the Xs.

"I know," she said when I explained that it was worse than I imagined. Oconee was overwhelmed. Dogs were dying. Ski could be dead tomorrow. We have to do something. When I'd finished, she told me to contact the rescue's shelter puller for Oconee.

I had already messaged her and gotten no answer, so I messaged again.

"I can't find foster homes for the dogs we've already committed to—sorry," was her reply.

There was nothing I could do. We had to get to Georgia. Frustration gnawed at me as we drove the monotonous road lined with scrub pine trees and hopelessness. By the time we arrived at Melanie's, I was itching to write. I had to tell this story. People needed to know about Ski and the Xs. If I couldn't save her, maybe someone else would.

Melanie is a tiny, efficient, quiet woman married to a man twice her height who is equally quiet and efficient. Their farm was beautiful, expansive, and seriously organized. Melanie drove Lisa and me around the property in her golf cart. We met the herd—more than fifty horses Melanie had rescued. A gifted artist, Melanie used her writing, photography, and artistic skills to fund the operation, along with a lot of donations. The animals she took in had nowhere else to go, and they had been lucky enough to land in north Georgia with a woman who would protect them all the days of their lives. These horses lived as naturally as horses can—functioning as a herd, spending their days grazing and napping. They would never again wear a saddle or feel a harsh or neglectful human hand.

Proud Spirit was a peaceful place, but my heart was anything but peaceful. I sent another message badgering our shelter puller. And then I sat at Melanie's counter and typed out an impassioned blog post, but my meager words couldn't begin to explain the fire burning in my heart. When I'd finished, I was spent. I watched as Lisa, my non-dog-loving friend, played with Melanie and Jim's eight (yes eight!) dogs. After seeing so many dogs through chain-link kennel doors, it was wonderful to finally get our hands on a few.

In the morning, just before we left, I got a message that Gala was being returned. Those wonderful adopters who seemed like the answer to my prayer, the ones I never met but who had posted pictures of Gala happy in their home, had decided to return her. They'd moved to a new place and Gala kept getting loose. They worried that she would be hit by a car.

I stared at the message and my heart sank. I wished I could drop everything and drive north and comfort this sweet, sweet dog who deserved so much better. On this trip I was meeting lots of Galas. As hard as it was to foster her, as much as she pushed me past the point of no return emotionally and made me question how we could continue to rescue, that was nothing compared to the heartache I was seeing now, up close. Maybe that year with Gala was Gala's chance to prepare me for this, to teach me I did have the emotional bandwidth to take this on.

Dog training and behavior modification were not my skill set. That was clear in my time with Gala, but I had something else in my bag of tricks. I could write about dogs. My blog had helped over one hundred dogs find forever homes. Could a blog help the dogs in the shelters? Could a book?

I didn't feel I was qualified to rescue Gala, any more than I felt qualified now to do something about what I was seeing in the shelters. That didn't mean I shouldn't try. How does anyone become qualified to fix this? Even if I tried and it didn't change anything, I couldn't not try. I couldn't simply walk away from this unchanged and do nothing. I owed it to Gala and every dog I was meeting that week to try and to use the only gifts I had to offer: words and a deep passion to rescue.

I didn't think we could foster Gala again, but I knew she was confused and needed someone who loved her now more than ever. Thankfully, Pam volunteered to foster Gala. She told me she was in for the long haul. I said a silent prayer of thanks for the size of Pam's heart and set out for our two shelter visits scheduled for that day hoping there was room in my own for whatever we might encounter.

23

Hope

It was the last day Lisa would be with me on the tour. She had to get back to her family and the start of the new school year, so she would fly home the next day, and Nick would arrive to be with me for the remaining days of the tour. We backtracked to South Carolina for two more shelter visits before we headed to Atlanta to stay with an old friend of ours who had recently relocated there. I met Heather when her husband, Scott, coached Addie for middle school basketball. They'd moved to our town from New Jersey.* Heather and Scott were persistently positive people with a great sense of humor, and I think I speak for all of southern York County when I say we were sad to see them leave. Heather had invited her book club to join us that night to talk about my book, and both Lisa and I were really looking forward to seeing the whole family.

But first, we had two more stops to make. Our first was at the Humane Society of Greenwood. They had just moved into their brand-new building, which would open officially the next day. OPH had been a critical piece in

---

* They were Eagles fans and instantly popular in my family's book.

their transformation. In 2012, the rescue created the documentary *600 Miles Home* about Greenwood, telling the visual story of what it was like to be a dog at Greenwood.

As Lisa and I strolled through the state-of-the-art shelter, still littered with boxes of new equipment and supplies, I asked Tammy, the rescue coordinator, how it came to be. How did Greenwood go from outdoor kennels with tarps over them, patched fences, and dripping roofs, a place where they destroyed as many as 70 percent of the dogs, to the beautiful shelter we were standing in now?

She said it was that documentary. When it was shown to the county council, they decided something had to change. The money for the shelter came in part from the county, but the rest from donations and fundraising. It took six years, but Greenwood now had a facility that would allow them to house dogs humanely and change the community's perception about adoption.

A shelter facility has a powerful impact not just on the care given to the animals, but on the community as well. Dark, overcrowded, noisy, desperate places do not attract adopters, volunteers, or quality staff. Employees who work in overcrowded, underfunded places, inevitably built as an afterthought close to the dump, play a desperate shell game trying to keep as many animals alive as they can. But a facility like Greenwood changes the game. The new building was bright, spacious, well equipped, and well staffed; it was a place where animals would be given first-class care.

Yes, there were still too many dogs being dumped and abandoned, but walking through the bright, endless halls, we could hear and see a new attitude at Greenwood. They were no longer alone trying to keep dogs alive—their government and their community were on their side. It was a step. A big one.

And it happened because of the documentary. When people learned of the conditions at their shelter, they were moved to change. This was a perfect illustration of my whole point! I was convinced that if people just knew what was happening, they would demand change. But how could I show them? I could write until my fingers fell off, and it might only reach a few thousand people, and maybe not the people who could make a Greenwood-type change happen at other shelters.

We didn't linger long at Greenwood as everyone was busy (and exhausted) getting ready for their big opening the next day. They still had a long road ahead (we passed a man arriving to surrender his dog as we were leaving), but they were moving in the right direction. The energy at Greenwood was exciting and so different from the other shelters we'd visited. Hope was in the air.

We were still riding high on the hope we'd felt at Greenwood when we arrived at Anderson County P.A.W.S. (Pets Are Worth Saving), a shelter we'd almost skipped. We were anxious to get to Atlanta and see Heather, and the only thing I knew about Anderson came from someone at OPH who said, "They aren't killing dogs there anymore, so we probably won't be pulling there much longer."

Those words would come back to haunt me by the end of the day.

We arrived at the shelter on another brutally hot day in South Carolina. We were greeted by Cheyenne, the rescue coordinator. Impossibly young, blond, and pretty, Cheyenne was dressed in scrubs and greeted us with a twinkly smile. "I'm so glad you're here," she said. "Let me see if Dr. Sanders has a second." She disappeared through one of the doors.

The lobby at P.A.W.S. was bright and open and had two glass-walled spaces on either side of the entrance, like display windows at a department store. Lisa and I watched several adoptable dogs lounging on beds and playing with toys in those spaces while we waited.

Cheyenne reappeared with Dr. Kim Sanders. She grinned as she shook our hands; Lisa and I were immediately impressed with her friendly demeanor and calm confidence. This was not the stressed and overwhelmed director we met at nearly every other shelter. Ambitious, smart, and Ivory Girl pretty, Dr. Sanders left her private practice as a vet to run P.A.W.S. It hadn't been an easy transition, and she questioned her decision plenty, she would later tell me, but her ideas and dedication changed Anderson. Two years before, Anderson County P.A.W.S. was a high-intake, high-kill shelter. In just six months, Dr. Sanders turned P.A.W.S. into a managed-intake, "no-kill" shelter.*

---

* Dr. Sanders said, and I agree, that "no-kill" is really a bad label. Every shelter has to euthanize a few animals because they are untreatable medically or behaviorally, and Anderson is no exception.

Cheyenne had worked at the shelter prior to Dr. Sanders's arrival and told us it wasn't unusual for her to come to work on any given day and be forced to euthanize dozens of animals. That was the norm. It made her sick and broke her heart on a daily basis; she hated her job. "Dr. Sanders changed everything," she said.

Dr. Sanders nodded and then excused herself but promised to spend some time with us when she had a break between surgeries. Meanwhile, Cheyenne gave us a tour of the huge facility, organized in seven colorful pods that each hold up to twenty-seven dogs. It was a vast facility, full to bursting with dogs. Later, Dr. Sanders would tell us it was too big, acknowledging that no matter the space size, it will always fill up. A smaller space would allow them to give better attention to fewer dogs at a time. At the time of our visit, P.A.W.S. had over 170 medium and large dogs and only a dozen or so small dogs. As was the case everywhere we visited, small dogs were in much higher demand.

Many of the kennels held more than one dog. Not only did this help them to hold more dogs at one time, as pack animals I imagine many of the dogs were happy to have a buddy sharing their space. Outside the kennels hung small metal buckets full of treats for visitors and staff to hand out. When Lisa realized they were free for the giving, she began handing out treats to every single dog, slowing our progress but giving Cheyenne and me a chance to talk. The treats were a brilliant idea—they trained the dogs to come to the front of their kennel when people appeared and to sit for a treat, two things that would help to get them adopted.

Cheyenne showed us the grooming room, the food prep room, the laundry room with its mound of bedding as big as a dumpster, and even a room to hold the donated newspaper the shelter used to line the cages of small dogs, puppies, and cats. She showed us the intake area where Animal Control trucks pulled right in, the quarantine room, the surgery suite, and the euthanasia room. P.A.W.S. only euthanized for extreme aggression. If she can fix an animal, Dr. Sanders will. As she put it later, "Whatever you can scrape off the pavement, I'll put back together. You name it, I'll save it."

Dr. Sanders was not only saving dogs in Anderson County with her programs, trained staff, and commitment, she was reaching out to the shelters in the counties that touch Anderson and pulling dogs from their kill lists too. She performed about forty surgeries four days a week, spaying and neutering countless animals and dealing with many of the issues that were fixable but would get a dog euthanized at an underequipped shelter. P.A.W.S. even treated heartworm-positive dogs at the shelter before they went home or to rescue.

I asked about the changes she made. One of the first things she did was ask the county to change how the shelter's Animal Services were run. Instead of an open-intake shelter, which allowed residents to dump a dog anytime for any reason, P.A.W.S, became a managed-intake shelter. While they were obligated to take animals brought in by ACOs and they accepted strays, residents who wished to surrender their dog had to make an appointment and as of the day we visited, the wait time was three weeks to surrender a dog. That gave the resident and the shelter time to figure out if the problem was fixable. Was it economic? Was it behavioral? Did the dog need medical treatment its owners couldn't afford? Training help? Sort of like with abortion or gun purchases, an enforced wait time helped the person make an informed, responsible decision, instead of an emotional one. And taking away the option of simply dumping your animal gives the shelter staff time to work with the animal's owner to figure out how to keep that animal in its home.

What was really remarkable about P.A.W.S. was that they didn't make all these changes by quadrupling their budget or mandating spay and neuter. They did it by practicing smart business. On a second visit I made to P.A.W.S. six months later with a team of volunteers, Dr. Sanders talked about the importance of transparency when it came to saving dogs. Transparency is a quality I've always valued in people, but it's also smart business in an industry where trust is not always easy to come by and passions run high.

Dr. Sanders demanded transparency of her staff and her shelter, and everyone involved in the business of saving dogs. There was no lying, no deceiving, no pretending the situation wasn't what it was. When I posed the question again, "How did you turn this shelter into no-kill in just a few months?" she replied, "We just stopped killing dogs." As if it was as easy as that.

And it had been for P.A.W.S. They weren't afraid to think outside the box to address issues. Obviously what our country has been doing in the name of saving dogs has not been working. It is time for a better plan, and P.A.W.S. just might have it.

Attitudes are a powerful force. From the moment anyone walks into P.A.W.S. they feel welcome. There are stacks of clipboards with adoption applications on a small table and several staff members quick to ask, "How can we help you?" By making P.A.W.S. a welcoming place they became a community center in a part of the South that could desperately use some community. In fact, they'd just received a grant to build a $100,000 dog park that would draw even more of the community to P.A.W.S. on a regular basis.

Dr. Sanders explained that they held a staff meeting every month to go over their intake/outcome numbers—how many adopted, how many to rescue, how many treated, how many euthanized. She never hid those numbers from the public or the staff. This was a problem they were solving together. There was no us and them. I studied the month's tally on the whiteboard in their conference room. I knew the numbers hadn't always been this great, but for a poor county in South Carolina, P.A.W.S. was proving that the problem was solvable. But first, you have to acknowledge the situation.

Pretending we aren't killing dogs in our southern states or qualifying those deaths by saying it's a lack of spay/neuter or ignorance or a shortage of resources isn't helpful and enables a horrific situation to continue unabated, as if the entire country has just thrown up its collective hands and said, "What can you do? It's the South."

At P.A.W.S., the staff had implemented numerous programs with the goal of saving dogs and, whenever possible, keeping them in the home they had. Most people who come to surrender dogs feel as if they have no choice. At P.A.W.S., they offered choices, and by doing that, they became partners rather than passing judgment. They knew the person forced to surrender their pet wanted to keep their pet, and P.A.W.S. wanted them to keep their pet, so they worked together to figure out how to make that happen. And in many cases they were successful.

For instance, if a pet owner was forced to surrender their pet because they had been evicted, had a family crisis, or lost a job and had to move houses or even had to serve a short prison sentence, P.A.W.S. had a program to temporarily house the pet while its owner was in transition. They'd hold an animal for up to forty-five days, sometimes longer in certain circumstances. Sure, Dr. Sanders said, sometimes people took advantage of this, but they worked with each situation individually, with the ultimate goal being to keep the person and pet together.

While visiting with my volunteer team the following spring, we met a large, happy pit bull mama and her six puppies so fat their legs looked like toothpicks jutting out of sausages on a tray of hors d'oeuvres. The mama had been brought in alone two days prior, teats heavy with milk. The Animal Control officer said he couldn't find any puppies.

Dr. Sanders sent her staff back out to the area with the mama dog in tow to find the puppies. The dog led them directly to the home where the puppies were. The mama dog was overjoyed to see her human and her puppies. It was obvious to the staff that the owner loved his dogs but simply didn't have enough knowledge or resources to care for his animals. The staff took all his dogs and the puppies back to P.A.W.S. The puppies were ready to be weaned and they would get them adopted out. They would also attend to the other dogs—have them spayed or neutered, vaccinated, microchipped, and checked for heartworm before returning them to the owner. And while all that was happening, Dr. Sanders directed the staff to take straw, dog food, and kennels to the owner so he would have what he needed to properly care for the dogs when they returned.

I thought about what would have happened to the mama dog had she been brought into another shelter without a proactive director. She would have been placed in Animal Control custody on a stray hold. With no microchip, there would be no way of knowing whose dog she was. And if her owner did come for her and couldn't afford the fee to collect her, he would likely leave her there. She would mourn the loss of her puppies and her person. She would be frightened and confused. She would probably not be the happy, friendly dog who jumped at the kennel fence to greet us at P.A.W.S. Instead, as a scared dog with bully breeding* who carried the physical evidence of

---

* Most shelters consider rottweilers, American Staffordshire Terriers, American Bull Dog Terriers, Staffordshire Bull Terriers, bull mastiffs, and English bulldogs or any dog that looks somewhat like one of those breeds a "bully breed."

multiple litters of puppies, she would have likely had an X on her kennel card. Or, if she was lucky and made it to the Humane Society side of the building, she might linger there for months, since bully breeds take longer to adopt out than most dogs. And her puppies? They would have been sold or given to friends, likely not spayed or neutered, and ultimately come back to the shelter.

"It's a business decision," said Dr. Sanders. "It costs us less to treat the dog and return it to its owner and give him what he needs to care for it than to confiscate the dog, do the necessary vet work, and then house it for weeks or months to get it adopted." Beyond that, she pointed out, "They're bonded. Why should I break them apart? He loves the dog, and it was clear she loved him."

Which brought me to one of the complicating factors in all of this, and perhaps one of the reasons rural shelters were so full—cost. It costs a lot to properly care for a pet. According to Petfinder, owning a dog can cost up to $2,000 a year. Should people be denied a dog simply because they're poor? Was it possible to quantify the value of how much a dog could enrich and inspire a life? Are pets so necessary to a life that the government should subsidize their care for individuals who can't afford it? While that is probably a question that could touch off a firestorm of political opinions, the huge increase in support animals at schools, in businesses, and on airplanes might argue that many people feel they are a necessity.

Dr. Sanders told us about a homeless man who brought his dog to P.A.W.S. each month to get its heartworm preventative. The shelter had offered to give him a six-month supply of preventatives, but he had nowhere to keep it. So he dropped by each month for the preventative and a small donated bag of dog food. Sometimes when he came in, he asked if he could bathe the dog and the staff directed him to their well-equipped grooming room. "That dog has such a great life; he lives better than my own dogs," said Dr. Sanders, wistfully. "He's with his person 24/7 and never wears a leash."

It's a heartwarming story, and do the math—it's cheaper for P.A.W.S. to give this man his heartworm preventative each month than to deny him because he can't afford it. Without preventatives in the hot, humid climate, this man's dog would eventually develop heartworms, and the dog would end up back at P.A.W.S. for expensive treatment and a lengthy stay.

Saving dogs, like pretty much everything in this world, comes down to business. What we need is a better business plan. Too many dogs are dying for want of it.

Plenty of other practices at P.A.W.S. cost the shelter little and saved money in the long run. Their foster-to-adopt program was a great model for other shelters. But it was the simple, nearly free things they did that impressed me. Playgroups, doubling up dogs, and copious treats outside each kennel all helped prevent dogs from breaking down from shelter stress and helped the staff get to know the dogs and prepare them to be successful in their future homes.

The biggest key to the success at P.A.W.S. was making the animal shelter a community center and a partner for animal-loving people. Many shelters are placed in out-of-the-way locations where no one goes or wants to go. They are near the public utilities, the train tracks, and many times, the dump. In fact, one shelter in Alabama is literally in the dump, and another shelter in Virginia is located next to the landfill, making disposing of dead animals convenient. In contrast, Anderson County P.A.W.S. has a large grassy campus just off the interstate and is easily accessible. On both of my visits, it was a bustling, busy place full of people and pets.

There were several adoptions that happened while we visited, but P.A.W.S. still depended on rescues like OPH. Cheyenne spent her days coordinating with rescues all over the country to move dogs out of Anderson County. Anderson was not a wealthy county and, like the others we'd seen that week, depended on rescues to take their surplus of dogs and move them to places in the country where they could be adopted.

Both Cheyenne and Dr. Sanders told me, "We couldn't do this without rescue."

P.A.W.S. was at capacity, and Dr. Sanders confessed that she was always anxious knowing that at any given moment an Animal Control officer could show up with twenty dogs from a drug bust or hoarding case, and what would she do? I didn't know, but I was pretty sure she wouldn't kill them; she'd come up with something.

In a sad catch-22, as P.A.W.S. had become no-kill, they'd experienced rescue groups ceasing to pull from them. It was precisely their success that could hamstring their efforts to save dogs in Anderson County and elsewhere. I made a mental note to share this situation with whoever I could at OPH. We should support a shelter like this—one that was paving the way and sharing all that they knew with other shelters.*

I wished I could clone Dr. Sanders; luckily, she wasn't a stingy person and she willingly and generously shared her knowledge and the programs and policies of P.A.W.S. with anyone who asked.

The situation in the rural South (and I'd wager most of rural America) is a desperate one. One that most of us don't believe (or don't want to believe) is real. Before traveling south, I was up to my neck in rescue, having saved over one hundred dogs, and yet I had no idea it was this bad. As we pulled out of Anderson and headed to Atlanta, I felt revived and thoroughly convinced that this was a fixable problem.

---

* Dr. Sanders and her staff regularly host directors and staff from other facilities to share their programs. They even close the shelter occasionally and travel to other shelters to offer hands-on help and in-facility training. Beyond that, Dr. Sanders told me that she welcomes e-mails and phone calls from other directors who need help.

24

New Co-pilot

Thank goodness for Lisa; she'd been the perfect traveling companion, taking copious notes, asking the questions I forgot to ask, and handing me crackers with cheese as I drove the behemoth van between stops. Our days and hearts were filled to the brim. We cried plenty, but we also laughed a lot. Much like anyone subjected to painful situations, sometimes laughter was necessary for survival. We found plenty to laugh about as we rolled across state lines—the signage, the yard décor, the implied frustration of our GPS app's voice at every missed turn, and the shifting mass of donations behind our seats, while maybe not high humor, still triggered the giggles and provided an escape from the heavy sadness we carried away with us as we left each shelter.

If you knew Lisa you would be surprised and not surprised that she was traveling on this journey with me. Lisa is not a dog person, but she is a Cara person. She has been my persistently optimistic cheerleader on my journey to becoming a novelist, reading too many versions of the same story and always assuring me it was only a matter of time before I hit the best-seller list. She was the friend who listened to my heartbreak when my four-year-old son developed the autoimmune disorder alopecia areata and all his beautiful red curls fell out and I wrestled with the unanswerable questions of why and what will come. I can't even begin to count how many bottles of wine we've shared on my screened-in porch talking through the challenges of parenting clever and creative children in this now-now-now world. When she visited my dog-filled house, the dogs flocked to her, and she would inevitably say, "I don't even like dogs, but this one is nice." (Every time.)

I watched as our trip affected her. Often, she was the last one out of the kennels, lingering in front of cages, tears on her face, her hand pressed to the fence. One dog, at Anson, stole her heart—an older dog, scrawny and white, not one likely to be pulled by many rescues. One likely to spend its final days there. She kept bringing her up, and just the day before she said tentatively, "I would foster her."

On Wednesday night at Melanie's, she sat on the floor surrounded by dogs—in her lap, pressed to her sides, even licking her toes. I captured that moment with my camera, and the smile on her face said it all—she looks tired, worn through, but her face is hopeful. Lisa is possibly the most hopeful person I know.

We spent our last night together at Heather's in Atlanta, catching up, meeting her neighbors, filling our tummies and catching our breath—finally. The range of emotions on the trip had swung wildly from devastation and hopelessness to joy and gratefulness. Almost every night we'd stayed with friends. It had been wonderful to catch up with them, and they'd proved a delightful distraction from the reality of rescue in the rural South. There hadn't been time in the evening to dwell on what we'd seen during the day; there also hadn't been time to write.

I mentioned this to Lisa, and she said, "But it would be really hard to go back to a dark hotel room after what we've seen." And she was right. Without the blessing of so many wonderful hosts and hostesses all week long, sharing their food and homes and hearts, the journey might have been too much.

Lisa and I said a teary good-bye the next morning in Heather's driveway. I couldn't imagine continuing without her. It felt like we had been through combat together, and now she was going home on leave and I was headed back into battle. I watched her smiling face disappear in the rearview mirror as I headed to the airport to pick up Nick, who would join me for the rest of the tour.

I circled the enormous Atlanta airport, wondering if my large, white, unmarked cargo van idling in the Arrivals zone, only to zoom off whenever the security officers headed my way, was raising any suspicions. Finally, Nick appeared on the sidewalk, and I climbed out of the van for a long hug. We'd hardly talked all week—I was too tired every night, and it was impossible to tell him about our days. I didn't realize how much I missed him, how badly I needed his strength and his competence and his fresh heart until he put his arms around me. The tears came.

With Nick at the wheel, I found a second wind. I tapped my phone furiously, sending out tweets and images and posts. Trying to "be Lisa," which was a much bigger job than I'd realized. She had acted as my publicist, working magic on social media, tagging the shelters and bookstores we visited, searching for popular hashtags, filming live Facebook videos, making sure as many people as possible saw what we were seeing.

She had been the one getting the word out, which I later realized was probably the most critical part of the trip. People needed to know what was happening. If they didn't, they couldn't help; they couldn't even know what needed to change. More than anything, people needed to know the struggles of the shelters, how the dogs were living (and dying), and the truth of what we all wished were not true. The images and thoughts Lisa posted touched hearts and hopefully inspired change.

In the days to come, Nick would attempt to help, and I would say, "You're no Lisa," so often that he began to preface his remarks with, "I know I'm not Lisa, but . . ."

We arrived in Chattanooga, Tennessee, a charming little city nestled in the mountains, just in time for a signing at Star Line Books, which was run by a sparkly, fun woman named, of course, Star. We partnered with the Humane

Educational Society of Chattanooga, and they brought out a gorgeous adoptable German Shepherd named Cruz and a Pack 'n Play full of kittens.

We had a lively discussion in which I tried to delicately, but not too delicately, share the realities of what I'd been seeing in my shelter visits and answered a few questions about the book and fostering. By the time we left, Star had decided that she would begin fostering adoptable kittens for HESC in her shop. It was exciting to see the magic of the book's message work right in front of my eyes.

The next day we trucked over to Franklin, Tennessee, for an event at Nashville Pet Products with Rural Animal Rescue Effort (RARE). We met Trisha as she was unloading animals and setting up. Trisha is the force behind RARE and fosters most of RARE's animals at her house. She was smart and committed, and her energy was admirable. We also met Laura, who volunteered with both RARE and the Maury County shelter, where we were headed that afternoon.

While I sold very few books, RARE did attract lots of potential adopters. I enjoyed getting to know Trisha and Laura and was astounded at all they accomplished while maintaining full-time jobs. Besides volunteering at several shelters and with RARE, Laura often drove transports with her own massive van. Her boyfriend (now fiancé) bought the van for her after watching her drive her own vehicle or rent others to drive animals from Tennessee all over the country to meet rescues on her own dime and with her own time. I connected easily with Laura, a thin, attractive woman with a warm smile and a nurturing spirit.

Trisha was competent and confident and quite a force to be reckoned with; her passion and commitment to the animals were enormous. I imagined they could also be intimidating. There were hundreds, if not thousands of animals that owed their lives to this incredible woman who rescued animals from overcrowded shelters and tiny municipal pounds, often hours away.

In addition to caring for many animals at her home, Trisha processed all the applications that came into RARE and drove animals to potential adopters' homes. That way she could see if the home and adopters were appropriate for the dog (or cat or bunny!). And she did this (very well) on a shoestring budget made up of donations and (I was sure, but she didn't say this) her own money.

These women were quite a team, an amazing, compassionate, animal-hearted duo who were saving many, many lives in rural Tennessee.

After the event, we followed Laura to Trisha's house to unload (Trisha was taking several dogs to a potential adopter's house) and met even more dogs, puppies, cats, and bunnies filling Trisha's garage, living room, driveway, and every available inch of her property. There were two dogs who ran in circles in the shady fenced front yard. Laura told me they had neurological issues; they would likely live out their lives with Trisha. A volunteer was cleaning out a puppy pen and introduced us to a sweet pit bull mother and her brood. More dogs were housed in large, shady pens and there was a grassy, fenced area for exercise and playgroups. It was quite an operation, and observing the well-kept spaces, I imagined it took every spare moment of Trisha's time. I asked Laura if Trisha had a husband and a family, and she shook her head. "She has a boyfriend on and off."

Nick said nothing, but I was sure I knew what he was thinking. It would take a special guy to sign on for this life. As my husband, Nick certainly put up with a lot in terms of the demands of the dogs and my crazy commitment to them. Later, driving on to Nashville, Nick would say, "I hope you don't ever want to live like that," about Trisha's world.*

After leaving Trisha's, we followed Laura to Maury County/Columbia Animal Services, where Laura introduced us to some of the staff and we got a tour of the large facility. Once again, we were told that the shelter was at capacity and once again we met many, many gorgeous adoptable dogs. It was a Saturday afternoon, so Maury County was buzzing with visitors and adopters and even a few volunteers.

Maury County is an open-intake shelter. We met a woman who had worked there for twenty years and currently handled intake. I asked if they questioned people who dropped off their animals. She shrugged and said, "I ask 'em, but it doesn't matter, we still take the animals." As an open-intake shelter, she told me Maury had no choice. I thought of Anderson County P.A.W.S. and silently wondered how true that was.

---

* Which nixed any plans I had to sublet our garage to a cat rescue.

At Maury, dogs brought in by Animal Control or the public as strays were held in a "stray hold" area, often for four to six weeks or longer before the shelter was able to process them* and move them to the adoptable room. Laura expressed her frustration with this timeline. As we had learned and Laura well knew, a dog kept in a shelter setting for four to six weeks with no real human interaction will often break down or suffer irreparable damage. The stray hold area was noisy and stressful, and the only exercise the dogs got was when they were removed from their kennel while it was sprayed out. The kennels were about four feet by six feet. There were no toys, no bedding, only a hard plastic shelf a few inches off the concrete that allowed them to stay out of their own urine and feces.

I met an adorable dog in the stray hold area with beautiful markings—a ruler-straight line dividing his face between black and gray with speckles of white. He had a big, friendly smile and the lithe build of a border collie; I decided to call him Bandit. He'd been at Maury over a month and didn't even have a name yet. I slipped my hand through the kennel fence to scratch his ears. It hurt my heart that this gorgeous, adoptable, friendly, sweet dog had been living in a tiny space with nearly no human or canine interaction for a month with no end in sight. I knew that if he were my foster dog, adopters would line up for him. I asked if our rescue knew about him, and Laura told me that she wasn't allowed to assess or pull dogs from the stray hold area.

Bandit and all the other dogs in stray hold would sit and wait and perhaps become sick physically or mentally from the harsh conditions. Maury County didn't even have a website with pictures of the animals on it, so until he moved to the adoptable room, at which time Laura would be able to take his picture and post it on Petfinder, no one would even know he existed beyond the inmate who cleaned his kennel and the employee who (finally) assessed him and moved him to the adoptable room.

As we walked down row after row, I swallowed tears and offered what little comfort I could to sad face after sad face. I asked our tour guide why the dogs

---

* Processing them meant evaluating for behavior and getting their vaccinations current.

ABOVE: Gala running on her long line. *Photo by Nancy Slattery.*
BELOW: Gala with Nancy after her photo shoot.

ABOVE: Van loaded up with donations for the shelters on the book tour.
BELOW: Lenoir County SPCA. *Photo by Nancy Slattery.*

ABOVE: Cara walking a shelter dog at Lenoir County SPCA. RIGHT: Visiting with one of the pit bulls at Newberry County Animal Control. BELOW: One of the OPH Rescue Road Trip team members with Casper, a deaf dog at Lenoir County SPCA. *All photos by Nancy Slattery.*

ABOVE: Estelle with her puppies. BELOW: Billy Jean. *Photo by Nancy Slattery.*

TOP: Dogs loaded up at Scott County for the ride home. CENTER: Cara meeting one of Brindlee Mountain Rescue's Great Danes. *Photo by Nancy Slattery.* BOTTOM: Aging dog at Red Fern Animal Shelter. *Photo by Ian Achterberg.*

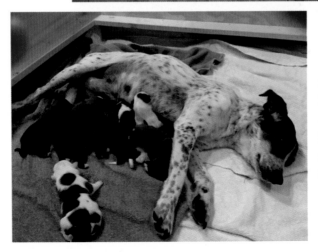

TOP: Dog cooling off from the heat at the Shelbyville City Shelter. *Photo by Nancy Slattery.* CENTER: Five of the Highway puppies. BOTTOM: Dixieland and her newborn puppies.

ABOVE: Fruitcake, the Swimmer puppy. BELOW: Hula Hoop and the Playground Pups.

ABOVE LEFT: Daisy Duke. ABOVE RIGHT: The Huntingdon Pound, Carroll County, Tennessee. *Photo by Ian Achterberg.* BELOW LEFT: Image Ian took of dog named Sky at the Greenfield Pound. *Photo by Ian Achterberg.* BELOW RIGHT: One of the dogs on the Animal Control side of Oconee Shelter whose kennel card was marked with an X. *Photo by Nancy Slattery.*

ABOVE: Oreo in the Anson County Shelter. BELOW: Oreo with Cara. *Photo by Nancy Slattery.*

ABOVE: Cara with Dave Rice, director of SHARK, and adoptable dog Lola. *Photo by Nancy Slattery.* BELOW: SHARK's main kennels located deep inside the landfill.

ABOVE: The original shelter for Abbeville County just inside the dump, where SHARK began.
BELOW: Laura Prechel with a RARE dog. *Both photos by Nancy Slattery.*

ABOVE: Nelson, the one-eyed heeler. BELOW: Buford.

LEFT: Lisa surrounded by dogs at Proud Spirit Horse Sanctuary. BELOW: Mama pit bull and pups at Anderson County P.A.W.S.

ABOVE: Hops. *Photo by Nancy Slattery.* BELOW: Greenfield City Pound. *Photo by Ian Achterberg.*

ABOVE: Playing with Sheba, the pitbull puppy with the X at the Oconee shelter. *Photo by Nancy Slattery*. BELOW LEFT: Sheba's intake sheet with the X. BELOW RIGHT: Meathead, one of the adoptable dogs at Karin' 4 Kritters.

ABOVE: Our unicorns—the Suess boys. BELOW: OPH Rescue Road Trip team meeting the inside dogs at Lenoir County SPCA. *Both photos by Nancy Slattery.*

ABOVE: The OPH Rescue Road Trip Team picking up their dogs at P.A.W.S. BELOW: Signing books with former foster dog Rollie (now Molly). *Photo by Steve Jones.*

ABOVE: The Chocolate Factory pups.
BELOW: The Giving Tuesday Puppies enjoying the woodstove.

ABOVE: The Pepper Pupper litter. BELOW: The Songs of the South litter.

ABOVE: Thelma and Louise at P.A.W.S. BELOW: Thelma and her newborn puppies.

TOP: Touring the Franklin County Shelter with ACO Heather. CENTER: Touring the Cheatham Shelter with director Kristin. BOTTOM: Visiting with Tito, an adoptable dog at Giles County Animal Shelter. *All photos by Nancy Slattery.*

ABOVE: Vanna (aka OPH Sweet Tea) in her foster home in Pennsylvania.
BELOW: Willow Wonka perched on top of her crate.

ABOVE: Fanny, "the little brown pit bull" in the Huntingdon Pound. *Photo by Ian Achterberg.* BELOW: Fanny in Pennsylvania. *Photo by Nancy Slattery.*

Houdini and Fanny.

had no toys or bedding and she explained that they got ripped up and then clogged the drains running under the kennels.

We followed her outside to a small area with two fenced enclosures with mulch covering the ground. She explained that dogs were taken out individually and could play (again with no toys and no playmates) for the time it took the inmates* to clean their kennel. When I asked if the dogs got any other exercise, she told me the inmates sometimes walked the dogs through the halls of the shelter when it was closed.

Maury was able to adopt out quite a few dogs because they were so close to Nashville, but they couldn't keep up with the influx and relied on rescue to move the others. That's where Laura came in. Laura got to know the dogs in the adoptable area, contacted rescues (all over the country), and drove dogs to meet rescue transports, sometimes hundreds of miles away.

To her credit, Laura was professional as she listened in on our tour, most likely biting her tongue at the deplorable situation. She wisely stayed focused on the dogs, despite what must be a frustrating situation for her at Maury County. It put her in a tough place. If she spoke up and criticized the situation too loudly,† she would be denied access to the dogs, and then even more would suffer and perish.

What struck me the most about this shelter was the defeated attitude of the staff. They didn't feel there was any way to improve the situation for the dogs. I'd only popped in briefly, so obviously I wasn't privy to the history there. Maybe they'd tried before and failed, but for a large, well-built facility with a large staff (none of which had to clean kennels since the local inmates were brought in to do that), plenty of open space outside,‡ and what seemed like a willing volunteer pool, the living conditions for the dogs should have been better. I kept thinking what Sherry and Helen from Lenoir County would do with a space and staff like this.

---

* Maury County used inmates to do the cleaning at the shelter, a practice I've discovered is not uncommon in shelters.

† Something Trisha had done, which resulted in her no longer being allowed to volunteer or pull dogs from the shelter.

‡ The shelter was surrounded by grassy fields.

I offered to secure Kuranda beds for the dogs so they would have something softer than the hard shelf they currently had but was told the director wouldn't allow them.* The employee who gave us the tour explained why the beds wouldn't work—something to do with the drains again. Spotting a problem he could finally address, my engineer husband took a look at the situation and quickly sketched out a way to modify the space to fit the beds and protect the drains, but the employee just shook her head and moved on with the tour.

I asked about toys to help ease the boredom of the dogs held so long, isolated in stray hold, and again was told they would block the drains. Finally, the employee relented that large Kongs might be okay. The knowing look from Laura and the tired expression on the employee's face made it clear that the bedding/toy situation was not something that would change, and I was not the first person to bring it up. Our tour guide was only humoring me, likely hoping I would shut up with my suggestions. The whole situation was maddening, and it was the dogs who suffered for it. Offering the dogs the smallest comfort would not break the bank and could make all the difference, and yet, it wasn't done.

I was disappointed that the director wasn't at the shelter to meet us, but maybe it was for the best. I tried hard to be an advocate and not an adversary for the shelters. I would have been hard-pressed to find something to say that would be supportive and helpful, not judgmental. She'd been at Maury County for over a decade and from what I could tell was decidedly set in her ways, believing she was doing all that could be done at the shelter.

From the visits I'd already made on our tour, I understood the impossible job she had, but Maury County had as many or more resources as Anderson County P.A.W.S. They should not have been killing dogs. The differences between the two places in terms of the emotional health of the dogs and the attitudes of the staff were night and day. And I was certain that one affected the other. It had to be hard to see so many sad dogs day after day. It surely wore on a soul.

But something could be done here. Perceptions had to change before anything else would; the employees had to decide that the situation was fixable

---

* I'd been told the director would try to be there to see us, but she never turned up.

and that it was in their power to fix it. They had to be open to new ideas and let go of their defeated attitudes. I'd bet every one of them started their work at the shelter because they loved animals and wanted to help them find homes. But the never-ending onslaught of unwanted animals and their needs could crush just about anyone's spirit.

It was very tempting to call this shelter out on so much, but Laura had instead chosen to focus on the dogs and do all that was within her power for them. Her patience with the situation and her commitment to the dogs was remarkable. What she needed, what the dogs needed, was better leadership. The situation at Maury County was not acceptable. Didn't anyone beyond Laura and Trisha see this?

Did the community, the government, the country not know about the dogs being killed on their dime? What did it cost taxpayers to store these dogs in the dark, cramped space called stray hold, while they suffered too long and so many ended up dying in the end? Surely, it would cost less to move them out quickly through rescue and adoption. Six weeks of suffering, while the county paid employees to care for them, bought food for them, and eventually gave them medical attention, perhaps more than they would need if they'd been attended to the moment they appeared at the shelter. The business approach of P.A.W.S. was making more and more sense to me.

Somehow, I needed to spread this word. Once again, what I needed was a bigger microphone. My book might have only been out a month, but as we left Maury and headed into Nashville for some much-needed R & R, a new plan was forming in my head. A new book, one that would take the readers inside the shelters so they could see what I was seeing.

25

These Boots Are Made for Rescuing

Nick and I rolled into Nashville at the same time as everyone else. It was the first home game for the Vanderbilt Commodores, and the streets were crowded and the hotel full. After we checked in and watched our nearly empty van drive away with the valet, we got cleaned up and headed for the honky-tonks.

The streets were so packed that we had to walk about ten blocks before flagging down a vacant Uber willing to make cash on the side and getting a ride the rest of the way. The circus that is Broadway in Nashville is a writer's dream—so many characters, so many stories, such sights and smells and sounds. We squeezed into a narrow bar and drank a beer, unable to even have a conversation over the noise. I wondered if this was the way a dog felt upon arriving in a crowded shelter. The sights and smells were foreign, the noise deafening, and you couldn't see past the backs of the people surrounding you.

I shook off the shelter image and nodded toward the door, and we escaped back out into the hot sunshine. Hungry, we found another bar a few blocks off the main drag that featured painfully fresh new singers belting out top-ten country songs. Finally, some of the dirt and desperation of the shelters lifted, and we were able to laugh and talk. For a few minutes, I forgot to be furious about the situation at Maury or curious about the life of Trisha.

After we ate, our next stop was a boot store. Many months before, when I discovered the tour would land me in Nashville, I had vowed I would finally buy real cowboy boots, something to replace my cheap ones purchased at the local Tractor Supply with a sole so thin, it hurt to step on a pebble. The store was enormous, with boots of every color, style, vintage, and fancy stacked floor to ceiling, some costing as much as $10,000 a pair. I wandered down an aisle, running my fingers over the hand-tooled leather, breathing in that familiar scent. Having come of age training horses and teaching riding, the smell of leather has always meant comfort and adventure and happiness to me. Nick encouraged me to go ahead and put some on my feet.

"Not the cheap ones, pick something good," he said, but having been raised by a woman who grew up in the coal-mining hills of Mahaffey, Pennsylvania, I couldn't justify spending a fortune on boots, even boots as amazing as these.

I tried on three or four pairs that were under $200. Spending any more would feel obscene, I reasoned.

"They'll last your whole life," Nick said. "You should have real cowboy boots."

I wondered briefly if he was hoping the boots would put a smile back on my face or at the very least change the subject for a while. I couldn't seem to get the shelter dogs out of my mind or our conversation. I reminded myself that this was a lifelong quest. Real boots. From Nashville. I'd looked for some in Oklahoma while we were there a few months earlier for my nephew's wedding but couldn't justify the expense. I couldn't justify it now either.

I put on a pair with a light stitched pattern, not too flashy, mostly neutral, and despite the pointy toe, they felt like slippers. I twirled and admired them in the knee-high mirrors all over the store. The attendant told me they were on sale, too. Fifty bucks off. Nick looked at the price tag and said, "You should try on some $1,000 boots, at least, to feel what the difference is."

Still wearing my boots, I walked up a different aisle and selected a $1,700 pair that looked similar to the pair on my feet. They were flashier with softer leather and a thicker sole. I slipped one boot on and walked awkwardly down the aisle like a kid with one foot on the curb. They were nice, but, honestly, I couldn't feel much of a difference.

We bought the less expensive pair, and it made me happy. They were beautiful and real and I loved them, but I'm my mother's daughter, and there's nothing like getting a good deal.

The next morning before leaving Nashville, we visited Ann Patchett's bookstore, Parnassus Books. I'd hoped to do a signing at Parnassus but had been turned down because not only was my book not a best-seller (yet), I also didn't have any local connections. It was a delightful store, just like I imagined, but when I spotted my book on their shelves, my heart soared. "Look!" I called to Nick. "It's here!" I posed for a photo and then took a copy to the register and told the woman working there that I was the author. She smiled indulgently at my glee and asked if I'd like to sign it. So I did, and I watched as she put a "signed copy" sticker on the cover and set it in a display. My book. At Ann Patchett's bookstore. Swoon.

After that, we got back in the van and headed out of town for the drive to Scott County, Virginia, our last stop. Scott County was the shelter that had inspired my first book. I'd only been fostering a year or so when I attended a presentation by two of the Scott County Humane Society's volunteers—two young, fresh-faced women named Rachel and Ashley. They'd come to an OPH training seminar to tell us what a difference we'd made in Scott County. Scott is more or less a dog pound in the mountains on the line between Virginia and Tennessee with a rural population tucked up narrow gravel drives that snake through the hollows between the hills. The shelter was only a holding space for dogs to be claimed by their owners or destroyed. Until the Humane Society got involved, they were not saving any dogs in Scott County.

In the year before OPH began working with Scott County Humane Society, the shelter had euthanized 68 percent of the dogs they took in. Rachel

ONE HUNDRED DOGS & COUNTING

and Ashley told us that six months into the year, they had euthanized less than 3 percent. That was the moment when I went all in on the belief that fostering could save lives. It was when I began conceiving the very book that was now taking me to Scott County.

I was excited to go to Scott County because this time instead of just delivering donations and touring the kennels, we were going to get to pull dogs! The van was almost empty, and Nick and I spent that night organizing what was left to give to Scott County and assembling crates for the passengers of our freedom ride. It was like putting together a jigsaw puzzle, figuring out how to place seven crates in the van so that no one was facing anyone.

After prepping the van, I headed back to our room, but Nick stopped to chat with a crowd of people who had arrived at the hotel on motor-tricycles.* They were drinking Diet Coke and playing some kind of game with dice in the common area of the hotel.

They were a friendly bunch and asked Nick why we were in Kingsport. When he heard what we were doing one man said, "They kill a lot of dogs in Alabama. No one wants to do it, but we ain't got no choice." Everyone nodded in agreement and began citing more atrocities.

When Nick shared their comments with me, I felt somewhat deflated. That's what things had come to in the rural South. Acceptance. The general population, at least the middle-aged, working-class, church-going, motor-tricycle-riding folks, saw the situation as inevitable. As if nothing could be done.

Maybe when I started this tour I believed there was no choice, but now I knew different. If I hadn't been so exhausted, I might have marched back down the hall and explained that to those nice folks. It was within their power to change the situation. I saw it firsthand. We can demand that our county governments build and maintain shelters that create the kind of atmosphere that encourages adoption, with the space and the staff to care for animals

---

* I don't know what else to call them—that's what they look like—motorcycles with two wheels in the back.

humanely. We can pay shelter staff the kind of salaries that will attract people like Kim Sanders who will save the county money in the long run by implementing programs and policies that educate and support their community's commitment to their animals, instead of wasting their money cruelly housing and then killing adoptable animals.

I knew it could be done, and just as soon as I got myself home and rested, I was gonna start beating that drum.

26

A Real Rescue

We found Scott County Animal Shelter down the same driveway as the dump. We arrived before the rescue coordinator or any of the volunteers who were fostering the animals we would be transporting for OPH. I guess I was eager.

While driving through Tennessee the day before, I'd learned that a pregnant dog had been turned in to Scott County by its owner. I'd contacted several people at OPH who said I couldn't pull her unless she had a rabies vaccine and a health certificate—the two things she'd need to cross a state line. Without them, she couldn't come to Pennsylvania with me.

I rolled around all night trying to imagine a scenario in which I'd miraculously find a vet open on Labor Day in the mountains of Virginia. And then I envisioned me just adopting her outright—for myself. Who would stop me?

That morning over breakfast, I'd told Nick, "I'm taking that dog."

He'd nodded and said, "I figured."

We knocked on the door and were met by Delta, one of the Humane Society's volunteers who was there to feed the dogs. We unloaded all our remaining donated food and supplies, filling several pallets with dog food. I'd saved quite a bit for Scott County, knowing the need there was large despite Scott's small size.

The county employee tasked with caring for the dogs at the shelter is not paid to come in on weekends or holidays, so if not for the SCHS volunteers, the dogs would simply go hungry and lie in their own waste. As it is, the volunteers spend countless hours cleaning the kennels, feeding and walking the dogs, taking pictures, and getting to know them in hopes that they can find a rescue to save them. They do some local adoptions, they told us, but most of those dogs come back.

The shelter had no cats or kittens because in Scott County cats were deemed "free-roaming animals," so the county was not obligated to deal with cats. I shook my head at this news. It seemed foreign to me, but it was the way of life in Scott, and likely many other rural places in our country. Delta helped out at a low-cost spay/neuter facility that spayed and neutered many cats, so she said she'd take the litter and cat food we had left in the van to donate there.

Ashley, one of the women I'd met a year earlier at the OPH training seminar, arrived. It was great to see a familiar face. She was a kindred spirit and a dog-hearted soul.

We also met Allison, a hound-loving SCHS volunteer who fostered many of the hounds who lingered at the shelter. Hound dogs are abundant in Scott County, especially this time of year, the start of hunting season. Plenty of backyard breeders produce litters in the hopes of creating one perfect hunting dog and have no use for the rest of the litter or the parents if they don't prove themselves. And getting another hound dog was as easy as wandering down the road to the neighbors. Nobody came to the county shelter for a hound dog.

Allison had so many foster hounds at her house that she was paying to board several others at a local kennel to keep them safe. Allison was a schoolteacher so likely couldn't afford to be doing that, but hounds, like pit bulls, can be difficult to move out through rescues or adoption, and they perish in large numbers at shelters.

It was a treat to catch up with Ashley, and she gave me a tour of the shelter. The original shelter burned down several years ago, so this shelter was relatively new. It was basically a large pole building with a concrete floor. A drain ran down the center of the building, and two sets of kennels faced each other. The noise was deafening when the dogs got going, and you had to lean close together to be heard.

I asked about the pregnant dog, the rescue coordinator, Billy, had told me about the day before. She was small—only twenty-seven pounds, fully loaded with puppies. Speckled like a coon hound, she huddled against the corner of her kennel, cringing from the noise, her eyes closed. Ashley and I went into her narrow kennel and I ran my hand over the dog, talking softly. She didn't move or acknowledge me. Her belly bulged.

There was no way I was leaving that dog to deliver puppies on a concrete floor amid the unbearable noise. I told Ashley, "I'm taking her," and then went outside away from the noise to figure out how. I called our puppy coordinator, Barb, and she said, "Gimme a few minutes to figure this out."

I didn't know what Barb would figure out, but I was absolutely not leaving without that dog. For the past nine days, I'd seen heartbreak after heartbreak and been unable to do anything except hand out a few donations and write about it. It was in my power to do something here. It was a chance to actually rescue, and I was sure as heck gonna rescue.

While I waited on Barb's call, I toured the rest of the shelter, but by now I knew what I'd find—large dogs, pit mixes, older dogs—the dogs no one wanted and few rescues would pull. SCHS worked hard to save every dog, and they nearly did. They were serious heroes. At the end of the row, I met two pit bulls eagerly lunging at the fence that separated us, seeking my attention. I snapped a picture, but then one of the volunteers pulled me aside and asked me not to post that picture. The two dogs were scheduled to be destroyed. They'd attacked a farm animal, and in this poor county, that was not a crime easily forgiven. By law, they had to be destroyed; it wasn't something the volunteers could do anything about as there were no rescues who would take a pit bull with a record of aggression. This was the part that none of us wanted to talk about or write about or post a picture of, but I spent a few extra minutes with those big dogs, memorizing their faces, acknowledging their lives, and wishing desperately this world was different.

The Scott County shelter budget only covered dog food—not vaccines or dewormers or flea meds/preventatives, not treats, bedding, not anything—just food. Everything else had to come by way of donations. Any and all vetting had to be covered by the rescue pulling the dogs or by the Humane Society's fundraising. After our visit, as we drove north, I posted a list of items they desperately needed, items you and I would consider essential, along with their dream wish—an animal scale to weigh the dogs so they could give rescues a more accurate assessment of the dogs they were trying to rescue.*

Barb called back and told me they had a plan. There was a twenty-four-hour clinic in Purcellville, Virginia, about six hours away. We could drive directly to the clinic (it was mostly on our way), and she would meet us there. If the clinic could do the health certificate and rabies vaccination, all would be well. If not, she'd take my little mama to her house (she lived about an hour away), and I would come back to get her in a day or so and take her to a vet.

We loaded everybody up and said a hasty good-bye, pausing to take a picture with the crew. Billy told me he'd listened to the audio version of my new book on his drive the day before and it had him in tears. I tried to imagine this large, affable mountain man in tears driving down the highway to deliver more dogs for rescue. I pulled copies of my book out of the van and handed them to everyone who wanted one. These people were the unsung heroes working tirelessly to save dogs that mattered to so very few. They had seen and heard the worst humanity had to offer, and yet they kept showing up week after week to do the work even while there was no end in sight. The chant began in my heart: Something had to change. People need to know. I would have loved to have stayed longer with these wonderful people, but we had a long, now longer, drive ahead of us.

I looked behind us at the sea of crates with our luggage tucked around them. My heart swelled. It wasn't much, but like the heroes I had come to know on this trip, I was proud of the few we were able to save. As I watched the rolling hills pass by our window, I heard the words "Take care of the ones put on

---

* A few days later one of my readers donated the much-needed scale. When I told Billy the news he said, "That is freakin' awesome!"

your path," like a commandment from somewhere deep inside me. It's all I could do, for now, but my mind was already spinning. People needed to know.

One of the dogs in the van, Flannery O'Connor,* was going home with us to foster. Whenever she heard us talking, she would start barking. If we stayed quiet, she stayed quiet. "Figures," I told Nick, "the only noisy one in the van is going home with us." And then we spent the rest of the trip trying to communicate with hand signals. There wasn't much to say, though. We were tired. My heart was spun dry.

We made it to Purcellville, and Barb told us there was no one at the clinic who could do what we needed to be done, so we transferred our little mama, who I'd named Dixieland, to Barb's car. I told her good-bye and that I'd see her soon.

We dropped off the other dogs at two stops in Maryland and headed home with Flannery and another dog, Gimme Some Shuga, who was staying with us for a couple of days until her foster could pick her up.

Two days later, back I went to Virginia to fetch Dixie. By then, Barb had realized that something was seriously wrong with her leg. Dixie had been so terrified at the shelter, she'd refused to move or even stand, so I'd been forced to carry her to the van and hadn't noticed the problem. The vet thought the bent leg was probably an old fracture. The owner who had dumped her at the shelter last Friday had likely never gotten treatment for it. The bones were fused together and calcified, leaving a permanent bend to her leg and making it shorter than the other and unable to reach the ground when she stood. She had obviously adapted to it and could move on it surprisingly well.

We needed to take X-rays to verify this assessment for Dixie's eventual adoption, and the vet told me, "She's so little, with the right angle we can probably see the puppies."

---

* I'd been allowed to name the dogs on my transport and had given them all southern names.

Sure enough, she was right on both counts. It was an old break, fused together, nothing to be done except maybe give her glucosamine to make her more comfortable. One picture showed the puppies. "A whole mess of them," said the vet. It was hard to know for sure how many, as they weren't fully developed yet. Dixie would have another week or two, hopefully, to grow them.

At home, we installed Dixie in our puppy room and for several days she slept. I don't know if I've ever seen a dog so exhausted. When I checked on her, Dixie would thump her tail at the sound of my voice, but not move. She was gentle and sweet and so, so, quiet. She did get up to eat when I fed her, but then lay right back down.

I spent countless hours with Dixie, watching, wondering. She was a daily reminder of the other dogs I'd met on our tour—the ones I had to leave behind, the ones who might already be gone, the ones I couldn't help.

At least not yet.

I was thinking and scheming and dreaming and writing and planning. Something had to be done. It was not acceptable that in a country as rich and advanced as ours that so many dogs were dying unnecessary deaths. It was not acceptable that we housed them in cruel conditions that broke their spirits and wore down their souls.

The endless stream of unwanted animals continued no matter how many good people like those I met at Scott County, and all over the rural South, worked themselves to physical and emotional exhaustion trying to help. In many ways it seemed like those volunteers were the little boy with his finger in the dike, holding back an ocean but no one ever showed up to fix the hole. We should have fixed this problem a long time ago.

Bob Barker had been telling people to spay and neuter for fifty years.* Why hadn't people listened? What were the obstacles? What would it take to make them understand that their ignorance and defiance were what was killing

---

* The new host of *The Price Is Right*, Drew Carey, continues the tradition.

countless dogs and cats? What would it take to make shelters into places that acted as a community resource and offered temporary shelter for animals in crisis, rather than a holding pen for rescues? What kind of change of heart was necessary to make people value their animals enough to make responsible choices about their medical care and not give up at the first inconvenience or obstacle? When would county governments seek out solutions instead of hiding the problem in underfunded shelters built next to garbage dumps and railroad tracks?

So many questions. I would keep asking them.

27

Home Again, but Different

I was home again, but restless and impatient for change. I sent countless e-mails full of ideas to rescue leadership. We had to do more. Images of the dogs haunted me—their eyes full of sadness and confusion, their bodies tense and leaping with stress or shut down and still. They scrolled through my mind when I woke in the night and when I sat down at the computer to write. I wrote articles and blog posts about the situation. Whenever I had the opportunity to talk about my new book, which was often as I drove hundreds of miles to signings or speaking opportunities, I always found my way back to the shelters.

I told people what I'd seen and they would shake their heads, unbelieving. They'd ask about fostering, wanting the funny stories of the dogs chewing through our house or having babies in our mudroom. The heartwarming stuff. There was plenty of that on our end, but what was so hard to convey was what happened to the dogs before they came to us and what happened to the dogs that never came to us.

In one situation, I remarked, "I met good dogs who are dead now," and the listener physically recoiled and said, "You can't say that."

And it seemed I couldn't. At many signings, people would pick up my book and ask, "Will it make me cry? I can't read it if it will make me cry."*

We don't want to be sad. That's the bottom line. There was plenty of awful stuff happening in the world, and the last thing people wanted to hear about was good dogs dying needlessly. But if they didn't know, nothing would change. People would keep buying dogs from puppy mills and pet stores, instead of choosing to rescue. In her book *The Dog Merchants*, Kim Kavin wrote that if just one-third of the people planning to buy a dog would instead choose to adopt a rescue, our shelters would be emptied in one day. One day!

I puzzled how I could share what I saw without frightening people away. I was convinced that if I wrote a book about the shelters, no one would read it. Or the people who needed to read it wouldn't. The media was beginning to gain momentum with television shows like *Pit Bulls & Parolees*, *Puppy Bowl*, and *The Dog Bowl* featuring rescues, and late-night hosts who bring out rescue puppies. But more had to be done to help the people and the dogs I had met in the shelters. I wanted to tell their stories. I wanted to take people inside the shelters. But how?

Dixie's huge belly had begun to limit her movement. She spent her days trying to find a comfortable position in the whelping box. Anybody who's been that pregnant knows the challenge of simply getting up and down.

When anyone entered the room, Dixie ducked her head and thumped her tail. If the broken leg that was never treated hadn't tipped you off to her past, the way she cowered upon introduction would. Someone was not kind to this pup. Since she'd been here, we'd had to carry her outside to potty. Once outside, she hunkered down and shook. If she did move, it was to pull toward a bush or

---

* For the record, *Another Good Dog* might make you cry, but most of those tears will be happy tears. Mostly it will make you laugh and wonder if you could ever foster a dog.

the woods—somewhere to hide. I'd yet to see her pee. She held it all day and used the puppy pads I lined her room with at night. It was clear she knew she shouldn't go in the house and the entire time I was cleaning up, she lumbered along the edge of her box, whimpering an apology.

"It's okay, sweet girl," I told her.

Watching her cringe at every sound and sudden movement, I ran my hand over her tiny head and assured her. "I promise, never again. Only love from here on out."

I couldn't imagine her getting any bigger, her belly was so taut with puppies, but if the vet's guess was right, she still had a week to go. For the puppies' sake, I hoped she'd hold off. Meanwhile, I did everything I could to spoil her rotten. She was happiest when I sat in the box with her and rubbed her belly while I read a book; I passed several evenings this way.

Later that week I got some good news. Vanna, the black-and-white pit bull I met in Lenoir County, was coming to OPH! Another foster had agreed to take her. Her new name was Sweet Tea,* and on Tuesday night, on a special transport bringing dogs north out of the way of Hurricane Florence, she arrived. I had a quick reunion with her at the transport drop before she headed off to her new foster home.

There was one more dog from North Carolina I was fighting hard to save—Oreo from the Anson shelter. Anson was also in the path of Florence, and before OPH could get him on a transport, his entire shelter was evacuated and he was taken farther south, to South Carolina. Rescuing Oreo would prove my greatest challenge yet.

The last time I'd whelped puppies had been with a dog named Darlin'. She'd lost five of nine puppies within days of their birth, and another a few weeks later when he succumbed to congestive heart failure. It had taken a Herculean

---

* Another name from my southern tour.

effort from scores of friends and OPH volunteers to save the remaining three puppies, but we did. That was eighteen months earlier, but that tragic weekend still crept into the back of my mind when I watched Dixieland in the whelping box. I wanted this to go well. I needed it to.

Fostering a pregnant dog was exciting and amazing, but it was also terrifying. The dogs came with no history, no prenatal care, lots of stress (theirs and yours), and normally no timeline. I was lucky to have a general idea of when Dixie's pups were due because of the X-ray she'd had, but that was still just a guess.

As the days ticked past the "due date," I got even more nervous. It began to look like I was going to miss the birth altogether because of travel plans. Back in the spring, when we were putting together the book tour, I thought it would be nice to work in a little vacation with Nick, to thank him for the countless dogs he would have to care for (and clean up after) while I was out pushing my book. When I got an invitation to go to a fundraiser for the Floyd County Humane Society at one of our favorite wineries (and possibly the most dog-friendly winery in Virginia), I jumped at it, even though it was six hours from home.

Chateau Morrisette is nestled at the bottom of the Blue Ridge Mountains. Going there would be the perfect excuse to drive my little convertible down the Blue Ridge Parkway with my favorite guy in peak leaf season. We'd stay in an Airbnb, hike in the mountains, drink great wine, and escape for a few days after the Floyd County gig. Sounds nice, doesn't it?

But then my book tour became a shelter tour.

And then I brought a pregnant dog home.

And then she didn't have her puppies.

Two days before the Floyd County event, I realized my little vacation fantasy was going to conflict with Dixie's whelping, so I prepared my second string.* Chris, Caitlyn, Juanita, and Katie came over to meet Dixie and get the lay of the land. They also checked in with Ian who would be the (reluctant) first responder while we were gone.

---

* Who were anything but, since two of them were nurses and Chris had mentored me for my first whelping—they were actually much more qualified birthing attendants than I was.

I knew Dixie was in good hands, but still, I was relieved when the organizer of the Floyd County event e-mailed to say I shouldn't come since the forecast was for heavy rain and wind and they had no way to move the event indoors. Books and weather like that don't mix.

We'd get down to Floyd County one day, I promised Nick. He was just happy we weren't leaving our sixteen-year-old with Dixie—we both hoped he was at least a decade away from participating in a birthing.*

Now Dixie just had to get through the ten-hour window when I would be gone for Bark Wag & Wine on Saturday, OPH's biggest fundraiser of the year and an opportunity to see some of my former foster dogs and sign books.

Dixie was nothing if not considerate. Not only did she have her babes before I left, but she was also kind enough to do it during daylight hours. Her labor began at 11 A.M. on Friday. Actually, it began (in my mind) the night before, at 1 A.M., when she got up and began making a nest of the towels and blankets that lined the box.

I saw the activity on our puppy cam and grabbed a book, pulled on some sweats, and joined her in the puppy room. She wagged her tail at the sight of me and hopped out of the box. We toured the yard in the dark and I reassured her (which was mostly reassuring me, since Dixie had definitely done this before).

I slept on the bench outside the puppy room, jumping up each time she got up for a drink or to rearrange the bedding again. By morning there were no puppies, just one exhausted me.

She gave me mixed messages—eating her breakfast while her temperature sunk even lower.† But then, just around eleven, Dixie began whining. She wanted me near. Our two weeks together had secured our bond. She nudged my hand and lay down beside me when I climbed in the box. I messaged Chris and Juanita to let them know puppies were happening.

Puppy number one arrived quickly—a brown-colored baby girl with a white stripe down her nose and white paws. She was perfect and just the right size for Dixie, thank goodness. I was relieved that instead of a limp noodle,

---

* I thought it would have been a great life experience though!

† A pregnant dog's temperature will dip drastically just before labor begins.

as Darlin's pups had been, this one arrived thrashing and mewling and was suckling as soon as Dixie finished cleaning her up.

The next one arrived a half hour later—a duplicate of the first, only much tinier. While I watched the two puppies nurse, the third one arrived. This one was bigger than the first two and covered in brown and black splotches, simply gorgeous. Another girl.

Juanita arrived and we waited.

And waited.

Juanita and I caught up and tried not to worry that the long wait between puppies meant something was wrong. This was not Darlin', this was Dixie, I reminded myself. She was much younger, had at least two weeks of good food and safety, and was delivering pups that were fully ready. All things that Darlin' didn't have working in her favor.

I fed Dixie some boiled chicken and she gobbled it down. It had been well over an hour since the last pup. Just as my internal panic was ramping up, puppy number four, a white girl pup with a big black spot on her back, arrived, butt first. Two more puppies popped out in quick succession—a tiny black male puppy and another brown girl puppy with a remarkable black mustache.

We could feel at least one if not two more puppies in the lineup, but Dixie seemed exhausted. I fed her more chicken, but no puppies seemed imminent, so Juanita and I decided that maybe Dixie needed a rest. She'd been dozing off between little clusters of contractions. We turned off the lights and went to the kitchen to spend a little time with Flannery.

Flannery smooched on Juanita, and for a few minutes we forgot about the drama unfolding in the other room, until I glanced at the puppy cam and realized a puppy was arriving. Puppy number seven was a brown male pup with four white socks.

Checking Dixieland, we could feel a large firm lump waiting to come out. It was either a whopper of a puppy or several queued up. Time dragged on and on. Juanita needed to go to pick up her daughter, but she hung around in anticipation each time Dixie had a series of contractions.

Finally, Juanita had no choice but to leave. Now I sat alone with Dixie in the box, watching and waiting. It was approaching two hours between puppies and I was just about to call Tracy (the OPH medical coordinator) for some reassurance when Dixie started contracting hard.

Nothing came out. She stood up and changed positions, pushing, but nothing. I put on a pair of surgical gloves, unsure how I could help but wanting to be ready. Dixie squatted upright and pushed, and then stood again. I lifted her tail and looked. My heart sank when I saw a tiny tail. The puppy needed to come out. Now.

I waited for Dixie to push, and when the puppy's hips appeared, I grabbed them. As Dixie pushed again, I gently pulled and the puppy finally slipped out. She was enormous—much bigger than the other pups. I was pretty sure Dixie would have gotten her out without my help, but I was glad I was there, glad I didn't melt into a sniveling, panicked mess, glad I could do something this time.

Eight puppies. Eight beautiful, healthy puppies. I couldn't feel anymore inside her, but I didn't want to say she was done since I'd done that twice with Darlin' only to have more puppies appear (seven hours later!). I watched Dixie for two more hours, feeling nothing but fluid in her belly. She was resting and seemed content. The puppies were adorable and fine, and Dixie was too. And in about two months, after the puppies were weaned and adopted, I would drive her to the vet to be spayed. And then the life she should have had would finally begin. I told her all this as I fed her more chicken and scratched her ears.

This sweet little dog, who flinched when you touched her by surprise and cowered at loud noises, who looked away in embarrassment when I had to clean up an unavoidable potty accident, who muttered softly in what seemed like gratitude when I rubbed behind her ears and leaned into me when I ran a gentle hand over her sides, who gave birth to eight gorgeous puppies, whose leg was broken and fused back together, but whose heart was healing—this lovely dog. She deserved to have the best life.

Dixie's first two years had been hard, but that life was over. My heart swelled at the win. I was still processing the trip, still sending e-mail after e-mail trying to save Oreo, but here in my mudroom, we had a win. A big one.

28
End of the Tour, Beginning of Something Else

s the last events of the three-month book tour approached, friends had said many times, "You must be exhausted!"

The truth? I wasn't. Not in the least.

I was energized and eager to keep working to spread this message, to save more dogs, to fix this oh-so-fixable problem.

The last week of October, I'd got word that Ski had been adopted. Ski was the little pit bull with the big red X I'd met at Oconee. After Lisa and I left Oconee, I'd continued to pester Jen, the shelter puller. Please, please, please. I knew Jen wanted to help, but she had the impossible job of deciding who came north and who didn't, and no matter how much she wanted to, she couldn't pull them all. Lynn, the rescue coordinator at Oconee, scrambled to get pictures and video documentation of Ski, and eventually, another foster, Annette, volunteered to foster her. She came north and became OPH Lilliana, and now she was in her new forever home, loved and adored. She could and likely would have died in that shelter. Others did. But I had to focus on the fact that Ski didn't. We'd saved a life.

And now I wanted the same for Oreo. He was the big white dog I'd met at Anson County Shelter. The one that had leaned his head against the fence that separated us. I was determined to bring Oreo north, but getting him here wasn't proving easy. First, there was the fact that he was a large, male dog with possible bully breeding. This required special permission and a committed foster. I agreed to be that foster, and eventually, OPH agreed to pull him.

But then Hurricane Florence had happened. Oreo and his entire shelter were evacuated in the middle of the night as the storm pounded. They were crammed in crates and vanned to Columbia, South Carolina, as the roof of their shelter fell in.

Another large rescue came to Columbia and pulled sixty dogs, but they didn't take Oreo because now he had two more strikes against him. He'd tested positive for heartworm. The previous year when he'd entered Anson shelter he'd tested negative, but Anson didn't have the funds to administer heartworm preventatives, and in the time since then, apparently he'd contracted heartworm.

But even worse news, he had also failed his dog-aggression test at the shelter in Columbia, which meant it was likely he'd be destroyed. At Anson, he was tested to be fine with other dogs, but a lot had happened to him in the interim, not the least of which was being evacuated on a chaotic night among frantic people and hauled farther south to a strange, crowded shelter.

In his test, he was fine with female dogs but reacted to dominant males. Why? I could talk your ear off with the possibilities, but it didn't matter because now OPH wouldn't pull him, as they, like most rescues, wouldn't knowingly bring up aggressive dogs.

"He's not aggressive," I insisted. I knew it in my soul. "I met him. I've talked to the shelter staff at Anson. That's not who he is, he must be stressed out." No one could see past the Columbia shelter's assessment* and his large size.

---

* There is no standard for assessing a dog's temperament at a shelter. Each shelter or rescue devises their own system. Many are outdated and unfair, but with no standard tool, it's impossible to know how accurate any shelter's assessment is.

Add to this new complication several layers of communication difficulties and the fact that everyone involved in rescue in North and South Carolina was beyond busy dealing with the hurricane aftermath, Oreo's fate hung in the balance for much too long.

I wasn't giving up. I was certain there was a reason I met Oreo on my book tour. Of the hundreds and hundreds of dogs I met, he stood out. Even if I could convince OPH to take this "dangerous" dog, finding him transport was proving impossible, and the shelter told us they couldn't get him ready in time to meet the transport even if we could arrange it because their vet had fallen and broken her leg.

At some point, all the excuses became motivation for me. Too many forces were lining up to kill this dog, and I couldn't let them. OPH would treat heartworm, but they couldn't get past the dangerous dog label; they needed assurances. I located more people who had met Oreo at the Anson shelter who vouched for him. They had known him in the long year he'd been in shelter care at Anson. None of them recognized this new Oreo that the shelter in South Carolina was so certain should be destroyed.

The Facebook messages and texts and e-mails flew back and forth up and down the coast between me, shelter volunteers and staff in Anson, our OPH shelter puller, the director of OPH, and the people in South Carolina. At one point, I grew weary. Why was it so hard to save this dog? I sat with Nick on our porch and tried to pick through the thousands of details I had, but too much made no sense. Finally, I closed my laptop and turned off my phone.

"There's nothing else I can do," I told him and went to walk Dixieland. It was a clear, beautiful night. We walked along the fence line of our pasture, the bats swooping low and the occasional fox crying on the ridge above us. Dixie's white shape glowed in the moonlight. She didn't want to go far, never wanting to leave her pups for long, so we headed back. I sent up a prayer as I walked. "Just get him here. Help me save him." I wasn't sure God would meddle with something as trivial as one dog among thousands in a shelter I'd never seen. Why that dog, and not another? A question I asked all too often but learned was futile. Was it chance or fate? I couldn't say, but for now I'd done all I could, and we would just have to wait. At that point, I didn't even know if Oreo was dead or alive.

The following Sunday my book tour officially ended. There were still a few more events scattered throughout the next month, and I was looking for more opportunities to talk about the book, its purpose, and all I'd learned in the shelters, but the three months of nonstop events and signings and travel was finally over.

My last event was sponsored by a woman named Karen Johnson. She designed and sold beautiful T-shirts with the message of rescue through her company PawsGo and gave away much of what she made to dog-related causes, many times OPH. She'd been a big cheerleader for me, sending encouragement and sharing my posts.

That night she hosted a book signing at Nectar Coffee and Wine Bistro in Alexandria, Virginia. Rooney, one of my previous foster dogs, joined me to sign books. It was a lovely event, but my nerves were ringing. I was all too aware of a certain dog heading north up I-95 at that very moment.

Oreo was safe. We'd found a way. I'd signed a contract with OPH acknowledging that if they pulled him, I would take this "potentially aggressive dog" into my home until he was adopted. I would handle the consequences if he truly was dangerous. I signed my name, certain that everyone else was wrong. No matter how hard I tried, I couldn't reconcile all that I was hearing with the dog I had met back in August. The dog with the sad, sad eyes who leaned against the kennel fence and reached his paw for my hand. The quiet dog who was starved for human contact. That's the dog I knew; he was not a dangerous dog.

But then I couldn't help but worry. What if I was wrong? I've lived long enough to know that I don't know everything, and in fact, many times I get things terribly wrong. What if the stress of shelter life, the relocation, and the crowded, chaotic situation had finally broken this beautiful dog? I told Nick that this was either going to be our biggest rescue or our biggest nightmare.

Even after I'd signed the contract, it proved nearly impossible to get Oreo north. The paperwork wasn't ready. There was no room on the transport. The meeting place was too far for a shelter worker to drive. My friend Matt was ready to drive down to South Carolina and get the dog himself. Finally, a volunteer from a different shelter said she could bring Oreo north with her. We made plans to meet her transport as it passed by on Route 95. That very night.

Finally. Finally. Because I had to be at my book event, my friends Nancy and Matt agreed to meet the transport and bring Oreo to our house.

Driving home from Nectar that night, I was overwhelmed by all that had happened in the previous months—the people and shelters and dogs, the book events, but mostly the outpouring of support and kindness I had experienced at every turn. It seemed fitting that it had culminated in this night arriving home to find Oreo in my driveway. Every time I thought about the struggle to get him here and how close he came to not getting out of the shelter ever, I swallowed tears.

When I reached our house, I was only moments behind Nancy and Matt. They were in the driveway with Nick. Oreo was here! I knelt down next to him and he leaned against me, just as he had in Anson, and it seemed the perfect final note of the book tour. We'd rescued another good dog.

This dog had my heart. I wasn't sure what would happen from here—I still didn't know what was true and what was not true about him, what lay ahead, or whether he would prove me right or just incredibly soft-hearted, but it didn't matter because now he was here. Now we could start getting him home.

We set Oreo up in our garage with deluxe accommodations. Nick hauled an area rug downstairs from the attic to set up a little mini living room for Oreo, and I pulled out all the best toys. We'd decided we would keep him separate from the other dogs, at least until the dust settled on all the mixed reports we'd gotten.

Plus, he needed to rest from his latest adventures: being neutered, vaccinated, microchipped, transported once again, and arriving here. We figured he'd need some quiet space away from the other dogs to decompress. When I visited him and sat in the chair in his living room, he climbed into my lap and put his paws on my shoulders like a hug. Oreo was not a small dog, and the chair I'd set up was a bungee chair, so when he did this we'd sink to the floor, but I usually stayed put until it got hard to breathe because I knew he needed this—he'd been living through an awful love drought.

Ian loved him on sight, and Nick was amazed at Oreo's impeccable manners—he didn't jump on you in greeting (the only dog on the property currently who didn't, since even Dixieland had begun jumping in greeting), he didn't pull on his leash, he didn't snatch treats out of your hand, and he hadn't made a peep yet. I knew that all could change as Oreo relaxed and realized he was safe, but for now, he was winning hearts and minds.

We were full up on dogs. I was officially that crazy dog lady, with four dogs and eight puppies living here with us. We hadn't had that many since we'd fostered Edith, a black Lab who had twelve puppies. I'd be embarrassed except, in light of all that I saw in the shelters down South, I was looking around wondering where else I could put a dog.

29

The Cost to a Heart

A h. I can't do this anymore!" I wailed at Nick after I cleaned up puppy
diarrhea coated on every square inch of the puppy pen, every toy, every
piece of fence.

"You know," Nick observed from where he sat with Oreo watching football
with a beer in his hand, "you reach this point with every litter."

He was right. I posted all the fun and cuteness and made it look like puppies were the best thing ever on my blog, but the God's honest truth?
Puppies are poopy. And puppies that have been wormed (again!) are plaster-
it-everywhere poopy. All eight needed a bath. I'd scrubbed the floor of the
puppy room at least twice daily ever since we'd begun our six-day course of
dewormer. And we were only halfway finished.

Fostering was not for the faint of heart. I did laundry nonstop, and had
walked miles in circles in the rain, and our latest foster, John-Jacob, ate the
tops off my dog-walking shoes. It took well over an hour from when I opened
my eyes in the morning until I could sit down with a cup of tea and the paper
because there were three dogs to walk, twelve to feed, and a puppy pen that

would require a serious scrubbing. And it wasn't just dogs that required my attention. Every morning, the cat followed me around mewling until I fed her, the chickens were waiting to be released from their house and fed, the horses stood in line for hay, and the barn cat darted from corner to corner, hoping I'd see her (but not see her) and fill her bowl with food.

But don't feel sorry for me—I loaded my own plate. And despite the poop and the mess and the endless cleanup, I still loved it.

🐕

Two weeks after he arrived, I took Oreo to his first adoption event. It was held at a jewelry store. OPH dogs would be featured in their holiday catalog, so to promote it they were hosting the event. Oreo was nervous at first—hair raised, clinging to me—but after he realized all that was expected of him was to sit calmly while people loved on him, he did great. He was such a gentle, well-mannered giant, it was easy to forget that he hadn't seen very much in his four years besides the rural countryside and the inside of a shelter.

Which was what made him so remarkable. For all he'd been through and the many, many ways that people had let him down, it amazed me that he was still a lover—leaning into people, climbing into laps, curling up beside me whenever I sat down. There weren't many dogs who could spend a year in an animal shelter, be adopted out and returned (twice), and still keep their faith in humanity.

Kid after kid hugged Oreo at the event. He leaned against every adult who stopped to meet him. One family of kids began a campaign to adopt him. Begging their parents who had come to the jewelry store unaware there would be adoptable dogs underfoot.

Oreo was special. I'd never been through so much to save a dog, so when he went home with his new family, the house felt empty. It was a great home and I was thrilled for him, but his adoption hurt more than most. Everyone asks how we can possibly let each foster dog leave, but I try not to think of it as them leaving us, more as them finding their family. We aren't their family. We are their foster family. We're here to keep them safe and help them get their hearts and bodies ready to be adopted.

But some dogs are just special. Not that I hadn't loved every dog we'd fostered, but some of them burrowed a little deeper into my heart. Oreo had cratered it. I saw something on Facebook about the pain you endure as a foster mom. It said: "I let my heart break a little so that theirs won't ever have to break again."

That just about summed it up, especially when it came to dogs like Oreo.

He got a great home with a family who already adored him. He would be an eleven-year-old only child's best friend, and there couldn't be a better job for Oreo. It had been a long and winding road, and he had literally escaped death multiple times, so I had no doubt that he was where he was meant to be. My sadness was not for Oreo; it was for me.

People told me all the time that they couldn't foster because it would hurt too much. As if I was some kind of superwoman who had no problem letting them go. So not true. While I was beyond happy for Oreo, it still really hurt. But my tears were not the point. To be blunt, the options are me being sad for a while or a dog like Oreo dying. When something matters to you, you're willing to sacrifice your money, time, comfort, and, yes, your heart.

Saving dogs mattered to me. So I never for a moment resented the emotions I invested or the pain I endured—it was part of the price I paid to do something that mattered to me (along with sacrificing a few shoes, experiencing an occasional sleepless night, and learning to live with multiple baby gates).

Feeling something—happiness, sadness, fear, joy, anything—makes us human; it propels us from spectator to participant in our world. I wanted to make a difference, I wanted to save dogs, and I never for a second imagined that wouldn't require pain on my part. The pain made me stronger and it only deepened my commitment to this mission.

That night after we'd said good-bye to Oreo and wandered around our empty house missing him, Nick and I drove through the rainy night to a winery in Maryland for OPH's Sip for a Cause.

And guess who was there, besides Santa?

Gala!

Another dog that broke my heart.

I'd shed more tears and had more laughs with Gala than any other dog we'd fostered. When I saw her, my emotions, which were already raw from saying good-bye to Oreo, overwhelmed me. I had to step into the bathroom to gather myself. I hadn't seen her since she left my house the previous March. I'd told myself it was because I didn't want to confuse her, but it was mostly because of the sadness I felt at being unable to save her myself.

While Gala greeted people and met Santa, I focused intently on the young woman pouring our wine tastes. "Yes, love that oaky Chardonnay," I said as my mind frittered through an entire series of worries. Would Gala remember me, would she remember Nick? Would she wonder if we'd finally come for her? Or would she be angry we'd deserted her?

I didn't really believe dogs processed (or obsessed over) things the way we do, but Gala was smart and complicated, and I put nothing past her. Finally, I couldn't stand it any longer and went to her.

Pam sat down with her, I sat beside her, and Gala gave me one sniff before launching herself on me and covering me with kisses.

This dog. She looked great. She'd gained a few pounds and looked happier and more settled. I was amazed at how good she was with everyone she met and how calm she was among so many strange dogs.

She had a similar reaction to Nick, and I noticed his eyes got misty at her greeting. Driving home, I was happy. Yes, I missed Oreo, and, yes, I worried that Gala still had no adopter, but the emotion that I felt was rich and real and simply evidence of my humanity.

There were so many more good dogs out there. And they needed us.

30

Rescue Road Trip

With Dixieland and her puppies all adopted, and Oreo gone now too, I looked over the list of potential foster dogs and spied a border collie coming from Scott County shelter. I e-mailed OPH.

"I'll take her!"

At her vetting in preparation for transport, it was discovered that my border collie, now OPH Hula Hoop, was pregnant. Did I still want her? Puppies for Christmas? Heck yes! The vet said she still had two or three weeks to go, but no one told that to Hula, who delivered three healthy puppies the very next day.

When Hula arrived, it was clear that she was only a puppy herself. She was more than happy to leave her babies to go outside for a romp at any opportunity (even four in the morning). And unlike so many of the other mamas I'd fostered, she was in no rush to get back inside. She loved exploring the woods and the cornfield. When she spotted Gracie, instead of growling protectively, she wagged her tail and whined, ready to play.

Her three pups (Scooter, Hopscotch, and Kickball) all grew quickly into adorable little butterballs. I knew they and their mom would be adopted fast, so I volunteered to take a returned dog named Daisy Duke. Daisy was returned for being an escape artist, but within days she was like Velcro with me, even waiting outside the bathroom door for me. You never know the real story when a dog comes back, but I try to assume the best. It just wasn't a good fit. Nothing wrong with this dog, just not the right dog for that adopter. Soon enough, though, she found her people and was adopted. Hula and her pups were not far behind.

On Christmas Day, we had another unexpected return: Flannery O'Connor. Unless you counted Gala,* Flannery was only the third foster of mine ever to be returned.† In the nearly three months that she'd been with her adopters, she'd begun snapping at the children. And as if to demonstrate this, she snapped at me when I reached for her collar to clip on a leash in our driveway.

"Oh no, we'll have none of that, missy," I told her and quickly escorted her inside and put her in a crate. She would definitely need a shutdown period while I sorted out where we went from here. When she'd left me, she was not a biting dog, but somehow in her life with five young kids and assumedly harried parents, she'd turned to nipping to protect herself. The family probably waited it out longer than they should have. I knew how impossible it was to predict/control/manage my three kids' behavior when they were young, so five only upped the ante. Inevitably training the dog landed low on the priority list. It certainly had when our Gracie was a puppy and my kids were seven, ten, and twelve. There was no time or energy or emotion to spare, and Gracie's early training suffered for it. Lucky for us, Gracie was a more patient dog than Flannery.

After a week or so of shutdown, Flannery returned to her former happy state, making us laugh with her expressions and her need to be in the middle of

---

* Who we'd fostered for nearly a year but who was not adopted from our home.

† I'd had one puppy and one dog returned within their first week trial, and one dog that lasted only a month, but Flannery was the first to be returned after more than two months with an adopter.

things. She was always invading my personal space, looking for a snuggle and following me around with looks I would translate as, Wanna play? Wanna play? I'm bored. Can we go out for another walk? How about a game of fetch? Here's the ball—psych! I'm keeping it—chase me!

The click-click-click of her nails on the hardwood floor followed me around the kitchen, her busy-ness mirroring my own. She nudged open doors, wormed her way over/under/through obstacles, and understood the dog door with no need for a demonstration. She nipped at new people and refused to be forced into doing anything. Luckily, she spoke the language of treats, and her stubbornness melted away when there was jerky in the mix. I had a feeling Flannery wouldn't be going anywhere anytime soon. Especially now that she had a bite addendum from her adopted family. Sadly, I would be right.

Winter is always hard for me—the unrelenting gray, the insistent cold, the short days, and ever-present ice that prevent me from taking my early morning walks. It just wears on my mood. Everything seems harder. To add to that, at least that winter, I was struggling to finish the gazillionth rewrite on a fiction manuscript I'd already poured years into, and I was beginning to wonder if I just wasn't ever going to publish another novel. I wanted to write more about the dogs, but what? How many foster dog stories can you tell? And what was the point? Dogs were still dying. The situation in the shelters had not abated. For all that I had written and shared, my trip south to the shelters hadn't produced any real results.

I kept coming back to the fact that people didn't know this was happening. Again and again, I would tell my stories of the shelter, and I'd get nods and blank stares that basically translated as, How terrible, I'm sorry there's nothing we can do about it.

But there was something people could do about it. It was crazy that the current situation in southern shelters persisted. I watched life go on around me and wanted to scream, How can you get in line at the Starbucks drive-thru or shop at Walmart or plan your next vacation when there are thousands of dogs lying on urine-coated concrete floors, waiting and dying? If they knew what I knew, I was certain they would understand the urgency. More people needed to know. That was the bottom line. Maybe I could take them there. I proposed to OPH that I take a team of volunteers back down to the shelters, only this time instead of just taking pictures, we would spend our days working in the shelters, doing whatever they wanted us to do. Their response? Do it!

I posted an open invitation to OPH volunteers and quickly signed up six people to join myself and Nancy, my friend and photographer who would document everything we did in pictures. Before we left, I warned everyone that it would be hard—not just physically, but emotionally. It had been hard to see when a fence separated me from most of the dogs. This time we'd actually get our hands on them, get to know them, and, more than likely, not be able to do more for them than lighten their load for a day and share their stories. But maybe, just maybe, with eight voices telling the story we could reach more people.

We created a Facebook page to share what we were doing, and donations rolled in for the trip and the shelters. I rented a big van and removed the back two seats so we could fit our gear and donations, plus crates to bring a few dogs back with us. We headed out on the last day of March.

The last time I'd visited the shelters with Lisa on my book tour, I'd been stunned. This time I knew what was coming, but arriving with a team of volunteers felt more substantial. We would join in the real work at six shelters, if only for a day.

It was a little awkward driving south with a van full of people I barely knew. Sure, we'd been OPH volunteers together, but we're an organization that has no physical building and communicates almost exclusively online, so while we knew each other, we don't "know" each other. We shared dog stories and lengthy silences, everyone likely as worried as I was about what the week would bring. I wanted this to go well. I wanted it to be the first of many. I was certain that if more people understood what the shelters were up against, change could happen.

Since the last time I visited the shelters, some of them had been ravaged by the flooding of Hurricane Florence, some had new buildings or new staff, and they all had new dogs and new stories, yet it was still, sadly, exactly as it was. Six months had not changed the situation. Dogs were still dying, shelter workers were still overwhelmed, and the public was still dumping dogs, filling the kennels with dogs they had no time, money, or love for.

At Lenoir County SPCA, it was great to see the familiar faces of Helen, the rescue coordinator/miracle worker, and Sherry, the shelter director/magician I had met the previous August. I hugged them and introduced our team. We met Debbie, the vice president of the board who was responsible for hands-on help at the shelter. She'd taken the day off from her real job to be with us. Her quick smile and positive attitude were contagious. We also met Laura, the assistant shelter director who did most of the dog assessments. Those of us who spent a good part of our day with Laura would come to appreciate her warm manner and how the dogs responded to her with great affection.

Helen gave us the tour, and we talked about our projects for the day. Matt, the engineer we'd brought with us, would spend his day designing and building a roof over the puppy play area so the puppies could have outside time even if it was raining or blazing hot. Erin would work with Helen to write dog bios and upload them to Petfinder. Nancy, with the help of Leslie, would set up a little photo studio, and they would get new pictures of every single dog in the shelter and even a few cats. Jen, Jess, and I would walk dogs and hold them for their pictures, sharing anything we noticed with Erin for their bios. And Jennifer, who was fluent in American Sign Language, would spend part of her day with a very special dog at Lenoir. Casper was deaf, and this made it tricky to get him adopted. Jennifer would try to teach him a few simple commands using sign language, and she would help to network him to the deaf community in the hope of getting him adopted.

Just before we set to work, a government inspector showed up for a surprise kennel inspection. I groaned inwardly. Of all the days. Poor Sherry. I experienced that stress on a much lower level when I had my inspections twice each year, but I only ever had anywhere from two to ten dogs, and Sherry had nearly a hundred. For inspections in Pennsylvania,* the dog warden needed

---

* Because I foster more than twenty-five dogs each year, I have to maintain a kennel license, and the county dog warden comes twice a year for surprise inspections.

to see proof of rabies vaccinations, copies of health certificates, and where I keep my fire extinguishers and hang my kennel license. She might walk my dog fence and inspect my puppy room. I could only imagine the work of inspecting Lenoir, with its staff and hundreds of records and a facility that likely had to meet certain codes. And, just to make it extra challenging, let's toss in eight strangers to get in the way!

It was a really good day and a good start to our trip. The staff at Lenoir impressed me again on this visit—they do so much with what little they have. Near the end of the day, I asked Helen how their numbers were so far this year, which is code for "How many dogs are you killing?"

She gave me a knowing look and asked, "Do you really want to know?"

I said that I did, and she waved me away from the others so we could talk in private. I braced myself, fearing the worst. Lenoir is a poor, poor county, and their kennels are full of pit bull mixes, more than half of them heartworm positive.

Helen leaned close. "None," she said. "We haven't had to euthanize any." She smiled, but then her face grew serious, stern even. "But you can't tell anyone," she said.

I knew why I couldn't tell anyone. If word got out that Lenoir County was no longer euthanizing dogs, fewer rescues would pull from them and donations might dry up. This was a sad truth, and I understood why Helen wanted me to keep the news to myself, even as I wished I could high-five her or do a little dance. She had worked so hard for this, sacrificing so much. What was most remarkable to me, and what made me revere her as a hero, was the fact that she was not an employee. All she did for Lenoir she did on her own time. If only there were more heroes like Helen.

As we finished up and prepared to leave, a pickup truck pulled up outside the shelter with two dogs in the back. Sherry frowned as she watched the man cross the parking lot. He'd come to surrender his pets. He said he got a new job and no longer wanted the dogs, which he'd adopted in another county. Sherry told him they were full, and he should surrender the dogs to the county where he got them. She knew this man; these weren't the first dogs he'd surrendered. She asked him why he adopted them in the first place. He shook his head and left, and I watched Sherry swallow her fury and move on to the next task.

Five minutes before closing, a couple arrived with a toddler in tow. The father wanted to adopt two dogs—a male and a female, he said, but he'd be happy if he could get the "gray female." He announced this in the parking lot loudly, and I wondered who he was speaking to and how he knew about the gray pit bull mama and her tiny puppy that was still nursing.* They were new arrivals and hadn't been posted publicly yet. It was too late in the day for an adoption, but Laura told him he could look around. His daughter began to cry and was frightened by the barking and the loud noise of the shelter.

We posed for a picture with the staff just as another car pulled in with a kitten to surrender. Just another day at Lenoir. A day that made me marvel at Sherry, Helen, Laura, and Debbie. How was it they weren't beaten down by the relentless onslaught of ignorance and apathy?

On our way south the day before, at the urging of Laurie, our OPH director, we'd made an impromptu stop at a tiny shelter in Essex County, Virginia, a place few people even knew existed.† At the shelter, we met another remarkable woman who was saving dogs through sheer will and resourcefulness. Ellen was a former college professor who took over a shelter with a high kill rate and turned it around. A fraction of the size of Lenoir, with just as few adopters, Tappahannock/Essex County Animal Shelter (TECAS) was fighting an uphill battle but was blessed to have a warrior at its helm.

I commended Ellen on the job she was doing at TECAS, and she said, "But for every five we send out, we take in six more." The same worry was etched on Helen's face. Two years ago, Lenoir County was euthanizing more than 50 percent of their dogs, TECAS the same. They have come so far, but today, when we visited on April Fool's Day, they were already full. The busy season had yet to begin. They were holding their own at Lenoir and at TECAS, but

---

* I never did find out how he knew the dog was there; likely he knew because it was a small town. One thing I have learned since, though, is blue pit bulls are popular, and many people breed them because they hope to get more money for their blue puppies. So it's very possible this was the case here.

† Myself included.

that could all change the next week—one hoarding case, one emergency, one violation from the inspector, or, heaven forbid, a health crisis for any of these women working so hard, and they could be back where they started.

I wanted to be hopeful about the situation in the southern shelters. I'm a hopeful person. They were making progress; it was just that from my vantage point, that progress seemed tentative, fragile, the thinnest of fabric that could easily tear. It was a toehold on better but a long way from good.

We still had so far to go.

31

It Was the Pitties That Broke My Heart

It was the pitties that broke my heart. I'd recently been told that I shouldn't call them pitties. But what else to call them? I'd been reading about the pit bull situation in rescue and in our country. The advocates advocate that we stop using this term because it's become an ignition switch for too many people. Mentally, I understand that there is no such thing as "pit bull"—no breed, no DNA test that can designate them this, and yet these were the dogs, with wide foreheads, tiny ears, and muscular builds, most likely to die in a shelter. Calling them anything else was tricky. I'd pressed Laurie, OPH's director, to start labeling our dogs "mixed breed" or "American shelter dog," or even "All-American dogs," as the AKC did. We didn't know what breed they were, so why call them anything? We might as well label them unicorns, I argued.

Laurie told me that while on a personal level, she completely agreed, OPH wasn't big enough to lead this charge. Adopters search Petfinder by breed. The first question they ask is, "What is it?" and by "it" they mean breed. But without DNA tests and not knowing the parents, we are all guessing—every shelter, rescue, humane society, all of us. We don't really know. As a writer, I have to call them something. For me, pit bull is an endearing term—I love this type of dog. I love their solidness, their enormous hearts, their big grins. And I hate what the ignorant public and click-greedy media has done to them.

Everywhere we looked in the shelters, it was the pit bulls that suffered the most. Or maybe it was just that they had such expressive faces. The next day, we were in South Carolina in Newberry County. We walked past row after row of pit bulls living in concrete kennels with no view except the metal wall in front of them or another kennel with another sad face.

The staff at Newberry County Animal Control seemed surprised to see us, despite the e-mails I'd sent confirming our visit. The large pole building was quiet when we arrived, just the shelter director and one other employee. They seemed unsure what to do with us but ultimately directed us to spend time with the dogs. We were free to walk them or take them into the gravel play yards. Nancy asked for a list of dogs that needed updated bio pictures and was handed a list of seven or eight dogs.

I led Kimbo, a large white pit bull with brown patches, into a play yard. I threw a ball for him and he dodged after it but then left it where it lay to come back again and again in search of my touch, so I spent most of my time "exercising" him by holding him in a hug. Next, I sat with Hazel, another pit bull mix, who was so frightened I had to coax her out of the dark building into the sunlight and once outside she wouldn't go any farther than a pile of gravel just outside the door. So we sat down and chatted for fifteen minutes until Katrina, the rescue coordinator, came looking for us.

I talked to Katrina, and then Leslie, the shelter director, and asked about their live release rate (LRR) but got fudgy answers. It was always an awkward moment when I asked this question at shelters. I knew they were wary of being painted as the bad guys, and, certainly, there had been plenty of people who have blamed the shelters, but without the facts, how could the situation ever get better? I understand that no one who works in a shelter wants to kill the animals, but too often they find themselves in a seemingly impossible position.

The public doesn't want animals to die here, but they seem oblivious to the superhuman effort it takes to find rescues and adopters and space for the endless stream of animals. They don't connect the fact that it's their tax dollars paying to kill adoptable animals. Pit bulls only made the situation more challenging. Some adopters can't adopt them because of breed restrictions in their insurance or housing situation. Others buy into the image portrayed by the media of pit bulls as dangerous dogs. Many rescues won't take pit bulls because they have an equally hard time placing them in foster homes or with adopters. The northern shelters are full of pit bulls already and less likely to take more of them from the South. But pit bulls are a popular breed, prone to large litters, and, consequently, arrive at shelters in large numbers.

When I asked about the odds for a pit bull or any of the bully breeds at Newberry, Leslie first told me they work really hard to save them, but then she sighed and glanced at the paperwork on her desk, and said, "But it's not fair for them to live their lives here. That's not a life."

She was right. I knew that, but there had to be another option beyond killing them. It seemed crazy to me—so many dogs being killed simply because of the way they looked. That was what it came down to. Rescues didn't take them and adopters didn't choose them not because they had a behavior problem or a medical issue but because of their appearance and an invalid assumption. The really crazy part, though, was that having rarely met the parents, it was impossible to know if they were or weren't this mythical breed that didn't exist! So their destiny was decided by a guess or a bad picture or a person who might be predisposed to call every beefy, big-mouthed dog a pit.

Again and again, researchers have shown that visual breed identification is extremely inaccurate, and more than that, scientists have known for decades that even first-generation crossbreeds usually look wildly different from either parent. So, labeling a dog of any breed is impossible to do simply based on a visual assessment.

The next day we headed to Abbeville, South Carolina. Abbeville's history was a hard one. I'd read articles dating back to 2010 about the city's shelter, which not only served the city, but also provided kennels for Abbeville County. The dogs were basically held in what amounted to a pound with no public access, no quality of care, and very little oversight. The conditions had been horrendous, and thousands of dogs had died there. The situation finally became public when a resident tracked down her lost dog at the city shelter and witnessed the cruel conditions and contacted a reporter. Thus began the journey that had landed us in Abbeville today—standing outside a brand-new building, once again a pole barn, being welcomed by a local councilman who seemed honestly hopeful they had licked their problem.

We met Jessica, the new director who had come from Anderson County P.A.W.S. Jessica was soft-spoken, young, and pretty, and seemed more than aware of how big the challenge would be here. Coming from P.A.W.S., she was well trained, but the struggle would be the same as it was everywhere—educating the public and creating a shelter that worked as a community resource and not a holding facility.

We toured the building and helped assemble new dog beds and cat condos before following Jessica's Animal Control truck to the city pound, the notorious place I'd been reading about, to meet the dogs who would move into their new digs soon. The new shelter was for Abbeville County, but they were currently paying Abbeville city shelter to house their dogs.*

The shelter was a concrete building surrounded by a tall chain-link fence topped by barbed wire. It was hidden down a country road that required passing vehicles to negotiate who would pull off the road to allow the other to pass. If you were looking for a set for a thriller movie, it would make a good one. There was no air-conditioning, and the only heat source appeared to be a single heater, similar to the kind you find on restaurant porches, hanging from the ceiling in the center of the dark space. I wouldn't have wanted to spend a night there, especially knowing that thousands of dogs had died in

---

* And here I have to note that nowhere that we traveled in or around Abbeville appeared to be a "city."

the dank, depressing space over the last several decades, and I wondered if the current dogs could sense the tragic past of the place. A shiver ran up my spine when I stepped inside.

There were fourteen kennels, one row for city dogs and one for county dogs. The dogs themselves, besides being dirty and covered in ticks, looked pretty healthy and were very glad to see us. We met a volunteer, a petite teen with a lilting southern accent whose mother waited in a car near the road. She was there to walk dogs in exchange for service hours. I startled when she called the city shelter director, Bryson (who seemed barely older than the teen), "ma'am."

Bryson gave us a broad smile and, at our request, said, sure we could get the dogs out to walk. The longer we spent at the city shelter, the more I worried about Bryson working out there all alone, handling the Animal Control calls and caring for the dogs. Clearly, she was dedicated, but her training came by way of 4-H, where she'd been showing cows for a decade. She wore cowboy boots and a big buckle on her low-slung jeans; she personified my image of a cowgirl.

The shelter was bare bones and it was easy to imagine that it looked the same as it did forty years ago. The supply room held Purina Dog Chow and Dawn dish soap, and beyond a few skinny nylon slip leads that cut your hand when a dog pulls, there were no supplies—no toys or treats and very little bedding beyond some worn Kuranda beds on the county side.

I asked Bryson what would happen to the remaining city dogs when the county dogs moved to their new shelter, and she shrugged. "They haven't said yet." I shuddered to think what would become of the place when the county wasn't paying to house their dogs with the city.

One of our team members fell in love with a small hound and asked to pull him to take back with us, so we made arrangements to move him to Anderson County P.A.W.S., where we would be on our last day so that we could take him with us in the van. There was also a black Lab who was gentle and sweet and appeared pregnant.* Her name was Baby and she'd come in with her "brother" Freckles. Jessica told me that she expected her owner would relinquish her and

---

* This was later confirmed and a few weeks after that OPH pulled her.

his other dog when he showed up and discovered he would have to pay $250 to collect them. I questioned the steep cost, and she and Bryson exchanged a look before she told me, "This is the third time Animal Control has brought them in."

I told her that I thought OPH might be willing to pull them, despite their size, and asked her to keep me in the loop on the owner's decision. They looked highly adoptable to me and certainly deserved a better home. And they weren't pit bulls, which, bottom line, was their best chance at getting out of the frightening shelter in which they had landed.

The treatment of pit bulls in the shelter system and in general is clearly breed racism. And like human racism, it is complicated and messy and wrong on every level. But unlike human racism, pit bull racism is not part of history. Pit bulls were beloved farm dogs and family pets, and a pit bull named Stubby is still the most decorated war dog in US history. I don't know when the tide turned, but it is well beyond time for it to turn back. Of all the dogs we met that week, the ones I carried home in my heart were the pit bulls. I knew that some of the beautiful dogs I'd met would die in those shelters. It didn't matter that they were sweet and playful and so very happy to see every visitor. It didn't matter that they were bastions of love and loyalty, who offered devotion on a level most humans didn't deserve. They would die simply because they had been labeled a pit bull, a breed that didn't even exist. Maybe we needed to start calling them "land seals," as I recently heard them referred to on the internet. Everybody wants to save the seals.

32

Which Dogs Will Die?

A t the shelter we visited the next day, it was no mystery which dogs would be killed when their time ran out. I had warned the team before we arrived at Oconee Humane Society and Animal Control that this would be the case. I told them about the visit Lisa and I had made there, the big Xs, and little Ski, the dog OPH had saved.

We spent our morning working on the Humane Society side of the building—bathing dogs, trimming nails, walking dogs, and photographing them. Then we were treated to a delicious lunch provided by the Humane Society. Lynn, the rescue coordinator, thanked us for coming and answered our questions. Then she introduced a volunteer to talk to us about their spay and neuter program. Oconee had received $80,000 from the county (yes—eighty thousand!) to offer free and reduced-cost spay and neuter services to their community. Janet explained that while that sounded great, it had been a frustrating situation. They were struggling to convince the public to bring in their animals for the surgery, and even when they went out to the communities and offered to transport the animals themselves, they were met with reluctance and disbelief.

"Why wouldn't they let you help their animals if it was free and convenient?" one of the OPH team members asked.

Janet shook her head, "Many of them said, 'It's just a dog, why would you do that?'"

And here was a key to much of the struggle for shelters in the South. Too many people did not value their animals—they weren't as much pets as property. "It's just a dog/cat" was a phrase we heard again and again, as if expending money or effort on them was ridiculous. Sure, there were a handful of people who claimed that they "wouldn't want to do that to him," when it came to altering their animal, but most people who didn't spay or neuter their animal simply didn't see the point.

Shelter workers will tell you that the biggest barrier to spay/neuter is cost and convenience. There are not enough low- or no-cost veterinary services available in many rural areas. But listening to Janet tell us how they literally knocked on doors and offered to ferry the pets to and from the clinic and offered the operation for free and were still turned down, my heart sank. It truly was an uphill battle they were facing. Attitudes had to change. What would change them? I surely didn't know, but the first step was awareness of the problem. People needed to know that their reluctance to care for or spay/neuter their animal resulted in dogs dying. Too many dogs.

After we finished lunch, we toured the "dark side." We all struggled with emotions as we walked down the row, pausing at the kennels with the Xs to give extra treats or reach a hand around the bars to touch these condemned dogs. One dog, Allen, was only a year old, and received his X because he was "dog aggressive." His owner turned him in to die. Allen was starved for attention and leaned against the fence, seeking any kind of human touch.

After about fifteen minutes, Lynn pulled me aside and said, "Your people are crying." Lynn is a big-hearted person and I knew it just about killed her that the situation was what it was, but she, like me, believed in letting people see the reality of the situation. It will never change if we protect people from the painful truth.

I lingered outside the kennel of Sheba, a cute black puppy with a white nose. She was friendly and eager and grateful for the treats I passed through the fence. I looked past the enormous X scrawled across her kennel card and read that she was six months old and picked up as a stray and had no bite history. And then I saw her crime. She was a pit bull mix.

I asked Lynn if we could get her out, maybe play with her. I knew the healing power of playing with a puppy. She could dry a few tears. Already my mind was reeling back to the last time I'd visited Oconee in August when we'd met Ski, who looked a lot like this dog Sheba and was also condemned to death for being a black pit bull.

We led Sheba out to a narrow area at the end of the kennels and let her off-leash. She was excited to be out of the kennel and jumped on everyone, licking their tear-streaked faces. She zoomed back and forth in the small space and pounced on tennis balls we tossed. She was just a happy puppy.

After we put her away, I walked three kennels down to study another young black puppy who looked so much like Sheba she could have been her littermate.* This dog's name was Thea. Her card said she was ten months old and a lab mix. Across her kennel card, instead of an X, was a sticky note indicating that a rescue would be picking her up on Tuesday. She was safe.

I was stunned. How could this dog live because she was labeled a lab mix and Sheba die because she was labeled a pit bull mix, when both were strays and no one really knew what either of them were? I made a short video of each dog and later posted it on Facebook, which caused some people to worry that I would get the rescue or the Humane Society in trouble. I left the video up, though, because it was true, and I was tired of shielding people from that truth out of some misguided idea that it might offend someone or get the shelter in trouble. One label—a label that wasn't even real and couldn't be proven—was the difference between life and death.

Ultimately, OPH would save Sheba. She would come north, prove to be a delightful foster dog, and get adopted faster than most. But would we have been as commited to saving Sheba if she didn't have an X on her kennel card?

---

* Later that night when Nancy and I were studying their pictures, we would struggle to tell them apart, finally resorting to the color of the bed and the placement of the water bowl in their kennels to sort it out.

And what about the dogs with the invisible Xs in the other shelters? I worried for Ghost and Shorty and Kimbo, pit bulls we played with at the Newberry shelter. Despite their loving, happy energy, their kennel cards could very likely be marked with invisible Xs. If they had instead been covered with that hand-scrawled X, would it give them a better shot at rescue? Would it make somebody do something?

This is what kept me awake that night at the hotel. Why, why, why wasn't anyone doing anything about this? And could I, a relatively amateur writer with few contacts and pitiful social media skills, do anything about it? I didn't know, but I had to try. I could not be quiet. I had to write about it and talk about it and find a bigger microphone. Somehow.

This had been my struggle from the beginning—finding that bigger microphone and convincing myself I could handle it. A few months after *Another Good Dog* was released, my publisher called to share an invitation to be a guest on the Hallmark Channel's *Home & Family*. My knee-jerk reaction was no. I can't possibly fly by myself across the country, navigate LA by myself, and be a guest on a television show. There was pretty much nothing more outside my comfort zone than every piece of that idea. I'm a nervous flyer, even in good company. LA is a city I had only ever visited long enough to know I never wanted to go back—the traffic and the crowds and the "coolness" of it left me feeling lost and made me want to move to a mountain in Virginia and become a hermit. And I'd had to google *"Home & Family* show" because I'd never heard of it, having never in my life subscribed to cable TV.

And, yet, it was what I asked for—that bigger microphone. So I did it, and plenty of other things that pushed me far outside my little box, because if that stressful experience could remotely change the situation I was witnessing firsthand, I was ready to do it.*

---

* In the end, my experience on the Hallmark Channel did bring in donations for the rescue and e-mails from viewers who wanted to know how they could foster. It also brought lots of questions about the show and Cameron, the attractive male host of the show. FYI, Cameron is very nice, and Larissa, the dog reporter, is a rock star, and the set of *Home & Family* really is a New England house built on the Universal lot. They change the seasons by gluing fall leaves on the fake trees in the backyard.

The deeper I get into dog rescue, the more willing I become to put myself out there if it will help. If flying across the country, facing my travel anxieties, and stumbling through a few questions under lots of pressure and makeup will help save more dogs, than I would be happy to do it every day.

Really.

Well, not every day. Maybe just once a week.

I was excited to finish our rescue road trip at Anderson County P.A.W.S. I knew that while everyone felt beaten down after our day at Oconee, the next day they would meet Dr. Sanders and see that there was every reason to hope. There was every reason to believe that things could change.

The next day's visit would also be different because several of us would be able to pick dogs out to bring home. After we'd showered off our day at Oconee, we gathered on a concrete balcony in the no-frills motel and shared chocolate and cheap wine and talked about our week. We had donation money to spend, and we divvied up who should get what, surfing the shelters' Amazon wish lists and playing Santa. It had been a good week. A hard week. I could tell that everyone was changed. Now they knew. It was a start.

The next day, just like I knew they would, the team found new hope at Anderson County P.A.W.S. The energy there was contagious. They had answers. The team met Cheyenne, the rescue coordinator, and Dr. Sanders. We toured the enormous facility and I spent a little time with two pregnant dogs—sisters who had recently been surrendered. I dubbed them Thelma and Louise. I could bring one home to foster, but not both. I did spend a quick ten minutes fantasizing about taking both, but no matter how I framed it, bringing home two pregnant dogs would be the first step toward divorce. I checked in with Barb, the OPH puppy coordinator, to clear Thelma and then posted pictures and videos on the OPH family page begging for another foster to step up. In the end, there wasn't a home available and so we would leave without Louise.*

In addition to bathing dogs and working on bios and taking lots of pictures, as we had at the other shelters, the team also got to spend some time with Dr. Sanders. She told them her story—how she took Anderson County from open-intake, high-kill to managed-intake, no-kill in just a few months. Granted, though being a veterinarian made that timetable easier, it did come down to the same thing she'd told Lisa and me six months before: "You just stop killing animals."

It was long past time for our country to stop killing animals. We left P.A.W.S., tired but inspired, and went in search of real southern barbecue. Over sloppy sandwiches and coleslaw, we talked about the week, what had worked (spending time with dogs, learning about the situation, making a difference) and what hadn't (cheap hotel with no breakfast or meeting place,† pulling dogs at the last minute). Everyone said they were glad they came and would do it again. I told them what I'd been telling them from the very beginning, "Tell someone about what you saw. That's the only way this will ever change."

The next morning, we were up early to load our dogs at P.A.W.S. and hit the road for the long drive home. We were serenaded by one little dog the entire drive and got stranded in DC traffic during the National Cherry Blossom Festival, but we made it home safely. Nick had already prepared the puppy room and set up the whelping box for Thelma. She delivered her puppies only a few days later—six beautiful, brown babes. I named them after my team. Since there were only six puppies and there were seven team members, I named one of them Jen Squared after the two Jens.

---

* Who left with another rescue a few days later.

† Or, in the case of Nancy's and my room, no bathroom door. To be fair, we'd insisted on staying in one of the rooms under renovation because the other room we'd been assigned smelled awful. The only room available was waiting on a bathroom door to be installed. It's truly a test of friendship to spend a week with someone in a hotel room with no bathroom door.

33

Mother and Son
Rescue Road Trip

A s the end of the school year approached, Ian had an idea for a summer project. Ever since I returned from the first trip south in the fall, Ian had said he wanted to go. His desire to travel south and see the situation had not dissipated. As soon as I returned from the volunteer trip, he said again, "I want to go."

Here's the thing about Ian: at six foot two and two hundred pounds, he seems formidable, but he has always been a sensitive soul. So when he asked again, that May, I again hesitated. I knew how hard it would be to see the situation in our rural shelters and be helpless to do anything about it.

He'd listened to me say again and again of the situation in the South, "It can't be that people don't care, they simply don't know." It was my mantra of sorts. He insisted that he could do something about it—he could document it in pictures. He was a talented photographer and had recently spent every penny he had on a quality camera. He'd been using it for a class at school and for an Instagram project in which he posted one image every day and planned to continue for a year, eventually creating an exhibit for his senior art show. Now he wanted me to take him south to see where the dogs came from, so that he could photograph them and share those images with the world.

Ian had been a partner in this foster adventure from the very beginning. He had walked dogs, cleaned up after many of them, and fallen in love with dog after dog, saying good-bye again and again. I owed him this. Plain and simple. He had a right to see where the dogs had come from and whether he could do anything about it.

And yet, I worried for him. I explained again how long the drive was, how exhausting the situation, that it would be hot, not fun, and mostly just painful, endlessly so because there was so little we could do. But Ian was convinced he could make a difference. That spring, he had a plan. It was a good one. One I would embrace fully and carry on long after he was back to school in the fall and immersed in swim season.

He told me he wanted to photograph the dogs—their expressions, their situations—and use those photographs to raise awareness. That year he had truly come into his own as a photographer, and he knew a picture could be much more powerful than all the words in the world. He wanted to take his new camera and go down there. To risk his heart, knowing it would be hard.

Finally, I relented. We considered many options, but eventually decided we would focus on western Tennessee, a place I hadn't seen. We would stop first at a bigger shelter so Ian could see what the "normal" public shelter situation was like before setting out to see a few private rescues and the tiny municipal dog pounds in western Tennessee, forgotten places where animals are in desperate need of rescue. We would count on Laura and Trisha, who I'd met when Nick and I were in Tennessee. Laura would arrange for some of our visits, and Trisha would drive west with us to find the dog pounds* that you couldn't find without a guide, places with no signs and no adopters, not marked on a map. Dog pounds still run by "dogcatchers."

---

* These were actually called "dog pounds," a phrase I thought had been abandoned decades ago in favor of "animal shelters."

Before we left, we created the site WhoWillLetTheDogsOut.org, where I would share our stories and Ian would share his pictures. I started a Facebook page by the same name, and Ian launched an Instagram account with that title. We loaded up our Honda Element with the few donations we'd managed to gather and headed south for the long, long drive to Tennessee.

Beyond the task at hand, I was excited to take a road trip with my son. In just a year, he'd be leaving for college, completely emptying my nest. I was looking forward to having uninterrupted time with him. He controlled the soundtrack of our trip—a lot of classic rock, the seventies and eighties music of my own youth. When we tired of rock music, we listened to the entire soundtrack of *Hamilton.* The drive down I-81 was a pretty one, through the mountains I hoped to someday call home.

We spent one night in a town on the Virginia-Tennessee border and got up early to get to Maury County shelter in Columbia, Tennessee. I visited Maury nine months before and I'd heard it had improved since I'd been there. They had a new director, had expanded their volunteer program, and, while there was still plenty of room for improvement, they were headed in the right direction.

Visiting Maury County (a public shelter whose numbers were improving but still not great) and then Williamson County Animal Center (a well-funded, no-kill shelter) that afternoon was an opportunity to set a bar. I was curious to see the changes at Maury County, but I also wanted Ian to see a typical municipal shelter before we set off the next day for our first pound visit.

At the Maury County shelter we met the new director, Jack, a bearded, baseball hat–wearing bear of a man who listened intently and shared his history, experience, and plans for the shelter as he walked us around. Ian pulled out his camera and disappeared into the kennels, snapping hundreds of pictures. When he found a particularly appealing dog (almost always a big one), he'd catch my eye and nod toward it with a grin.

We also met volunteer leader Maily, a beautiful, thoughtful young woman who stayed busy with her own tasks as Jack talked at length of his experience

---

* Twice.

and his plans for Maury. Since then, I've been impressed by Maily's steady, quiet, hands-on influence not just at the Maury County shelter, but in the rescuing of lots of dogs from Tennessee.

Instead of the barren kennels and isolation I'd seen the last time I'd visited, now the adoptable dogs had blankets and Kong toys filled with peanut butter, plus as many as three walks or playtime with volunteers each day. Maily had created a board with a list of volunteer jobs and room for volunteers to make notes about what they learned about a dog while interacting with it. There were shelves crammed with boxes of treats for the volunteers to share with the dogs. It was quite a different scene from the previous fall when I'd visited under the old director.

Dogs were still spending too much time in stray hold, but Jack seemed aware of this and assured me he was working to not only speed up the process but allow volunteers access to the dogs in stray hold. He was also trying to phase out the use of prisoners to care for the dogs and adding those responsibilities to the staff work, a move that may not have been popular with the employees but made sense for the dogs because they would have a more consistent standard of care.*

When I visited before, it was hard to pin down the live release rate, partly because the director did not show up to meet with me. To be honest, I never knew for sure what that number meant because there were many different interpretations of it. Was it the number of treatable, adoptable animals that made it safely out of the shelter through return-to-owner, adoptions, or rescue out of the total number of animals that landed there for any reason? Or was it the number of all intakes that made it out alive? And what constituted "treatable, adoptable," and who made that judgment?

One big difference between then and now was that Jack seemed willing to talk about just about everything. He'd been in shelter work for over twenty

---

* When prisoners do the work of cleaning kennels, there is no opportunity to train them beyond a rudimentary set of directions, as the staff never knows which prisoners will be working each day. The prisoners are cycled through work assignments, and the shelter cannot request certain prisoners because a predetermined schedule could create a security threat or enable contraband to be passed along from civilians.

years. He'd seen a lot. He'd learned a lot. Shelters were much better now than when he first started, but better didn't mean that too many dogs weren't still dying. We cannot settle for better. Any improvement would have been better when you considered that twenty years ago, the live release rate at many shelters was as low as 10 percent, which meant that as many as 90 percent of shelter dogs were being destroyed.

Jack seemed frustrated with people with far less experience than him pushing him to try new ideas, but to his credit, he seemed willing to at least consider those ideas. He agreed that live release rate was very open to interpretation. He didn't know the numbers off the top of his head, but later he e-mailed them to me. Maury had euthanized 108 of the 1,096 animals they'd taken in since January 1; more than half of those were very sick kittens. That put their live release rate at 90 percent, the gold standard for no-kill. Pretty good so far for that year as far as municipal shelters go, but not nearly as good as Williamson County Animal Center, just thirty minutes away.

To be fair, though, Williamson was smack dab in the middle of some of the poshest suburbs you'd encounter in the east. There were volunteers and money and community support to spare at Williamson. There was a large staff, a well-equipped building (with "catios" and a full veterinary suite), a full-time vet (and two techs), and a full-time volunteer coordinator (to organize the plethora of volunteers we were literally tripping over). This created an atmosphere that was positive and bustling with activity. Williamson's live release rate was somewhere around 97 percent, and Chris, the kennel manager who gave us a tour, told me that they really stressed over that last 3 percent.

Williamson was an example of all a shelter could be—engaging with its community, caring expertly for its animals, and saving every possible animal they could save. I asked Chris if their numbers were going up or down in terms of intake and without hesitation, he said, "Up."

So a great building, full staff, veterinary access, and lots of money still didn't stem the flow of unwanted animals. I asked Jack at Maury what he thought the problem was, and while he told me that he believed it was a complicated, many-pronged situation, he thought the biggest change that was needed was a "paradigm shift" in terms of how people thought about animals. For all his tough-guy appearance, he was a vegan who loved animals, especially cats. And like so many other people I meet in the world of rescue, he was baffled as to why other people didn't care about animals the way he does.

"This is a work in progress," Jack said to me many times on our tour. Maury does still have a ways to go in terms of care and in terms of shifting that paradigm, but so does this country. That much was still clear.

34

Tennessee Heroes

Our host that week in Tennessee was Laura. She didn't have a title per se, but in my mind she was the Rescue Wizard of Tennessee. Since meeting her on the book/shelter tour last fall, I'd gotten to know more about her and realized that she was the "man behind the curtain" when it came to rescue in Tennessee. Laura is an extremely humble genius who spends all her free hours connecting dogs whose lives are in danger in the South with rescues all over the country, and then facilitating their transport.

One night while Ian and I were visiting, Laura and I were up late talking rescue. I mentioned that she had a unique talent for knowing every detail about so many rescues and shelters and an uncanny ability to match up the right dog to the right rescue and then take care of every tiny detail. She was so calm and cool on the surface, hiding a mind that had to be spinning.

She nodded and ducked her head before laughing and saying, "I'm really good at manipulating everyone."

Which made it sound like what she did was something less than miraculous—which it wasn't. She had single-handedly, on her own dime, with no rescue or nonprofit or wealthy benefactor, saved the lives of tens of thousands of animals. No lie. Every week, she gathered the stats from shelters and rescues in Tennessee on dogs and cats who desperately needed to be moved as their time was up, and she sent the information out to rescues and shelters all over the country—somehow, magically knowing who had room, who would take a pit bull, who could handle a tripod shepherd or a litter of Dobermans or an aging hound dog. She made sure all the vet work was done and located a transport headed that way or transported the animals herself, many times first hosting them for a night or two at her house in a sort of rescue transport layover, so that they could catch their freedom ride usually north and sometimes west. And she did this not because she was an employee or even a volunteer of a particular organization; she did it because it needed to be done and she could do it. It started with helping a few dogs at one shelter and then it grew and grew and grew. Like with so many of the people I was meeting in rescue, I wondered: What happens if—heaven forbid—she gets tired of doing this or has to stop for some reason? There's no backfilling or chain of command, or even a job description for what Laura was doing. If not for her incredible mind and her vast heart, it wouldn't happen. Dogs would die.

Staying with her for the week and watching her juggle so many details effortlessly was inspiring. Laura has one dog of her own, Cadence, a large, goofy dog who always made me smile. She weighs fifty-five pounds and looks like she was put together from the spare parts of multiple breeds with a beard and an underbite and a scruffy coat. Whatever her DNA said, she was adorable. Cadence has laryngeal paralysis caused by an unknown neurological condition that compromises her breathing; hanging out with Cadence is a bit like having Darth Vader in the room. There is little to be done and Cadence's condition will eventually deteriorate, but for now, she is vastly loved by a woman with a heart as big as the state of Tennessee, so she is one lucky pup.

Laura had gotten married that summer, although her new husband had yet to move in. They're in their early forties and have a lot to consolidate, not the least of which is separate grown-up lives and homes nearly an hour apart. "Brent wants to finish up the job he's working on, then he'll be here.

He says he can't wait to help me with the dogs." She grinned wickedly and then added, "He has no idea."

🐕

The next morning, we headed west from Nashville, driving a long slog down US 40 and then several smaller highways that took us through Paris and Pillowville until we reached our destination: the police station in Greenfield, Tennessee. Greenfield reminded me of towns in Idaho—a wide, dusty main street divided by train tracks, where the cars parked diagonally, noses angled to the sidewalk, rimming storefronts that likely looked exactly the same way they'd looked forty years ago.

We found the police department beside the city hall. It was hard to imagine a town as tiny as Greenfield needing either. There was a Jeep Cherokee parked out front with the back end open so the occupant of the tiny dog carrier wouldn't overheat. We went inside to meet Tabi, officially the records clerk for the Greenfield Police Department, unofficially the keeper of the Greenfield city dog pound.

In this part of Tennessee, they use the word "pound" in the truest sense of the word. The dogs are impounded until their owners claim them, and if they are not claimed they are destroyed as the public nuisance they are assumed to be either by a veterinarian's needle or a dogcatcher's gun.

Tabi was a friendly, cheerful soul, despite the situations she faced every day regarding the dogs in her care and the dogs abandoned, abused, injured, or confiscated that soon would be. She greeted us warmly from behind her partition and then waved us outside to follow her to the city pound just a few blocks away. The pound was beside the water tower, next to a few unmarked pole buildings, presumably the town maintenance department. Six chain-link kennels sat on a concrete slab under a small corrugated roof. Five of the kennels each held a dog; one was kept empty at all times in case a police officer needed a place to put a dog. Each had an igloo doghouse or a hollowed-out plastic barrel for shelter.

"They're out here? All the time?" I asked. "Even in storms? Even in winter?"

Tabi nodded and explained that these kennels were much better than the old kennels, which she pointed to across the road. Literally beneath the water tower sat a small clutch of kennels that were falling apart, with rusting fence and barbed wire that looked like the trash can holders some of the people in our rural area built to keep wild animals from getting to their trash before the trash collectors.

"How long have these dogs been here?" I asked as the dogs threw themselves at the fence that separated us, begging for attention. There was a black Lab-looking dog, three hound dogs, and a gorgeous blue pit bull named Sky. Ian picked his way through the mucky ground behind the kennels. Spraying out the accumulated poop had created a feces-filled marshland behind the kennels. I wondered what his motivation was for braving the conditions, but one of the pictures he took that morning would later make him a finalist in an art competition and earn him a Scholastic Arts & Writing Contest nod.

I fed the dogs treats through the fence as Tabi rattled off the stats for each dog; several had been living in the kennels for more than a year. I asked if they ever got out of the kennels for a walk. Tabi scrunched up her face and said, "Sometimes I let them out to run. They race around, but they don't go nowhere. They always come right back." I glanced in the direction of the highway I could hear and the train tracks that crisscrossed Greenfield proper.

"Do you have any volunteers to help you?"

She shook her head. "The police officers are supposed to take care of the dogs, but they aren't trained to do it and don't like to get their uniforms dirty, so I do it. And they were just feeding them crap from the dollar store, so I bring the food too." Tabi cleaned the kennels each day, made sure the dogs had water, and fed them.

"How did it come to be like this?" I asked, swallowing my horror that a town, even one as small as Greenfield, could shirk its responsibilities and leave it all to one kind-hearted, well-meaning woman whose only real qualification for being the town's unofficial shelter director and de facto Animal Control officer is that she loves dogs.

Tabi started with the police department twelve years ago. Back then the officers put the dogs in the pound (the original falling-apart one under the water tower), held them three to five days, and when no one came for them (because no one ever did), had them destroyed at the vet in Paris. Tabi volunteered to look after the dogs so the officers wouldn't have to; she enjoyed it at first, but soon the kennels filled up. When another dog came in, she was told she should take one of the others to the vet to be euthanized.

"When they said that, I got pissed. So I took the dog home instead," she said. Only Tabi didn't have room to keep all the dogs that kept coming. She found another resident who would allow her to use a piece of property along the highway just outside of town. She moved the growing number of dogs there into makeshift kennels or staked out on lines. This worked for a little while, but then the public began complaining. It was an eyesore. The mayor told Tabi she'd have to move her dogs (who were really Greenfield's dogs). She told him she would but she had nowhere to put them, so he gave her a small spot just outside of town, down a narrow road, out of sight.

That's where we followed Tabi next to meet the rest of the dogs. The ones at the pound, she explained, escaped too easily from the kennels we were headed to see.

"So, the city pound is really the high-security dog prison?" I asked.

She laughed. "Yeah, pretty much."

At Tabi's rescue, Karin' 4 Kritters (K4K), there were fifty-four more dogs in outdoor kennels on a narrow, partially wooded lot. The walls were cobbled together from leftover chain-link fence pieces plus a few donated chain-link kennels and covered by a sturdy metal roof. Once again, Ian quietly disappeared with his camera, capturing breathtaking images that spoke volumes.

Each dog had a raised bed and an igloo doghouse or a plastic barrel, just like at the pound. They greeted us, jumping and barking, but then settled back down and waited for Tabi to visit with them, which she did, one by one, introducing us.

We met Amber and Brandon and their four kids, the family who took care of the dogs every day, all year long, as volunteers. There was no money to pay them. I didn't want to be rude and ask how they could afford to do this; they didn't strike me as the independently wealthy type.*

Maybe they did it for love, because clearly these dogs were loved. When Amber told us about each one, her voice softened and her affection was obvious. She introduced each dog to us, addressing it directly and prefacing its name with Mr. or Ms. When she answered my questions, she always began with, "Yes, ma'am," before telling me about the dog as if it were an old friend or a favorite nephew. The kids were in and out of the kennels, helping when asked, visiting with their favorite dogs. Amber applied flea/tick preventative to a big coonhound and a small pit bull who shared a kennel, dividing the application between them. All the dogs looked healthy and, considering their situation, happy.

I asked Tabi why they didn't go to the city or county for money to support the dogs, which were technically their responsibility, and she said, "I'm afraid if I did, they'd just go back to killing them."

Like so many people I have met in rescue and in shelters, she's afraid to make waves. Afraid demands will be met with not just resistance, but interference, or if the demands are too difficult, the county might just shut the shelter down and go back to killing the dogs. If the county or city took over, put up a real building, set up guidelines, they might tell Tabi that she had to euthanize Maxine, who was gray all over now but had a sweet smile and a happy attitude. Her only crime was being a large elderly dog in a county that doesn't care.†

During one of their encounters, the mayor told Tabi to write a business plan. Her response? "I don't know how to do that, and I don't have time to do it either—I'm too busy taking care of dogs." And keeping the records for the police department. And scrambling to find enough money each month. And driving dogs to vet appointments or to meet rescues. And loving fifty-nine dogs. And answering calls about stray dogs or dogs living in dangerous conditions or dogs people want to dump. With no Animal Control department

---

* Although I really hoped they were.

† As I was finishing this manuscript, I learned that Maxine was finally adopted after two years at K4K.

in Greenfield, Tabi, Amber, and Brandon act as the informal ACOs. No one calls the police about a problem dog; they call them.

Tabi could never do what she does without Amber and her family. I enjoyed talking with them, listening to them joke with each other, sharing their plans for a large outdoor play space, and laughing with them at the newest guest, a skinny brown dog lounging in a baby pool to cool off in the oppressive heat, his head poking over the rim, giving us the side-eye.

Some of the dogs had been living at K4K for two years or longer, most at least several months. I asked if anyone ever came to adopt dogs, and Amber laughed and said, "We get someone out here maybe every couple of months." The rest of the dogs are moved out through rescues, mostly out of state, thanks to Laura.

As we got ready to leave, Tabi asked if we could take the tiny Chihuahua in the back of her Cherokee to Laura's house. Her name was Helen and her tongue lolled permanently out of the side of her mouth, making us laugh and instantly endearing us to her. Tabi had picked her up in the middle of the highway and Laura was sending her to a rescue in Chicago.

We left K4K with a few donations of treats, dewormers, toys, and flea/tick preventatives. Despite their meager budget, Amber did manage to give the dogs heartworm preventatives, a rarity in too many southern shelters and rescues despite the risk of infection in the warm climate.* Most of the dogs were not neutered or spayed. There was no vet in Greenfield and the closest ones were not willing to give any discount to the rescue, so they traveled forty minutes to the vet in Paris who would help them.

As I took all of this in, I couldn't help but think of the shelter we'd seen the day before in Williamson County, with their well-stocked in-house veterinary suite, on-staff vet (and two techs), and their army of volunteers. I wondered if they could be a big-sister shelter to K4K, sharing some of their wealth and perhaps taking a few of their dogs.

The other thing I wondered as we drove away was, What if something happens to Tabi or Amber? What then? How can there be a place in this

---

* Heartworm is transmitted by mosquito bite.

country—a place with an adorable downtown with its own police department and a city hall with a flag flying out front—that doesn't spend a single penny to take care of its lost dogs? Instead, it depends on two women with limited incomes to care for all the unwanted animals in their town, pick up the strays, respond to calls for help, and deal with abuse and neglect. How can this town do nothing to help or change the situation? Is it because they don't care or because they don't know?

35

Where Is the Line between Caring and Killing?

The next day, after plying Ian with eggs and bagels, we drove out to Trisha's place, home of her rescue, Rural Animal Rescue Effort (RARE). Nick and I had visited briefly on the last trip, so I knew what to expect. RARE is foster-based, but most of that fostering is done by Trisha herself in her little brick rancher home she's converted to a shelter of sorts. The bunnies and kitties live in the garage, and the dogs are kept either outside in covered indoor/outdoor kennels or inside in Trisha's living room in large crates. There is a large fenced-in play area and several other fenced areas that allow the dogs to get playtime and exercise every day.

Trisha struggled to trust other people with her animals and found many times it was easier to do it herself than farm out the dogs and cats and bunnies. Because she transports dogs to the homes of potential adopters, having them all in one location makes her work easier. Having that many animals at her house though makes for one mountain of work.

"I'm not really a human person," she told me. "I'm a dog person."

Trisha is a pretty brunette with an expansive heart for animals, a well-honed mistrust of people, and a get-it-done personality. She does not suffer fools easily and has no qualms about calling a spade, a spade. We waited while she finished up her morning chores, and then we climbed in our car for the drive west.

It was hard to keep up with Trisha's busy mind as she rattled off the situations we might encounter, depending on how our day went. Listening to her take calls and deal with rescue business in the back seat as we drove gave me a glimpse of the chaos that is her life. I continued to be amazed at what so many (mostly women) were willing to do to save dogs in the rural South. No one I knew in my little rural-suburban life would believe it if I told them. Even a loose dog is pretty much unheard of in our parts.

Recently, a dog was spotted loose and unattended in a yard in a fairly affluent part of Baltimore County, just over the state line from where we live. People on the site Nextdoor explained that they'd spotted the loose dog and stopped. It had jumped right in their car, and they were now keeping it safe until its owners were found. There were over thirty-five comments and suggestions for what to do with the dog, and it was posted on multiple sites as a lost dog within the hour. It turned out the dog lived at the house where they'd found it. If I explained that situation to some of the people I encountered in Tennessee they'd probably wonder what I was smoking. They'd never believe that one loose dog in its own yard could cause so much worry. Down here, loose dogs were commonplace. Most people didn't give a second thought to a loose dog wandering in their neighborhood. Surely, it belonged to someone, and if it didn't, well, it would probably just move along.

Unless that person was Trisha or Amber or any of the heroes who assumed the responsibility the county was shirking.

🐕

Our first stop was the Huntingdon dog pound in Carroll County. Trisha explained that she hoped we'd be able to get in but hadn't gotten confirmation from the dogcatchers she'd contacted. I know you think I'm making it up (because I thought Trisha was calling them that out of disgust), but "dog-catcher" is really what they're called. It's a paid position in many of the counties in Tennessee. In fact, Carroll County and Huntingdon city each have a paid dogcatcher, and they are both responsible for the Huntingdon pound.

Trisha checked her phone again. No response. "They don't give a shit," she said. Ian smiled and shook his head. He, like I, had been listening to Trisha's side of many colorful conversations for the last few hours. Later he would describe Trisha as a New Yorker, which she was, but he meant it more because of her language and her attitude. She was my kind of rescuer, though: determined, passionate, and not afraid to say what she really thought.

The truth of her pronouncement was clear when we arrived. Quite literally, the dogcatchers did not give a shit. The Huntingdon pound was a small concrete building surrounded by a tall chain-link fence with three strings of barbed wire on top. The only sign on the road in didn't mention a dog pound; it said, You are Entering a Firing Range and Will Be Prosecuted for Trespassing. I wondered if we were trespassing, but Trisha knew where the key was, so I assumed she had some kind of tacit approval for our visit.

There were no dogcatchers or kennel attendants, just four dogs in kennels that were piled with feces, flooded with urine, and swarming with flies. There were no beds or doghouses or even a blanket to lie on, so the dogs had no choice but to lay in their own filth. They barked at the sight of us, jumping against the fence excitedly. One small brown pit bull was emaciated and crusted with poop, but wiggled and wagged, eager for our attention. A few kennels down were two dogs together in one kennel with twice as much filth. One had a belly likely bloated with worms; the other Trisha was pretty sure was a sibling of a dog back at her house she had rescued a few weeks before. Around the other side of the building, we found a sweet yellow dog with doe eyes and a nylon collar, also frighteningly thin, who had a soft cough.

"He's heartworm positive," Trisha said when she heard his cough. "I'm positive of it."

"What will happen to them?" I asked as Ian snapped pictures. I'd never seen such a sad situation and wondered what Ian thought, but he kept the camera in front of his eyes, documenting everything and saying nothing.

Trisha shrugged. "They'll stay here until the guys get tired of taking care of them. Then they'll take them to the vet to be killed."

"But what if you say you're going to pull the dogs?" I asked.

She shook her head. "Doesn't matter, but one of the techs there will call me if they show up, and then I try to get over there in time."

It's twenty-five dollars to have a dog euthanized in these parts. Trisha assured me that they had it good; she knew of another pound where they just shot the dogs and saved the money.

I thought of the two-and-a-half-hour drive we'd just made to get here, the thirty-five other animals presently at Trisha's house. As if reading my mind, she muttered, "I just know they're gonna kill these guys soon, and I can't get out here until Sunday. I've got to get some dogs adopted."

I glanced back at my little Honda Element. We hadn't even brought a crate, but I briefly considered just packing the dogs in the car and taking them away, anywhere, even loose would be better than starving to death, lying in their own filth, awaiting certain death.

Trisha went back to the car for the supplies she'd brought. I held each dog while she tested for heartworm, dewormed each dog, fed it heartworm preventatives, and applied flea/tick preventative. All the dogs, except the bloated hound dog, were sweet and submissive, not even flinching at the needle stick. The little brown dog rolled on her back and sighed contentedly at our touch, then wagged her tail through the whole ordeal. I could feel her bones poking me as I held her, and a lump formed in my throat. When we finished, I didn't want to release her. I wanted to tuck her into my back seat and take her home with me. What were her chances? I'd seen enough on my shelter tours to know they weren't good.

She wiggled her butt and danced around as I led her back to her kennel, as if trying to convince me to take her somewhere else instead. On a whim, I asked Trisha if we could get a video of her with another dog, just in case I could talk somebody at OPH into rescuing her, even though I knew that person would likely be me. Trisha pulled out the blond dog from the back and we introduced them. My little girl, who I was calling Fanny, only wanted to play. We caught it on video, and I hoped it would be enough to convince the powers that be that she was dog-friendly.

Ian had disappeared around the back of the building. I knew from his silence that he was having a hard time emotionally. I was struggling too, and this was my third trip south. Had it been a mistake to bring him here? Would this nightmare follow him home? It was reality, but that didn't mean it didn't hurt terribly to see it up close, to touch these dogs and know what their likely end would be. I didn't want to put Fanny back in her kennel to die. Why couldn't I just take her with me? Sensing my hesitation, she glanced up at me with impossibly sad eyes, even though her tail never wavered.

"I'm sorry, girl," I whispered as I opened her kennel gate. She walked slowly inside and then lay down against the fence, watching as Trisha sprayed out another kennel. We moved all the dogs to clean runs, gave them fresh water, and fed them before reluctantly leaving.

Later, when I talked to Nick on the phone, I told him about the little brown dog. There was something about her that touched my heart, it was as if I knew her already. Her pain was my pain. I would study the pictures Ian took of her and those eyes would haunt me for months.

As sad as I felt leaving the Huntingdon pound, I had to buck up. I couldn't do anything about the problem if I let it stun me into inaction. These dogs needed more advocates, and if I was going to be one, then I needed to be able to see their situation clearly, and we still had more visits to make.

When we stopped to grab a quick lunch, Ian confided to me, "I've had enough."

I'd told him before we left that if it got to be too much, we would cut and run. I'd worried this would be too much. Like everyone else I've told about what I've seen on my trips, he hadn't believed it could be that bad. It was that bad. But this was even worse.

"We have to go to Red Fern, they're expecting us," I told him. "You can stay in the car, but you'll be bored and hot, you might as well get out and take pictures. But we'll leave tomorrow."

He didn't say anything. As we drove to Red Fern, Trisha left a message on the voice mail of each dogcatcher. "Don't kill them, I'm coming to get them," she said. Then she called the vet clinic and asked them to call her if the dogs were brought in. When she hung up, I asked if they would really call, and she said, "It depends on which vet tech is working."

Red Fern Animal Shelter is a lot like K4K: privately run on best intentions, humongous hearts, and never enough money. Anne and Kim are sisters in their sixties who care for seventy dogs and 145 cats at their property in Dresden. Weakley County has no real shelter, just a dog pound like Huntingdon. Anne and Kim were not actively taking in dogs since so few ever left, but that didn't stop dogs from finding their way to them.

Trisha met Anne and Kim while she was living in Buffalo, New York, working for a rescue that pulled from Red Fern. She couldn't believe the things they told her and had to come down to see for herself. Not long after, she moved down here and began rescuing independently.

Anne and Kim were happy to see us, hugging Trisha and introducing us to dog after dog. Kim is a teacher with a warm smile and a soft voice, the kind of teacher who former students mention when they talk about the influences in their lives. Anne is a nurse—sharp and thoughtful; she told me about hammering in the last nail on Thanksgiving Day when she finished designing and building the kennels. Both women were intelligent and interesting and passionately committed to saving animals.

All the dogs at Red Fern lived outside in large, homemade kennels with worn tarps attached to the sides and roofs to offer shade and protection. It was a lush, shady spot, but it was still unbearably warm that day. Ian mumbled a hello and disappeared to photograph the dogs. I asked Anne if they had volunteers, and she mentioned one regular volunteer who helped out. Looking around at the sprawling grounds covered with kennels, it was hard to imagine these older women cared for all of it, but they did and had been doing it for years.

I asked Anne how they got into this business. She told me about Tiger, her beloved dog who died fifteen years ago. When he passed, she decided she wanted to give something back. "It was the first time I ever had that feeling in my life," she said.

So, she volunteered to foster for another organization, and they brought her nine dogs and some cattle panels to keep them in. "The dogs all got out," she laughed. Nine? And here I was thinking it was such a trial when I cared for my first foster dog, a tiny beagle who ate all the kids' stuffed animals.

After a while, Anne and Kim decided they could do better themselves. So they created Red Fern Animal Shelter. Like Tabi and Karin' 4 Kritters, they began doing what the county should have been doing, paying for it out of their own pocket and now with their Social Security.

It was clear that Anne and Kim loved these dogs. In fact, that seemed to be part of the problem. They couldn't imagine letting them go to just anybody. There were very few adoptions. Trisha pulled some of their dogs, the ones she thought she could place. "If we could just find homes for the young ones, the old ones could stay," Anne told me.

I leaned into the kennel of an adorable, tiger-striped puppy with a beautiful boxer face, and Kim decided to let him out to bound around the yard for a bit. He was only six months old and came to Red Fern suffering from Demodex mange but was strikingly handsome now.

Trisha called Ian over to try to get pictures of Chance, a huge white six-year-old pit bull with an equally huge smile. He'd been there too long, and with his great personality, she was certain there must be a home for him.

I spent a few moments with Lyric, a young black dog who looked like the standard-issue OPH dog, the kind we seemed to pull by the dozens. She was thrilled for my attention and happily gobbled up the treats I passed her. I snapped a few pictures and made a note to mention her to Laura.

We couldn't stay long; we still had the long drive back to Laura's, and Trisha needed to get home to begin her four-hour evening feeding/cleaning. We gave Anne and Kim a few donations and promised to spread the word, but a hopelessness washed over me. How could we help these women? To my mind, if they kept going the way they were, the situation was just one health crisis for Anne or Kim away from a national headline: SENIOR CITIZENS WITH TWO HUNDRED ANIMALS. Really, this situation was simply too hard to explain. I was certain they didn't set out to do this. They set out to help a handful of animals, but then, like water finding the gully, more and more washed up. And how do you say no? No wasn't a word Kim and Anne could say to a helpless creature in Dresden, Tennessee.

I used the frog in the kettle analogy a lot to explain how my house had become such a dog-centric place where I find it not the least bit odd to walk through two baby gates to get to the kitchen every day. The same applied here. Probably, when they began, the shelter was manageable, the workload reasonable, but little by little the heat increased until now, when they should be retiring and slowing down, they were boiling in a pot of their own making and the temperature was only rising.

Back at Laura's, Ian disappeared into his bedroom, likely to text his girlfriend or play a game on his phone to decompress. I began packing up our car and rearranging to accommodate our extra passengers.* Laura was busy preparing for a transport leaving from her house the next morning at five. Ian seemed stunned by all that we had seen, but when Laura called him downstairs to see an enormous Great Dane who was one of the dozen dogs spending the night to catch the early transport, his smile returned. Ian loves the big dogs.

As I loaded our car to head home, I wished I could stay. There were so many stories here. So much happening that seemed impossible. I knew that most people, at least people I knew, wouldn't believe what was happening down here. I couldn't imagine my little town tolerating Animal Control Officers who allowed dogs to suffer and starve before they eventually killed them, having made no effort to find them a home. Why was it possible here? Where was the outrage?

I'd asked this question of Kim that afternoon, and she'd said, "People don't care. It's just a dog."

Those were the same words I'd heard a few months ago in South Carolina. Was there a line somewhere between North and South, like the Mason-Dixon line, where people stopped caring about animals? Where dogs were regarded as a nuisance rather than pets? Where you couldn't be bothered to spay or neuter or even vaccinate them? Where you only fed them garbage and didn't

---

* The regular transport for OPH had run into difficulty, and they'd asked me to transport two dogs north with us.

worry about exercise or enrichment? Where when you got tired of them or they became too much work, you dumped them on a local rescue or took them to the pound and left them to be euthanized?

At the same time, it was also hard to imagine anyone doing the things that Kim and Anne and Trisha and Tabi and Amber did to save dogs. Why was this work left to them? They were soldiers in this battle against apathy and cruelty that should not exist. That didn't have to be.

But how do you make people care? Why can they look the other way when these dogs were abandoned in a locked, lonely, barbed-wire place all alone to starve to death, only to be eventually dumped at a vet to be killed or, worse yet, shot to death by the hands that should be caring for them?

If I hadn't been there seeing it with my own eyes, running my hands over the bones of these dogs, looking into their desperate eyes, I wouldn't believe it.

36

Who Will Let
the Dogs Out?

Early the next morning, long after Laura had left with her van full of dogs, we loaded up our new passengers—Evie, a large red Doberman, and Shorty, a squat yellow dog who was still in shock from his second neutering the day before.* Shorty was content to hunker down in a crate, but Evie, once squashed into hers, commenced a lengthy soliloquy as to her unhappiness. Eventually, we would break down and release her, and she traveled most of the trip tethered in the back seat, silent.

Driving up Interstate 81, we passed my beloved Blue Ridge Mountains, and all I could think about was how soon I could get back down to Tennessee. There was so much more to see. So much more to share. People needed to

---

* No one could verify that he'd been neutered, and some dogs who are neutered later in life still had some "baggage," so he'd been sent for surgery, opened up, and verified that yes, he had already been neutered.

know. Thinking of the dogs that might already be dead at Huntingdon, especially Fanny, the little brown pittie pup, increased the urgency. People needed to know. That was the only way things would change.

But why was I the one to tell them? Certainly, there were journalists and celebrities with more talent and more reach than I. Why weren't they raising a ruckus? Yes, the number of dogs dying in our country had been reduced, but it was still too high. Who would speak for dogs like the hound dog with the belly full of worms or the poop-encrusted pittie pup? Would their deaths even be counted? After seeing what I saw and hearing the stories, I knew for certain that the numbers were not accurate. The big organizations pushing the no-kill agenda hadn't found these little pounds. At most of the shelters I visited, when I mentioned some of the organizations, like Best Friends Animal Society, they had never heard of them. They were too busy working like mad to save animals. They didn't have time to write grant applications, let alone report numbers anywhere they weren't legally bound to. The help needed to trickle down. Maybe these shelters only housed a few hundred dogs, but add all those shelters together and you had tens of thousands of dogs dying, unaccounted for and forgotten.

It was within our power to fix this. The evening when I returned to Laura's after visiting Tabi in Greenfield County and seeing K4K, I'd met with a woman named Robin. A physician by training, Robin also volunteered at the two shelters we'd visited on our first day in Tennessee. She had asked if we could visit another small shelter on the other side of Nashville, but there wasn't time, and I was pretty sure Ian's heart was at capacity. So I invited Robin to stop by to talk that Tuesday night at Laura's. Robin's specialty was organizing volunteers. She'd done it at the Williamson County Animal Center and Maury County and was now working with another shelter, the one she'd hoped we'd have time to see—Cheatham County Animal Control.

At Laura's we shared a bottle of wine and talked, enjoying the company of Helen, the tiny Chihuahua with the tongue stuck out. I told Robin about K4K, as it was fresh on my mind and heart. Robin was a good listener and she asked questions about K4K, looking up the rescue on her phone as we talked. She mentioned that there was a college not far from them. Finally, she asked, "Do you think they'd be open to some help?" Laura and I had looked at each other and nodded. Yes, Amber and Tabi would likely love help.

By the next afternoon, as we were leaving Huntingdon pound, I'd gotten a message from Robin. She'd already created a Facebook group for K4K volunteers. By that evening she had more than one hundred members. She told me that statistically probably only 10 percent would actually pan out, but that could mean a dozen regular volunteers for K4K.

In the weeks and months that followed, that group of volunteers would reenergize the rescue—raising money, volunteering time with the dogs, and, most importantly, sending pictures and information to another volunteer who uploaded the dogs to Petfinder. Local adoptions started to happen. Amber would message me on Facebook to tell me about them and thank me for the donations that had flooded in from readers of our blog. It was this experience at K4K that hooked me. I could help. I wasn't anybody, but I was somebody, and I could still do something.

Back in Pennsylvania, I wrote a proposal for a new book. One that would pick up where *Another Good Dog* left off with our foster family, but it wouldn't stop there. I would take my readers to the shelters. So often when I talked about what I saw in the southern shelters people shook their heads, and I was never sure if it was because they didn't believe me or they didn't want to believe me. But in my book, I could take them there. I could show them.

I began planning in earnest, expanding on the blog Ian and I had started, Who Will Let the Dogs Out, because now I knew—we could let the dogs out. But we couldn't do it alone.

37

Back to Tennessee

I spent the remainder of the summer preparing to go south again. In between contacting shelters and mapping out a route and writing, there were still my foster dogs. Flannery continued to snap unexpectedly at just about anyone, even people who had been contentedly petting her for a few minutes. She was unpredictable. But my kids and their friends loved her. Teenagers, at least my teenagers, are very accepting of odd behaviors from their friends. They looked the other way when she nipped, and, thankfully, she never injured anyone, so I continued to hold to my belief that she didn't mean it. If a dog wanted to bite you, it would. Flannery was just communicating; her nips meant "I've had enough" or "Don't boss me." We joked that she had small-dog disease, which caused her to feel the need to lord it over anyone and any dog she could to make up for her lack of height. She'd taken to lounging on the back of the sofa, and I was pretty sure she liked that spot because it gave her a higher vantage point, and thus superiority over the other dogs and a few humans.

For a long time, I'd been saying that I thought she could excel in agility, so I decided to spring for six weeks of intro classes at a facility just over the line in Maryland. She loved it! She bounded up the A-frame and the dog walk and zipped through the tunnels. She cleared the jumps by feet, not inches, bouncing between them with no stride. The class had several border collies in it who, as expected, excelled, but they didn't come close to Flannery for speed. I made videos and posted them, and still no applications. Would Flannery become our dog by default? I'd always called her a nudge for the way she pushed her way into everything, not waiting for permission. Is this how she would join our family?

I didn't want to adopt a dog that bit people for no apparent reason, but would anyone ever adopt her? I loved Flannery, but even I didn't trust her. All three of my kids wanted to adopt her, but none of them would be living here permanently.* Brady was at home temporarily, having recently graduated from college. He'd had an extremely stressful final semester, cramming in enough credits to graduate with two degrees but leaving no extra time for job hunting or even enjoying himself. When he'd finally finished, he'd spent two weeks in California with his grandmother, decompressing from college life. Now, the summer was slipping away with only a few interviews and, so far, no job offers. His friends came and went and never batted an eye at the little black dog that occasionally nipped them.

I forgot how wide and open and possible life seems in your early twenties. There was no rush because you had all your life before you. Now, in my early fifties, I felt an urgency. The faces of so many dogs click through my mind. Dogs lying on concrete floors or hard plastic shelves, with so little human contact; their eyes haunted me. They were confused and frightened and so incredibly vulnerable. I didn't have a minute to waste.

Nancy, the photographer who had adopted my fiftieth dog, Edith Wharton, and gone on the spring trip, volunteered to accompany me back to Tennessee. As I began planning, I kept hearing about Alabama. It was rumored to be worse. How could that be? I thought of Fanny, the skinny, brown, poop-covered dog at the Huntingdon pound. She was safe now with Trisha, who had named her Mocha, but I'd heard that more dogs had landed

---

* At least I hoped they wouldn't.

in that same pound. Trisha had pulled several more, and shortly after that she had a distemper outbreak at her house, which forced her to euthanize seven dogs. Thankfully, Fanny/Mocha wasn't one of them. Quarantined at Trisha's, now Fanny spent her days in a crate as Trisha worked to be sure no more dogs would contract distemper. She also contacted the dog-catchers at the pound to alert them that they had distemper, since it was dogs she'd rescued from their pound that infected her shelter, but they ignored her and did not disinfect or shut down the pound. So Trisha contacted the mayor of Huntingdon, but the only thing that happened was that the dogcatchers told her she could no longer rescue from the pound. Now the dogs had no one.

It was as if the pound didn't exist. I searched online and found no mention of it. Ian located it on Google Maps by searching for the fire road that led to it. He sent me a screenshot, but there was nothing I could do. The only weapon I had was my words, so I wrote an impassioned piece about all that I'd seen in Tennessee. Jessica, my editor at Pegasus Books, pitched it to the *Washington Post*. They were interested, but the entire summer passed without word about whether they would run it.

As the date for my next trip with Nancy approached, I asked Jessica to try a Tennessee paper. As much as I would have been thrilled to land a piece in the *Post*, mostly what I wanted was for the people of Tennessee to be furious about the Huntingdon pound, which to my mind was basically a death camp for dogs. Jessica approached *The Tennessean*, the largest paper in Tennessee, and they agreed to run an op-ed piece—just 550 words. I labored over every word and Jessica sent it in. *The Tennessean* ran the piece, and I only hoped it would cut through the noise of everything else in the news cycle that day to find readers who would be moved to act.

Meanwhile, I was busy preparing for the next trip, helping Ian get ready to start his senior year, and spending time with Addie, who was home from her summer spent working in New York City for just four days before she would leave for a semester in Greece.

On a gray Saturday morning, Nancy and I set off for Tennessee. I decided to rent a car for this trip since all our vehicles had well over a hundred thousand miles and couldn't be counted on for the three-thousand-mile trip we'd planned. I'd reserved a compact SUV, hoping to keep costs down, but when Nick dropped me off at the rental agency and noticed a big, black Jeep out front, he joked with the guy at the counter that I loved Jeeps.* I explained what I was doing and the guy offered to upgrade me, and that was how Nancy and I found ourselves driving south in a brand-new four-door Jeep with tinted glass and big tires. When I texted Nancy a picture of our ride, she typed back, We'll be totally bad-ass.

The Jeep had all the bells and whistles you'd expect in a Jeep, and from the massive key fob to the big plastic dials, it seemed like a Lego toy. It felt like driving a tank, and all week I would struggle to park it without dinging anyone.

Nancy was great company. She was smart and funny and easygoing. We'd both packed lots of food, expecting to eat on the run since we would be visiting thirteen shelters and rescues in six days. We stopped after eight hours of driving and spent the night in Bristol, Virginia, where we found a craft brewery near our hotel and drank a small flight to celebrate the upcoming adventure.

The next day, we made it to Laura's house. We would spend two nights there before heading to Alabama and then another night on the way back. Laura had invited Robin, plus a handful of other animal advocates, to join us that first night for cheese and crackers and wine to talk about how to address the issue of spay and neuter in Tennessee. For so many of the shelters, even the ones close to Nashville, it was a challenge and sometimes an impossibility to find low-cost veterinary services. Robin was determined to find a solution; she said she was "Men-in-black serious about this." After seeing the results of her efforts

---

* My beloved Honda Element was getting on in miles, and since Honda doesn't manufacture them anymore, I figured my next dog-friendly car would likely be a Jeep. I hadn't ridden in one since my college days, when my roommate Kimra had a classic Jeep, with huge tires, that could shake your teeth right out of your head on the highway.

to create volunteer programs at four shelters, I had no doubt in her ability to tackle this one, although it would not be as easy.

In the afternoon, before the women were to come for our powwow, Nancy and I went to visit Trisha at her house, the home of her rescue, RARE. I was anxious to see Fanny/Mocha, the little pit bull Trisha had rescued from the Huntingdon pound a few months back after Ian and I had visited. I didn't know much about her other than what I'd seen in the few hours at the pound. I'd felt an inexplicable pull then, but it had been an emotionally charged day as I juggled Ian's needs and my shock at what we saw. Would Fanny be the dog my heart remembered? Or was I just romanticizing the situation, looking for something good out of bad? Sometimes I caught myself narrating my life and experiences as if they were a film. Maybe Fanny wasn't Fanny; maybe she was just Mocha, another dog that Trisha rescued from the Huntingdon pound.

When we reached Trisha's we went inside to get Fanny, and I saw where she'd spent her summer—in a large crate next to another dog inside Trisha's living room. Compared to so many dogs in shelters and rescues in the South, she was lucky. As the week would go on, the majority of the dogs we'd meet lived outside in the hundred-degree heat that was dragging on now through September. Trisha was bonded with her and assured me that she was a great couch snuggler. Fanny bounded around the yard, cautiously creeping up to us to accept proffered treats.

After a little time with Fanny, we spent the next ninety minutes wrangling dogs so Nancy could take their pictures. A good adoption picture makes all the difference, and it was the first photo session of the dozen to follow that week. Each night after dinner, and sometimes in the Jeep as we drove, Nancy would spend hours editing the hundreds of photos she took each day and then e-mailing them to shelter directors so they could use them to get dogs adopted.

Trisha knew each of her dogs well and loved them ferociously, but I wondered why they stayed so long with her. Was it because no one wanted to adopt them or because Trisha had a hard time letting them go? I've realized that her dilemma is more common than you'd think. Shelter and rescue workers see the absolute worst in humanity. They see dogs who have been abused, neglected, and abandoned and many times meet the people at whose hands they have suffered. It can make a person bitter. Add to that the lack of resources and the frustration of not being able to change the situation or stop the abuse and it makes sense that it's easy to become jaded. It becomes hard to trust.

Trisha has an enormous heart and fiery spirit, both of which take a toll on a person doing her life's work. She rescued dogs from awful situations and then loved them back to life. Letting them go again and trusting the people who adopted them wasn't easy. I got that. But at the same time, like with my fosters, the faster you got them adopted, the more dogs you could save. And that involved a level of trust. For me, I had to trust the adoption coordinators who approved the person to adopt my dog. Trisha did all the jobs for her rescue, so she was not only the foster home, she was also the rescuer, the transporter, and the adoption coordinator. As I watched her interact with her dogs, I worried for her. How much room did she have in her heart and how long could she do this?

Later that week we would visit another foster-based rescue run by a woman who was older than Trisha but reminded me of her in some ways. Rhonda invested in her dogs. She didn't simply hold them until an adopter appeared. She ran Brindlee Mountain Animal Rescue in Joppa, Alabama, where she rescued a dozen dogs at a time, housing them in kennels on her property and rotating them through living with her in her house. She specialized in Great Danes, but the morning when we pulled up to her gates and two of the enormous beasts ran toward us, I didn't know that. They looked positively prehistoric to me. "What are those?" I asked. Nancy laughed and said, "I think they're Great Danes." Neither of us got out of the car until Rhonda had put them away and opened the gate.

Later we learned that Great Danes are anything but dangerous. Rhonda's Danes and all her dogs were well-mannered sweethearts. But she worked hard to make them that way. Her dogs, like Trisha's, stayed with her for months, not weeks, before she deemed them ready to be adopted. As she put it, "I want to be sure they're ready; I don't want them coming back." Her dozen dogs lived as family pets. The kennels were large and airy, and all of the dogs had time roaming free in her expansive yard or living with Rhonda and her husband, Billy, in their home, learning to go to "their place" at mealtimes and to have house manners.

Our morning at Rhonda's was eye-opening, learning not just about Great Danes but about how to run a quality private rescue operation. She noticed my wide eyes at all she was doing and said, "There's a fine line between rescuing and hoarding. I keep myself on track by making sure that every move I make improves the situation."

I liked that motto. Maybe it would be how I would keep myself from losing perspective on this journey to save dogs. It was beginning to take shape in my mind. I needed to do more, but to do more, I needed a bigger microphone and I needed the ability to raise money. Both would be necessary to be able to improve the situation.

38

Doing the Impossible

O n Monday morning we headed to Cheatham County Animal Control. This was the shelter both Laura and Robin had urged me to visit when I was in Tennessee with Ian in June, so I made it our first stop on this trip. If both women wanted me to see it, there must be a good reason.

Nancy and I set out early but realized thirty minutes into our drive that I was still operating on Eastern Standard Time and we were now in Central Standard Time so we would be an hour early. To kill time, we stopped at an exit near Cheatham County, in search of Wi-Fi. Nancy wanted to tinker with photos for Trisha and our Instagram account, and I wanted to get a blog post up about the start of our adventure. We were making a concerted effort to use our small but growing platform to raise awareness about what we were doing. Nancy was blitzing our Instagram and researching tags while I was trying to post to Facebook and to our blog. Neither of us were social media whiz kids, so all we could do was the best we could do and hope. I ended every blog post with a request that people share our content, and person by person our following was growing.

We stopped to buy gas and a Powerball ticket* and then drove to an Arby's that advertised free Wi-Fi. There wasn't anyone at the counter, but we could hear people in the back. We weren't hungry but figured we'd better at least buy a drink if we were going to squat on their Wi-Fi for the next hour. After a few minutes, no one had appeared, so we found seats and got to work. After twenty minutes, a uniformed employee appeared and stared at us. She didn't say anything, so we continued to work. Another employee appeared behind her and said, "We're not open."

Instead of pointing out that their door was unlocked and their lights on, we packed up and headed on to Cheatham, taking a scenic route that reaffirmed for us that the shelter was truly in the middle of nowhere.

At Cheatham, we met the new director, Kristin Reid. She'd been in charge a little over eighteen months, taking over the shelter, which had been deemed "atrocious" by the Middle Tennessee Shelter Directors group. Cheatham had a terrible record of killing animals. The previous director had been something of a hoarder, and when Kristin took the job, the eighty-three-acre property was littered with dozens of vehicles, equipment, machinery, rusted kennels, and hundreds of oddities whose purpose was long forgotten. Before she could do anything, she brought in dumpsters and started cleaning up.

She trained the staff, teaching them health protocols, animal care, and basic customer service. As we followed her through the facility, I was impressed with the staff we encountered; not only were they busy and professional, they also seemed happy. Kristin was a young, petite, red-headed woman with lots of tattoos, who dropped out of high school and worked her way up to director by learning every aspect of animal sheltering, but listening to her I was certain she could hold her own in any boardroom. She was knowledgeable, eloquent, open-minded, and confident, not to mention incredibly smart. I made a mental note that she would be a great person to interview if my idea of making a film about the southern shelters ever came to fruition.

---

*   The prize was over $200 million, and so we bought two tickets with our pooled money and spent many happy moments imagining how we would fix whatever problem we were looking at with the money we would win. Alas, we didn't win.

Cheatham is an open-intake shelter with a tiny budget of only $60,000 a year, yet for all intents and purposes, Kristin has managed to turn it into a no-kill shelter, even if she doesn't have that status officially. She works hard to move dogs out through rescues, which allows her to work with some of the harder-to-place dogs longer. She wants to figure out what their issues are and what each dog needs to be successful.

After tackling the shelter building, animal care, and staffing, Kristin set her sights on rebuilding the respect and support of her community. Instead of focusing on what she didn't have—volunteers, money, community support, or a fancy building—she instead looked at what she did have—plenty of land in a beautiful part of the country. The shelter sits on one side of the Cumberland River, and most of its community is on the other side. To reach the shelter, you have to drive over one of the bridges and follow the long, winding road that Nancy and I had just traveled. Kristin needed something to draw the people to the shelter.

She set to work creating trails through their woods and began a rock-painting program. The staff and fledgling volunteer program began painting and placing rocks with positive messages on the trails. Then they invited the public to come and hike, paint a rock and place it, or find a rock and take it home. She enlisted the local high school students to create storyboards and post them along the trails, giving young families even more incentive to come to the shelter. The only price for using their beautiful, interactive trails? Walking an adorable, adoptable shelter dog! Talk about a win-win. I loved it and was fast becoming a member of the Kristin Reid fan club.

Kristin's commonsense solutions and systems were obvious everywhere we looked, from the one-way paths in and out of the kennels so that volunteers walking dogs didn't unexpectedly run into another dog, to the volunteers with treats in hand who asked the dogs to sit before moving them in and out of doors or kennels, to the pharmaceutical rep setting up lunch in the employee work area to train her staff (for free with lunch!) about how and why to give vaccines.

We left Cheatham inspired and headed to what I considered the mecca of animal shelters—Nashville Humane Association (NHA). With a budget of $2.2 million, I was prepared to see the Ritz-Carlton of shelters.

NHA is completely privately funded. No Animal Control responsibilities for them, and no public funds. Private versus public status was the big difference from a shelter like Cheatham, whose hands are tied by the rules of public funds and whose intake is out of its control. Kristin can't fundraise and has little say over how much the county allots to Animal Control. She has to work within her means.

Nashville Humane saves over three thousand animals a year with a 99 percent save rate. In addition to dealing with Nashville's homeless dog population they also help many of their surrounding public shelters, pulling dogs, and offering veterinary access (they have a mobile unit that Robin dreams of accessing for her plans to make spay/neuter available to the underserved public in western Tennessee). Their director, like Kristin, was relatively new and had big plans and a can-do attitude. She was willing to partner with whoever she needed to in the name of saving more animals.

I was feeling a little guilty about this particular visit. Obviously, Nashville Humane didn't need our help raising awareness or funds for their operations. The previous Saturday they'd held their largest event of the year, and Laura, their director, had hoped to take a much-needed day off after working through the weekend. When I e-mailed, though, she didn't hesitate to offer to come in that Monday to meet me. I appreciated that she could have easily pawned off our visit on another member of her large staff but didn't.

I'd followed Nashville Humane in the news and on social media, marveling at their innovative programs, the number of animals they moved, and their impossibly clever marketing. In the weeks before our trip, there were two Nashville Humane stories that caught my eye and were stellar examples of their smart sheltering PR. In June, they'd airlifted ninety dogs from Puerto Rico ahead of hurricane season because it was more cost-effective than waiting to bring dogs in during a disaster that hadn't happened yet.

The second story, though, was a stroke of genius. The air-conditioning in their fifteen-year-old building broke in early August and couldn't be fixed for at least a day. Instead of letting the dogs suffer in the oppressive southern heat, they quickly sent out a plea for foster homes. They were inundated with volunteers, not only their current fosters (of which there were four hundred!) but new applicants ready to help. They streamlined their application process and got every single animal out of the hot building. Not only did the animals get a night out, but the shelter gained new fosters who could help them in the future. Taking lemons and making serious lemonade was what that was.

We followed our GPS to Nashville Humane Association down a narrow alley in perhaps not the nicest part of town.* The cheery, open, modern lobby smelled of pumpkin spice and hydrangeas, thanks to their latest fundraiser, scented candles. It was a Monday and the building was closed to the public, but much of the staff was there doing deep cleaning and preparing to receive a transport of animals to refill their kennels, which had been nearly emptied by adoptions from their big weekend.

Laura appeared with a wide smile, giving away no resentment of the fact that our visit had interrupted her much-needed day off. In fact, she made Nancy and me feel welcome from the moment we met her, radiating a warmth and confidence that was contagious. As she walked us through the facility explaining their programs and the intentionality of their setup, I found her to be smart, articulate, and deeply passionate about her work. In addition to an enormous staff that included two full-time vets (and seven assistants/vet techs), there were volunteers busy visiting with dogs. The facility had heated floors, plenty of natural light, and calming therapy music floating from tiny speakers. Volunteers administered a rotating selection of enrichment toys, used clickers and treats to train dogs to sit calmly at the front of their kennels, and taught the dogs to walk on leashes (many times a first experience for the dogs). The bright, airy spaces and thoughtful and intentional programs were designed to keep the thousands of animals that come through their doors each year calm and happy during their almost always brief stay at NHA.

Laura talked about their move toward open adoptions, making adoptions more of a conversation than an interrogation, addressing one of the biggest excuses I've heard from people as to why they didn't choose to adopt from

---

* The location for most shelters.

a shelter. "It's harder to adopt a dog than a kid" is a common complaint of rescues and shelters that require extensive background checks, home visits, and lengthy application processes. Even with their more lax application process, NHA was still under the national average for returned pets.*

Laura walked us outside to show us their newly redesigned "backyard." Formerly a steep, unusable space, they'd worked with Rescue Rebuild† to make the space inviting and useful, with stairs built into the hillside and outside enclosures that gave dogs an area to romp.

Wishing some of this wealth and creativity could be sent west to the shelters I'd visited in June, I shared what I'd seen at the Huntingdon pound. Laura's eyes grew wide. "Can you get me more information?" she asked. I told her about K4K and Red Fern and she said she would absolutely be interested in working with them. The very next day she e-mailed to thank us for visiting and to ask for contact information for the shelters in western Tennessee.

It had been a good start—two inspiring shelters, lots of sweet dogs, and first-class accommodations. The rest of our week would be cheap hotels, endless drives, long days in the amazing heat, and situations that would break a heart.

---

* NHA's return to shelter rate is about 7 percent, while the national return rate is hard to estimate, American Humane Association puts it at around 10 percent.

† Rescue Rebuild is basically Habitat for Humanity for shelters. They do amazing work under the umbrella of Greater Good.

39

The Fuzzy Definition
of No-Kill

W e set off that Tuesday morning to visit three shelters only an hour or
so southeast of Nashville. At each stop, I scribbled notes furiously so
that I wouldn't begin to blur all the dogs and directors together, but
inevitably I did and later I would pester Nancy with questions.

"Was there a school bus parked in the back of the Bedford shelter or am I
thinking of Cheatham?"

"Where was that big blue dog with the merle markings?"

I desperately wanted to get everything right. That felt important to me. I'm
not trained as an investigative reporter, but that's what I felt like I was doing.
At each shelter, I wanted the hard facts, but I also wanted the real story—what
was preventing the shelter from saving every last dog? Was it politics, personalities, history, budget, location? I was certain there was an answer, but more
and more it began to simply feel like the shelters were David and the task
before them was Goliath. Finding the effective slingshot seemed impossible.

We rolled into Shelbyville a few minutes late thanks to unexpected traffic. Nancy had messaged Jessica, a volunteer who together with her rescue partner, Kathy, started the Shelbyville Shelter Soldiers* to prevent the Shelbyville city shelter from having to destroy dogs for space. More and more, I couldn't bring myself to use the phrase, "euthanize for space," because it had become an oxymoron on my tongue. You euthanized dogs for mercy because not doing so would be cruel. Dogs dying because of lack of space, resources, and government apathy? That was killing. Jessica, Kathy, and Rhonda, the Animal Control Officer currently supervising the shelter, were working hard to change the situation in Shelbyville.

It was crazy hot as we stood and sweltered on the porch of the small pole building housing the shelter. Jessica's husband, Ashley, slowly walked a skinny, skittish brindle dog named Lola around the parking area as we talked. Lola had landed at the shelter after being hit by a car. Her leg was broken, and the Shelter Soldiers paid to have the leg treated and cast. Lola tore off four casts before the local vet gave up and advised crate rest and restricted movement. Lola's vet bills had already climbed into the thousands on top of the bills Jessica and Kathy had recently paid to try to save a litter of mastiffs who came down with coccidia and then parvo. Only two puppies survived.

Listening to Jessica and Rhonda talk about a community who would rather shoot its dog than pay the thirty-dollar surrender fee to the shelter, my heart sank. "They'll tell you a bullet is thirty-two cents. They'd rather shoot the dog than ask for help."

The idea of a government-funded shelter not being open-intake was new to me, but at our next stop, Bedford County Animal Control, we heard the same story. Both Bedford County and Shelbyville City Animal Control claimed they were "no-kill," but I wondered what happened to the dogs they turned away? Did they end up with a thirty-two-cent bullet or an even worse fate?

---

* The Shelbyville Shelter Soldiers is basically Jessica and Kathy. They collected donations for the shelter, secured vet care for shelter animals in distress, and paid for almost everything out of their own pockets.

I've learned that some shelters protect their no-kill status by turning away the hardest-luck cases. The Shelter Soldiers were doing their best to pick up the slack in Shelbyville. At Bedford County, the policy was to refuse owner-surrendered dogs that were not "adoptable." Instead, they suggested the owner take the dog to their vet and "have a conversation."

This seemed reasonable—why should a shelter have to kill a dog that a family deemed too dangerous to live in their home? But it made me wonder about the definition of "adoptable." If a shelter decides that dogs that look like pit bulls are "unadoptable," does that excuse turning them away or killing them when they turn up as strays? Do those dogs count in their live release rates? If you could filter which dogs landed in your shelter, it would be relatively easy to achieve no-kill status, and with it receive grant money from national organizations, plus community support and government funding. It seemed to me to be a slippery slope. I had a college statistics professor who told me, "Don't ever trust numbers. You can make the numbers say whatever you want."

Best Friends Animal Society has been leading the charge for a no-kill nation. Their dream is that one day animals will no longer be killed in America's shelters. It's a good dream, a great one, even. To achieve it, they've built a Best Friends network to bring animal shelters and rescue groups across the country together to save lives. They have a formula for determining who is "saving them all." They believe that any shelter that is saving 90 percent or more of the animals they are taking in is "no-kill."

Reading through the lengthy explanations on the Best Friends website, it's clear that their intention is to save every animal possible. The only reason they condone euthanizing an animal is if:

> A veterinarian has assessed that there is no chance of recovering an acceptable quality of life or it would be clearly inhumane or unsafe not to do something immediately or in cases of irremediable canine aggression when (1) a veterinarian has eliminated medical treatment as a solution; (2) rehabilitation by a specialist in canine behavior has failed; and (3) staff and public safety cannot

be reasonably assured, or other management protocols seriously compromise quality of life.*

That's a great definition for the average shelter in a city with immediately available and reasonable veterinary care, plus trained behaviorists at their disposal, but I can't read it and not think of the Anson shelter I visited in North Carolina, where they have to wait up to three weeks for a vet appointment, or the shelters we'd visited that couldn't afford distemper shots, let alone a behavioral assessment by a veterinarian or specialist in canine behavior. More than that, 90 percent seems like a great number, but I'm still left wondering 90 percent of what? Adoptable, treatable dogs? All the dogs brought to the shelter for any reason? Or just the ones the shelter chooses to accept? It seems way too easy to manipulate that number for your own purposes and, to my mind, distracts from the mission of rescue and sheltering—saving every animal that can be saved.

No-kill has become the gold standard that every shelter strives to achieve—they need it to win the public's trust and therefore support. A director may also need to achieve no-kill status for job security. I'm 100 percent behind the idea of not killing any animal unnecessarily. My beef then is with the pressure we put on shelters to achieve no-kill status without also giving them the resources, staff, facility, and budget to do it. Or with shelters that achieve no-kill by hand-selecting which dogs to admit to the shelter, regardless of what happens to the dogs they turn away. Not to mention the shelters who achieve no-kill by allowing dogs to languish for years on their concrete floors—not dying, but not really living either.

We walked through Shelbyville's small building out to the back, where most of the dogs were living in chain-link kennels on a dirt or gravel surface. Rhonda explained that the city had only recently granted them the money to build an addition to the shelter that would bring all the dogs inside, where they would have heat and air-conditioning. One smart dog sat inside his water bucket, panting in the heat. The others chased the shade created by

---

* https://bestfriends.org/about-best-friends/position-statements#euthanasiavkilling

tarps strung across the kennels. More indoor housing would be a good thing for them, and I hoped it was a sign that the community supported the work of the shelter.

As we were leaving, we met the deputy sheriff, who had arrived to meet with the architect designing the addition. We chatted for a few minutes, and I asked him what he thought was the reason so many dogs ended up at the shelter. He offered an interesting perspective I hadn't considered. He said that the history of dogs in rural areas was that people owned large pieces of land and the dogs roamed freely, but as development came to Shelbyville, open, unoccupied spaces filled up as neighborhoods and businesses came in. Yet many people continued to allow their dogs to roam free as they always had. More run-ins with people and more contact with other (unsterilized) dogs led to more Animal Control calls, more dogs seized, and more unwanted puppies.

I'd heard that same reasoning in the North about why we have occasional issues with wild animals, but I'd never heard it posed in regard to dogs. It made sense, but it came back to what so many other directors said to me—it's a mindset. People have to think of their animals differently. We need awareness, education, and examples.

We left Shelbyville Animal Control shelter at 10:20, and at 10:28 were navigating the tight, tiny parking lot of Bedford County Animal Control shelter. The story at Bedford was much the same as Shelbyville, and I couldn't help but wonder about the duplication of duties and the divvying up of resources and support. Couldn't they accomplish more together? In addition to Shelbyville Soldiers, Shelbyville city shelter and Bedford County shelter, there were two other organizations in town saving animals. There was a Humane Society and a rescue organization called New Destiny. There were a lot of people who cared about saving animals in this corner of Tennessee, that much was evident. Why they didn't work together was not.

I'm not naive enough to believe that there weren't conflicting agendas, practices, and personalities that might make combining their efforts impossible, but from a commonsense and for-the-animals'-sake standpoint, it seemed much smarter to pool resources and consolidate efforts into one shelter where all that passion and talent could do the most good.

Creating one new progressive shelter facility with a modern design and practices to meet the needs of the animals and the public would change the game. That would bring together a wealth of resources, ideas, energy, and volunteers. What a powerhouse they could be for animal sheltering in a state that sorely needed one.

Nancy snapped pictures and exchanged eyebrow raises with me as we listened to the director, Maria, and Josie, another ACO, tell us about the shelter. Bedford was a no-kill shelter, but as previously mentioned, they didn't accept many owner surrenders. There was much that was good at Bedford, and the two of them hoped to make it better. Their cat area was clever and interactive, the shelter had a surgical space so a local vet could operate at the shelter, and Maria hoped to make the shelter more ADA compliant* and to update the existing kennels. We suggested they apply to Rescue Rebuild for help reimagining their outside space so they could create a way for the dogs to get exercise.† Currently, there was nowhere for their one volunteer to walk dogs except the sidewalk of the busy roads surrounding the shelter because the small outside area was cluttered with unusable buildings, badly designed holding pens,‡ a "new" concrete kennel building modeled after traditional pounds that held a dozen dogs, and freestanding chain-link kennels used for quarantine.

We unloaded a few donated bags of toys and treats for the shelter and then hustled down the highway to Franklin County, our next stop. Laura had told

---

* ADA compliant means that all electronic and information technology must be accessible to people with disabilities. At the time, I thought Maria was referring to wheelchair access for people who wanted to see their dogs. Many shelters cannot accommodate a wheelchair thanks to their dated designs, gravel surfaces, and narrow kennels.

† I would get a message that evening from Maria that they'd already submitted an application to Rescue Rebuild.

‡ Maria told me that the pads of the larger hound dogs got stuck in the heavy metal grate flooring of the raised holding pens each time they moved the dogs there while cleaning their indoor kennel.

me that Heather, the Animal Control Officer at Franklin, worked harder than any director she knew to save dogs, but as Heather would explain to us, she couldn't save them all. As recently as three months before our visit, she'd been forced to kill twelve dogs for space and over fifty cats.

Franklin was a tiny, squat concrete building next to the town's sewage treatment plant. When we arrived, there were three ACOs in the tiny office (there was no lobby) adjacent to the shelter. Two bulky men, uniformed ACOs, remained seated as they shook our hands and then proceeded to ignore us as Heather gave us the tour.* She apologized for the fact that their no-longer-used gas chamber was currently housing a dachshund and her two pups. "She's pretty scared, and it was the only place I could put them to get them away from the noise and the other dogs."

We peered in the small opening that resembled a fireplace at the tiny dog, who immediately shielded her pups from our view. Heather closed the grate and I shivered to think of how many animals had perished in that space. In another small office, where I assumed they did adoptions if they ever had any (90 percent of the animals at Franklin left through rescue if they left at all), there were two more small dogs. One was a Chihuahua mix with a broken leg and the other a shih tzu with a crushed pelvis. Heather had found rescues for both dogs, and the rescues were paying their vet bills.

Which brings me to an important fact—small dogs rarely die in shelters. That doesn't mean rescues shouldn't pull them; of course, they should, and rescues happily pull as many small dogs as are available. They are easy to transport, foster, and adopt out. But the idea that pulling a small dog makes room for another dog isn't exactly accurate since nearly every shelter we visited kept small dogs, if they had any, in tiny kennels similar to the ones that held cats, not a space where you could house a pit bull. These two badly injured dogs, simply because of their size and appearance, would live, never mind that the thousands of dollars spent on their extensive veterinary care could save dozens of dogs. I'm not here to pass judgment, and I've wrestled

---

* Later, I asked if the other two ACOs helped her, since we didn't see them move in our time there, and she said, "They help, but they're not as invested as I am."

with how to say that, but there's no other way to say it. Small dogs rarely die in shelters.

Heather walked us through a cavernous garage-like space lined with kennels, and we talked as we looked at some of the dogs lucky to be housed indoors. She was practical and honest about her situation and eager for any contacts we could give her to help her save more dogs. Unlike Shelbyville and Bedford, Franklin is a true open-intake shelter. They take anything and everything. She introduced us to a pair of dogs who had arrived that morning after their owner committed suicide. They were older and mixed breed. One had blood spattered on its coat, likely faithful to its owner to the bitter end. "I'm hoping the relatives come for them," she said, but her tone said she doubted it.*

Most of the kennels were small chain-link outdoor spaces with concrete floors and plastic igloo doghouses that took up most of the floor space and became ovens in the relentless heat. A large black dog leaped against his fence, bounced off his igloo, and then did it again on endless repeat. "He never stops," said Heather, shaking her head. "He's crazy." I looked at his conditions and didn't doubt what made him that way.

The row of kennels where the black dog lived was exposed to the relentless afternoon sun with no shade of any kind. The heat seemed to come from the kennels like our convection oven at home, blowing in my face as we passed. I was uncomfortable just walking by. Heather told us the county planned to put up an awning to give the dogs a bit of shade for the summer, but it was September and they still hadn't sent anyone to do it.

We asked about the longest resident, and Heather had one of the inmates bring him out to make a video with us.† He was a rambunctious young dog of no obvious breed. Heather found a ball and showed us how much he loved to

---

* She texted me a few days later to say the family didn't take the dogs.

† Franklin County utilized inmates to do the cleaning, but their presence at the shelter meant that it was impossible for the shelter to have a volunteer program as residents were not allowed to have any contact with the inmates. As Nancy took pictures, she had to avoid taking any pictures of them as well. Without volunteers, the dogs at Franklin County got very little exercise, enrichment, or human contact. It was no wonder to me that dogs like the black dog we met were suffering from shelter stress.

fetch. I asked his name, thinking I would encourage OPH to consider pulling him, and Heather said, "He doesn't have a name. We don't name them. He's kennel seventeen."

She walked us through the crowded cat shed, remarking, "Nobody wants cats." When I asked about the budget, Heather avoided the number but said she'd heard it would be going down this year under the new mayor. The shelter budget didn't cover spay/neuter, deworming, or rabies vaccines, but it did cover distemper vaccines (after experiencing a distemper outbreak), plus the expensive drugs used to euthanize animals.

As we drove through the town of Winchester on our way to the shelter, there were lots of nice houses and stores; the shelter was not in the middle of nowhere like Cheatham County Animal Control. I had to wonder how the good people of this town could allow this situation to happen. It was obvious to me that if not for this one woman, every animal in that shelter not claimed by its owners or one of the handful selected by the rare person who adopted from the shelter would die. Every single one.

Instead, this amazing woman worked her tail off all day long, then went home and cared for her own family and spent her evenings editing pictures and badgering rescues to take her dogs. Or she drove dogs or cats to meet transports or get vetting, many times paying for that vetting out of her own pocket.*

Every time I came down here, it was the same story. Desperate dogs and heroic people standing between them and a veterinarian's needle (or sometimes an ACO's gun). This was crazy. People in this country spend nearly half a billion (yes, billion) dollars on Halloween costumes for their pets.† And, yet, dogs in many rural shelters lack even the basics like a distemper vaccine, flea/tick preventatives, and heartworm testing, never mind the fact that the dogs

---

* Laura pays the transport costs for Franklin because she knows Heather is already spending all she can on the health certificates and rabies shots dogs need to be transported out of state. A few days after we visited Heather, Laura told me that Heather had to hold off on moving dogs to rescue because she needed to pay down her vet bills at both vets in town before she could get more dogs vetted. I contacted one of the vet's offices to pay some of her bill. They sent me a copy of the billing record. Heather owed $701.

† According to Marketwatch.com

leave the shelter unneutered or unspayed only for their puppies to return to that same shelter.*

Later, I discovered that there is a no-kill Humane Society shelter in town. I called the director, a very nice woman who seemed to honestly care about the animals and the situation at Franklin County Animal Control. Her hands were tied, she insisted, because her shelter was almost always full, and she had a board to report to. They did occasionally pull a few dogs from Animal Control, she said.

The fact that the Humane Society was a privately funded managed-intake shelter and Animal Control was an open-intake shelter led to a natural sifting of more adoptable (younger, friendly, smaller, desirable breed) animals living in relative safety at the Humane Society and less-adoptable (older, sicker, larger, bully breed) animals fighting for their lives at Animal Control.

One sad side effect of this fact is that many people in the general public will choose to go to the no-kill, privately funded shelter to rescue their pet because they don't want to support the public shelter, "where they kill animals." But that public shelter won't ever be able to achieve no-kill status without their support. I've discovered there are many of these catch-22s in shelter work.†

I wrote a scathing but honest post about Franklin County's shelter, calling upon its residents to help, but then worried that I might get Heather in trouble, so I toned it down and sent it to her before I published it to be sure there was nothing I had written that could jeopardize her job since so many lives depended on her. She read it and wrote back that what I said was correct and that she suspected there would be backlash but she wanted me to post it.

I posted it and as far as I know, there was no backlash, but then again I didn't imagine that my little blog with its few thousand followers was actually going to reach any powerful ears. Once again, frustrated by my tiny microphone, we headed to Alabama.

---

* I've had foster dogs come from the same shelter years apart that I was certain could have been related, and they certainly might have been.

† Sometimes corporations or nonprofits refuse grant money to shelters that can't report no-kill numbers or evidence that they are working toward achieving them.

40

Alabama

e'd only been in Alabama for about twenty minutes when something hit the windshield. It left a milky blob larger than the average insect splatter. Before we could ascertain what it was, a steady pelting began. My first thought was hail, but it was sunny and near a hundred degrees outside. In minutes the entire windshield was covered with the guts of bugs—big bugs. When we stopped at our hotel for the night, the once spotless Jeep's front grille, hood, and windshield were speckled with inch-long blotches of bug guts. Nancy, the scientist among us, studied the remains of several bugs and took their pictures. Later she would inform me that they were lovebugs. We'd just driven through a storm of Alabama lovebugs. Too tired to do anything about the mess that night, we crashed for the night, and the next day we discovered that the bug guts were cemented on the vehicle and no amount of windshield wiper fluid would budge them. At least now we looked like we belonged there.

Gifted with a few free hours the next morning, I wrote blog posts about what we'd seen, and Nancy furiously edited pictures, but the whole week we felt like we were chasing our tails. There wasn't enough time and the needs were so big. If only we could stay put and help more, gather their stories and tell them, surely there was someone, somewhere who could fix this. I tried to beat back my doubts that what we were doing was having any impact. We had no choice but to cram in as much as we could in the eight days we would be on the road. It was expensive to travel, no matter how flimsy the hotel room or how much peanut butter and jelly you ate. We'd paid for this adventure out of our own pockets and with the meager money we'd raised through the Etsy shop that Nancy had set up to sell our Who Will Let the Dogs Out T-shirts.* It wasn't enough. At every turn, there was more to see, more need, more dogs suffering, more people struggling to save them.

Every time I opened my e-mail there was another message from another shelter director or volunteer saying, "Come here! Animals are dying!" or "There is no Animal Control, not any shelter, sometimes they just shoot the animals," or "Our shelter is crammed, we need your help!"

But what could we do? And why, I kept asking, were so few people concerned about it? Had they given up? The Humane Society and Best Friends and the ASPCA and other big organizations had been working on this problem for years and, yet, still, here in this place of lovebugs and Dollar General stores and teeth-shatteringly sweet tea, there was little evidence that progress had been made. I'd believed the dog pounds and dogcatchers were something we did away with fifty years ago. The idea that any government-funded shelter would allow dogs to die of distemper or leave unspayed or unneutered was crazy. Beyond crazy. And, yet, this was what was happening.

That afternoon, we traveled to Jasper, Alabama, to Walker County Humane and Adoption Center (also known as Walker County Animal Control). OPH partnered with Rescuers United For Furbabies (R.U.F.F.), a local foster-based rescue to bring dogs from Walker County north, and I was excited to meet Kara Jones, a R.U.F.F. volunteer I'd been e-mailing with about our visit.

Once you get out to the far reaches of Alabama, road signs seem to be a luxury they can't afford, and we were a few minutes late getting to the shelter. Kara teaches seventh graders, so we'd arranged to meet after school. When

---

* That income covered about two tanks of gas.

we arrived, Kara was waiting for us, along with Kay Farley, the new shelter director, one of the only two employees at Walker County, which handled about 1,500 animals each year. Both Kay and Kara were frank about their current situation and about the dark history of Walker County, where too many adoptable animals had died and the public was wary of getting involved. Only recently, after a distemper outbreak, did the county provide funds for distemper vaccines. Without a $5,000 grant that R.U.F.F. recently helped Walker County apply for and receive from Maddie's Fund, none of the animals would be spayed or neutered before being adopted. They weren't sure what would happen when that grant was depleted.

We toured the facility, which was bursting at the seams with dogs and puppies, many housed outdoors in chain-link kennels on dirt or gravel because the indoor kennels were full. Kay opened the door to the male dog play area and we were met with happy dogs who rushed past us to quickly streak through the indoor kennels, raising a ruckus. Once Kay and Kara had corralled them all back outside, we made a short video. There were so many adoptable dogs, yet only a quarter of them would be adopted locally. Walker County had no adoption fee, so all the dogs were free.* I puzzled at this because even in the poorest counties we'd visited there was usually at least a nominal fee of maybe twenty dollars or so.

Alabama no-kill advocate Aubrie Kavanaugh, the author of *Not Rocket Science: A Story of No Kill Animal Shelter Advocacy in Huntsville, Alabama*, told me time and again that one of the best ways to bring change was to approach sheltering from a fiscal standpoint. It is the county's responsibility to take care of these dogs with the taxpayers' money. If the taxpayers are unhappy with the way the government is using their money (i.e., killing dogs or offering subpar care), they can demand change. But first, they have to know how their money is being spent. I had to wonder if many people in the rural South who struggle to put food on their own tables were worrying about the animals at the shelter who die for want of an inexpensive vaccine.

---

* This is something Kara, Kay, and R.U.F.F. hope to change.

And, yet, we are an animal-loving nation. I read my local newspaper obituaries every day; it's a weird habit, but I find the words that people leave behind fascinating, even when I never knew the person. Just about every day, there's at least one obit that asks mourners to donate to the local SPCA in lieu of flowers. I believe that every community wants to believe their tax dollars are used to shelter dogs in a humane way and help them be adopted into loving homes. They do not want that money used to kill dogs or care for them inhumanely. Long ago, when we domesticated dogs, we made them our responsibility. And our tax dollars should cover that responsibility, but not everyone wants a dog,* so it also makes sense that by charging an adoption fee you are placing some of the burden on the part of the public that will most benefit from the shelter's services. To my mind, any county shelter operating without adoption fees (or pull fees for rescues) is simply fiscally irresponsible. Never mind that giving away dogs for free devalues the animal and inspires people to treat them as such.

The dogs at Walker seemed happy and well cared for, and it was clear that Kay and her coworker were likely working far more hours than they were paid for at the shelter. The task of feeding, cleaning, administering medications, evaluating, and exercising seventy-five to ninety dogs and twenty to forty cats seven days a week divided by two people was mind-numbing. Add to that the paperwork, phones, adoptions, vet visits, and heaven knows what other administrative tasks required of government workers, Kay was unlikely to keep up that kind of load long-term.

R.U.F.F. was working hard to help and handled most of the heavy lifting in terms of getting dogs out through rescue. Kara introduced us to a few animals that were headed north to OPH in just another week. I asked about a small dog we'd seen huddled in the corner of his kennel. Unlike the other dogs who were jumping and lunging at the fence, competing for our attention and the treats we handed out, Houdini was curled in a tight ball in the back of his kennel. He'd been at the shelter since May, and Kay explained that he was an escape artist. So desperate to get out of the shelter, he'd climbed tall

---

* Or should have a dog.

fences and broken through gates, hence the name Houdini. Now he'd finally been contained inside a kennel with a concrete floor he couldn't dig out of, surrounded by sturdy chain-link sides with a chain-link panel placed on top of his kennel and weighted down so he couldn't climb out.

I asked if we could bring him out, and Kay agreed to meet us in the lobby with him. Out of his kennel, Houdini brightened, climbing all over us, searching for treats. He was skeletal and covered with cuts from his escape attempts. Kay was worried about him, and Kara said she'd been unable to find rescue or even a foster home for him. Now, he was shutting down from shelter stress. All of me wanted to scoop him up, put him in the Jeep, and take him with us; after all, there was no adoption fee, right?

I messaged the shelter puller from OPH, asking if we could bring him back with us. She cautioned against simply taking him, worried that without following the proper procedures of allowing R.U.F.F. to have him vetted and neutered and in a foster home, we might miss something important. I understood that, but I also understood that if we didn't get this dog out now, he would die here, on the concrete, huddled in the corner of his kennel. The shelter puller insisted I needed to wait and said that if I would commit to fostering him, she would try to get him on the transport the following week.

That night, Nancy listened to me rant. "We've seen thousands of dogs this week, all of them need to get out, but Houdini needs to get out now. He won't last another week."

In the morning I called Kay. Desperate to help Houdini, she offered to foster him until we could get him, possibly on our return trip home. OPH sent him to the vet the next morning. After examining him, the vet said he was extremely frail—too weak to travel or to be neutered. He would need more than a week of careful care to recover, and if he recovered, we could bring him north in a month.

I was relieved. Houdini was safe and had his best chance of recovering. But at the same time, I felt bad that now Kay had to bring her work home. She had a family; the last thing she needed was to care for a sick dog who had a habit of escaping. I apologized to her and sent a care package of items to help fatten up Houdini. She assured me she was just happy that he was getting help.

Houdini became a symbol in my mind, like Fanny, of all that was wrong with the shelter system in the South. And I'm not trying to be an uppity northerner, I'm just going on what I had seen having now visited dozens of shelters and rescues in the rural South. Too many people are looking the other way. Too many people believe that this is not their problem. Too many people think that saving most of the dogs is okay. It isn't. We must save all of the dogs.

Alabama was breaking my heart, but the next day we visited another county shelter run by the Humane Society that would show me there was reason to hope, reason to believe they could fix this problem.

We found the Humane Society of Chilton County down a shady road near the train tracks. Inside we met Jennifer, the director, who started out years ago as a volunteer when she was a stay-at-home mom. Now, as the director, she was using the skills she honed as a mom to juggle and delegate and do five things at once with eyes in back of her head to manage this shelter that handled 1,500 to 2,000 animals a year, 90 percent of which left the shelter via rescues, but all of which left spayed/neutered, microchipped, and up to date on shots.

Chilton County enjoys immense community support, and despite their aging building, they manage to save every savable animal that comes through their doors. They are technically a managed-intake facility—not obligated to take every dog—but Jennifer told me that she does work with the police department to take dogs in need of help whenever she can.

The lobby was stacked with crates full of new arrivals, and Jennifer assured us that she would find a place for them. Chilton used a donated van to move animals out through rescue and was contemplating how to use a large donation to update and add on to their facility. Blessed with lots of outdoor space, all the dogs got outdoor playtime.

Instead of unloading some of our donations, Jennifer insisted on filling our Jeep back up with some of their plentiful donations, and employees loaded twelve cases of treats into the van. My faith restored that Alabama could ultimately fix their problems, we got ready to drive farther south.

41

The Shepherd and His Lambs

A few hours into our drive that afternoon, I confessed to Nancy that I hoped this wasn't a wild goose chase. We were headed to the very bottom of the state, the Wiregrass corner it was called, to meet a man named Dave, who led an organization called Safe Haven Animal Rescue and Kennel (SHARK). When I'd contacted a national Humane Society representative in Alabama, she'd told me that his was a story I'd want to hear. I hadn't been able to speak with Dave on the phone or even via e-mail, but through several Facebook messages, he'd given me an address and a time and promised to meet us.

As was becoming par for the course in Alabama, we drove back and forth past the entrance to SHARK multiple times searching for a road sign or a marker. Finally, I pulled over just past the landfill to call Dave. He answered immediately and asked if we were in the black Jeep. When I said we were, he said, "Look left, you see a truck with its lights on? That's me."

He was parked at the entrance to the landfill. I'd thought the shelter was next to the landfill, I didn't realize it was actually inside the landfill. We turned around and went to meet Dave. He jumped out of his truck and I was struck not by his age (Dave was seventy-six at that time), but by his youthfulness. He was spry and quick, and his eyes sparkled with mischief. I guess I was expecting something else. He wore a brown work uniform similar to other ACOs we'd met. Dave explained that he was a trained and certified Animal Control Officer; he just wasn't paid for it. "They told me I'm too old," he said with a chuckle. And yet, the Henry County and Abbeville city authorities called him for animal emergencies and stray dogs. "I'm supposed to bill them ten dollars for each call, but I never do," he said.

When Henry County and the city of Abbeville closed their shelter for budgetary reasons, SHARK volunteered to take over the shelter, and Dave stepped up to be the ACO. The county agreed to let them use the kennels and later allowed SHARK to build a larger kennel on a piece of land in the middle of the landfill.

Dave showed us around the original shelter, which was a leaning, open-air shack with ten narrow kennels inside. The shack walls were chain-link and boards that created a little shade but gave scant protection from the elements. We squeezed inside the narrow aisle with Dave as he explained that he took care of this bunch of dogs personally. They were dogs that needed special care; one was blind and another was struggling to hold any weight and needed a special diet. Others were new to SHARK, and he was holding them there until he assessed them and space opened up in the main kennel.

Nancy snapped pictures, struggling to capture the dogs in the dimly lit, cramped space. It was hard to believe that this was the county shelter. Abbeville seemed like a nice town. We'd driven through some obviously impoverished areas on our drive in, but once in Abbeville there were neighborhoods and shops and well-cared-for properties.

"You don't sound like you're from Alabama," I commented to Dave. Nancy guessed, correctly, that he was from Massachusetts. A town near Cape Cod, he told us.

"How'd you end up in Alabama?" I asked.

He chuckled and said, "I'm a disabled veteran, and my wife is disabled too, so we tried to retire in Florida. It wasn't the life for us, so we decided to try moving north a bit. We threw a dart at the map and it landed on a little town in Tennessee. On the way there we ran into some weather. We stopped in Abbeville, and then we never left."

Until recently, Dave had run a business restoring classic cars, but then someone offered him "stupid money"* for one of his cars at a car show, and he decided to sell the business and donate the money and land to SHARK so they could build a real shelter. Currently, the dogs were housed in four different locations, two of which were here at the dump.

We followed Dave down a long, rutted road into the landfill past Southeastern Alabama Youth Leadership Academy Therapeutic Resources (STR). "They call it that, but it's really a juvenile detention center," Dave said. It was a challenging drive, one deserving of a Jeep. It seemed somewhat symbolic that Henry County chose to house the abandoned dogs and the troubled young people down a dirt road in the dump. I hoped the decision to place them here was simply one of convenience and not intention.

The main kennels were on a grassy patch banked on one side by an enormous mound of land that had already been filled (and covered and vented) and the other side, where trash was actively being buried.

"It's only a matter of time before they want this spot, too," Dave remarked. "That's why we need to build a shelter on our own land."

At the main kennel, a devoted core of volunteers, mostly retired women, took care of the dogs—feeding, cleaning, and making sure each got out twice a day for a walk or a run around the large yard.

The kennels were basically a large, airy pavilion under which sat twelve large chain-link kennels. The dog chorus began as soon as they saw Dave. Dave introduced us, greeting each dog. The adoration in their eyes was mutual. The affection and deep respect he held for each animal radiated in his touch. As we walked down the aisle visiting with the dogs, who were almost all large dogs with possible bully breeding, Dave said affectionately, "They're all my lambs."[†]

---

* His words.

† LAMBS: Lower Alabama mixed breeds (a breed of Dave's creation).

In 2017, SHARK rescued about six hundred dogs, and in 2018 it was closer to seven hundred. It was now September of 2019 and Dave told us they'd just gotten their 1,107th dog the day before. "But the day is young," he quipped.

So many in this country believe that we are winning this battle, that the numbers are going down and we are killing fewer shelter animals, but once again I was reminded that we are not, and if we are, it is a precarious win that could backslide with just the slightest turn of events or dip in the economy. If not for Dave and SHARK, all these animals would have found their way to the landfill, but not to be lovingly cared for by devoted volunteers until they can be safely transported to new homes.

In Alabama, the law dictates that each county "provide a suitable county pound and impounding officer for the impoundment of dogs, cats, and ferrets found running at large."*

I'm not sure how the ferrets made the cut (and I had yet to see a ferret at a pound in Alabama), but I talked to one official in Alabama who told me that at least one-third of the counties are not in compliance with this law. They simply don't have the money to provide a pound, or the current leadership doesn't choose to allocate funds for it.

The law does allow for counties without a pound to "contribute their pro-rata share to the staffing and upkeep of the county pound" in a neighboring county. Henry County, where SHARK is located, is 568 square miles, but I imagine some of their animals come from surrounding counties that also have no pound, and no dedicated group like SHARK to shepherd their lambs.

"Does SHARK pay for everything?" I asked.

He laughed again. "The county gives me a stipend of $1,000 a year and the city gives me $1,200. You want to see our last vet bill?"†

The bill was for $27,000.

---

* Code of Alabama, Section 3-7A-7 (Acts 1990, No. 90-530, p. 816, 7; Act 2009-636, p. 1949, 1): Maintenance of Pound; Notice of Impoundment.

† Both the county and the city have increased their contribution to $2,000 annually as of this writing.

"We pay it, though, never run a balance. We find a way. People around here are good."

As he says this, I'm amazed, but I also wonder why the people of Henry County and Abbeville city allow this situation to go on. Why they throw away so many dogs. SHARK was currently housing seventy-eight dogs. Twenty-two hundred dollars wouldn't cover expenses for one month, let alone a year. And, yet, SHARK found a way. They also made sure that every dog that left, almost all through rescue that Dave secured, was vaccinated and spay or neutered, before Dave drove it wherever it needed to go to meet a transport or take it himself to safety. Sometimes that meant driving to Maine or Minnesota.

Dave opened the kennel of a little fireplug of a dog named Lola. She'd been at SHARK for six months. Most of the lambs stayed with SHARK for four months or more on average before he could find them rescue. Lola was a sweetheart with a wide grin and the snuffly breathing of a bulldog. She raced around the outside of the kennel a few times before Dave called her over and we made a short video that was interrupted by the sound of a Chinook helicopter from Fort Rucker, forty miles west. They flew through almost daily for training exercises over nearby Lake Eufaula.

Before we left, we unloaded donations, since SHARK relied on donations for everything. I asked Dave what I asked every director: "How do we fix this? How can we help?"

He said he is always hopeful that a new board of directors in their county will decide to make the animals a priority, but mostly what SHARK and the lambs needed was more awareness and more exposure so that people realized they were here, deep in the dump of Henry County.

For a man who quite definitely sees the worst of the worst, Dave was upbeat and positive and so, so inspiring. Later, he told me in an e-mail, "I shouldn't have lived past twenty-two, when I left some blood in the mud back in Vietnam. I always wondered why. Now I know the plan He had for me all along."

I promised to share his story and once again wished desperately we could do more.

That night, Nancy and I stopped in a little town an hour from Abbeville. We found a small brewpub, and over a flight of craft beer and a handmade pizza we hatched a plan. In order to do more, we had to come back, we had to go to more shelters and rescues, and we needed to travel farther to find the forgotten places. To do that we needed money. To raise money we needed nonprofit status; then we could apply for grants, have dedicated fundraisers, look for sponsors. Over the next few days as we traveled back to Tennessee and visited more shelters and rescues, our idea grew. There was so little we could do now, but we would be back. And we would be bigger.

42

One Last Stop

Our last night at Laura's was filled with dogs. Her basement and garage were crammed with crates of dogs preparing to leave the next day on a transport north. Laura's house often acted as the hub for multiple shelters and rescues. It took a day or two to gather all the dogs, get them vetted if necessary, and prepare them for transport. From her house outside of Columbia, Tennessee, the dogs were loaded into Laura's van or someone else's for the trip north or to meet up with another transport (like OPH's, which met them in Abingdon, Virginia, once a month). Only recently, Laura had acquired a plane for transports. It wasn't hers exactly, but the owner/pilot bought it for the specific purpose of flying transports for Laura.

It boggled my mind how she could keep so many dogs and shelters and rescues and transports straight. Nearly every week, she organized multiple transports, moving dog after dog out of danger to safety in shelters and rescues out of state. She had a full-time job and was recently married, and yet she was by far saving more dogs than anyone I knew. Literally thousands of dogs owed their lives to her, and yet very few people knew her name. She was a quiet, kind, unassuming woman with an uncanny ability to manage hundreds of details, dogs, and sometimes difficult people.

In her basement, above the crates and dog supplies, hang multiple platinum and double-platinum albums. The first time Ian and I stayed with Laura, we stumbled upon them by accident when we transported the tiny Chihuahua, Helen, from K4K to Laura's basement. As soon as she got home that night, we both had questions. Was she secretly a musical superstar? Most of the artists were Christian rock bands whose names I only knew from the Billboard charts. As it turned out, she came to Nashville from Minnesota when she was twenty years old with dreams of working in the music industry. She scored a job at EMI Records (later purchased by Universal), where she worked on the distribution team. When one of their artists' albums went gold or platinum, the whole team was gifted with their own awards. Laura worked there for sixteen years before she finally left that work to devote herself to the rescuing of dogs. Now she works for a realty group for a paycheck so she can rescue dogs.

After Nancy and I helped Laura get the dogs out for a potty break, we sat down and shared all that we had seen since we left her house on Tuesday morning. She nodded as we talked about the places she knew well and pulled out her phone to look up the rescues, like SHARK, that were new to her. We'd spent our day in Giles County, only an hour away from Columbia. She was eager to connect with leadership from Giles County Humane Association (GCHA) so she could help the newly reopened Giles County Animal Shelter, which had a dark history of killing dogs and had been closed down the previous October by the district attorney.

Nancy and I had driven the length of Alabama, arriving back in Tennessee in the early afternoon to tour the tiny Giles County shelter, formerly the Giles Dog Pound. We'd come there at the behest of another rescue advocate, Daphne, who had contacted me after my June visit with Ian to say, "You have to see what is happening in Giles County."

The rumors abounded as to why the shelter was closed, most having to do with the inhumane methods of killing dogs. The current ACOs told me the investigation was ongoing and they couldn't talk about it, so we focused on the shelter and its new director, Morgan. As was all too common at these small rural county shelters with a shallow tax base, Giles had a tiny budget. It didn't include much beyond rabies shots; only puppies got distemper shots.

When we arrived at the tiny concrete building, we were greeted by Morgan, plus Sherry, Margie, and Marcie from the GCHA. Sherry handed me a copy of a handwritten report from the previous director listing the intake numbers and outcomes during the years the previous director served, which was prior to being closed by the district attorney. About 80 percent of the animals were destroyed each year until the GCHA got more involved, but even then the numbers were heartbreaking.

While the shelter had only reopened two months ago, they'd already taken in more than 120 dogs. They only accepted strays and dogs seized by Animal Control, no owner surrenders.* The number of strays running around Tennessee and Alabama, and I suppose all of the South, continued to astound me. So far, Morgan told me she had only euthanized dogs for extreme aggression.

Morgan seemed nervous and later confessed that she'd been anxious about our visit, worried that we'd come to judge her, not help her. We assured her the opposite was the case. As was my habit, I asked Morgan about her thoughts on how we could fix this problem—the unending number of dogs that landed in the shelters and too many dying as a result.

She echoed what many had said, we need more low-cost/free access to spay and neuter, but she went on to say what they really needed was education. As an Animal Control Officer, she believed her job was not just to enforce, but to educate. "Some people just don't know how to properly care for their animals. If I can educate them and help them keep their animal, that's better than me bringing it back to the shelter."

She tried hard to give people the benefit of the doubt. Instead of citing them, she explained why a Chihuahua can't live outdoors in the winter or why it isn't okay to allow your unneutered male dog to run loose. Having just spent the week listening to the stories of so many dogs, I imagined that educating

---

* We ran into this policy many times, and each time I wondered if owners who couldn't surrender their pets simply dumped them for the ACOs to find somewhere so they had to accept them. I didn't want to think about the other alternatives.

the rural southern population must feel like an endless task. Morgan had been an Animal Control Officer for several years, she'd certainly seen the worst, so it was encouraging to listen to her talk about her hopes of making a difference here in Giles County by offering education and partnership instead of citations and seizures.

So often, ACOs got painted as the bad guys, but we had seen different. Like Morgan, most of them wanted to solve this problem. Like so many problems in our country, we can't punish and penalize our way out of this. We need to come at it from a different angle. I've listened to plenty of people say we have to make spaying and neutering a law, and that sounds like a simple solution. But if you make it the law, you have to enforce that law, and how in the heck do you enforce a law like that? Arrest every person who shows up at a shelter with a litter of puppies? Track down the owners of the dog with the balls and fine them? And if you make it a law, does it become Morgan's job to confiscate the dog and get it spayed or neutered? And who pays for that? The guy who lives in a shack and can't afford to have his dog altered? Or this community that already won't allow its tax dollars to be used to spay and neuter the dogs currently in their shelter? Legislating that all dogs be spayed and neutered is a ridiculous idea that will not solve the problem and will cost the taxpayers much more than simply funding shelters with a budget that includes spay and neuter (and distemper vaccines and deworming while you're at it). Perhaps a more reasonable law would require that all dogs in publicly funded shelters be spayed and neutered before they are adopted out or pulled by rescue. But that would require that counties fund the law and that there be veterinary access—two things we rarely saw in the shelters we visited.

Spay and neuter is only one piece of the problem. I came down here looking for the answer, but I left with only more questions. What I did know after talking to so many ACOs, shelter directors, rescue coordinators, volunteers, and advocates was that education and awareness are the first steps. You can't fix something you don't know is broken.

One director in Tennessee said to me, "Our local population has no idea what we're dealing with here. No idea."

When I set off on my first trip south in that van with Lisa, so full of excitement and ignorance, I had no idea of the scope of the problem either, even after fostering one hundred dogs. And now it was also apparent that the people living in these counties where the dogs were coming from don't realize the extent of the problem. Cleary, the place to start is telling people.

And that was what I planned to do. Now I just had to get home and get started. But before I left, there was one more dog I had to rescue.

Fanny had spent her entire summer in Trisha's living room. Since leaving the Huntingdon pound, where she should have died, her life had been very small. Trisha loved her, but Trisha's love was divided thirty-five ways on a daily basis. It was way past time for Fanny to have a home of her own.

On our way out of town, we stopped at Trisha's to pick up Fanny, who would come home with me, as a foster dog—for now. I could still picture her in that pound, her skinny poop-encrusted frame and her happy wiggles, even as we stuck her with a needle. I'd wanted to take her then and talked myself out of it. Now it seemed meant to be. Was she my dog? Or just another rescue? I didn't know, but I was going to take her home and find out.

43

It's Time

Once home, Fanny clung to me, but she was terrified of all the men in my life, which at that time were Nick, Ian, and Brady, who was still living at home, having yet to find a job. Fanny ran from all of them, slowly warming up to Nick, but only if he was sitting on the couch. I walked mile after mile with her, thinking about the trip, where she came from, whether she was my dog. She was skittish, slow to trust, and not always well behaved, peeing in the house, chewing up my favorite sandals, barking at the boys, running from me when it was time to go in her crate. All of this made sense considering her history. She would not be an easy dog. She would take a lot of work and training and, mostly, time. Maybe now wasn't the best time for me to adopt a dog, but then, would there ever be a best time?

Not long after arriving home, I had several opportunities to speak about what I'd seen in the South. I carefully crafted a PowerPoint presentation about my journey into fostering and rescue that ultimately led to the shelters in the South. Ian and Nancy's pictures were powerful, illustrating not just the desperate situation, but the beauty of the dogs trapped in it.

After my first presentation at our local Jewish Community Center, I asked Nancy, "Was it too much?" I knew my stories were shocking and upsetting, and I wanted them to be, but I tried to temper them with the hope I also felt and with the incredible stories of the people I met, like Dave at SHARK and Laura, who rescued thousands. I wanted people to be moved by their stories enough to tell someone else or to help or, at the very least, to consider adopting a rescue instead of buying a dog.

It was so intensely real to me, and I couldn't help myself. When I talked about the situation, my voice rose and rushed and I could not hold back. I'd run into someone in the grocery store, and they'd ask about the trip, and I'd start talking, unable to censor myself or tone it down. I'd watch as people's faces glazed over; they'd look away, anxious for me to finish. When I didn't, they made excuses or changed the subject. They didn't want to hear it, or they didn't want to hear so much of it. They, like me a year ago, didn't want to believe it. And even if they did, they didn't feel they could do anything about it.

But they can. I can. You can. If my trips south had taught me anything, it was that this problem was fixable. It will take all of us. Every person can do something. In this country, where we love dogs to an extreme, spending millions on grooming and dog walkers and day care, there is no shortage of people who care about dogs or have money to be spent on dogs.

There are solutions, but the first step is awareness. We have to recognize that while in many parts of this country, dogs in shelters do find homes, there are too many places where they will instead suffer and many of them die. And they don't have to. It's within our power to change.

While in Alabama, Nancy and I had a quick lunch with Aubrie Kavanaugh, the author and no-kill advocate I've mentioned. We talked about what we saw in Alabama, the fact that too many dogs suffered there, and how I wanted our rescue to pull more of them, and she reminded me of the story of the starfish she told in her book:*

You may know the tale of a boy on a beach, surrounded by starfish that have washed up on the shore. The boy reaches down, picks up

---

* Blatantly copying it here, but Aubrie said that was okay. From Aubrie Kavanaugh, *Not Rocket Science: A Story of No Kill Animal Shelter Advocacy in Huntsville, Alabama,* self-published, 2019, pages 185–186.

a starfish and throws it in the water. A man who sees the boy asks, "Don't you see how many there are? You'll never be able to make a difference." The boy picks up another starfish, throws it into the ocean and says, "I made a difference for that one."

Many in animal rescue circles refer to shelter animals as starfish. As they wash up on the beach, rescuers work individually or collectively to help them. Rescuers often say they cannot save them all, but they can save that one.

While it is noble to save those individual starfish, we can do so much more if we take a little time to look at the bigger picture. Where are all these starfish coming from in the first place? Can we keep them from washing up on the shore? Once they are onshore, are there more efficient ways to help them than by trying to do it all ourselves? Can we get the public and the media to help us get them off the beach and on to new lives?

I struggled to find an end for this book, just like I did for *Another Good Dog*. I thought maybe I'd find it if I took just one more trip south, but that trip only left me with more questions. I thought I'd find it if I brought Fanny home with me, but she was complicated, skittish, and needy, and only reminded me of the many I didn't bring home. I thought if I hiked miles in the mountains and thought long about it, the ending would reveal itself, but instead, I aggravated my runner's knee and returned no closer to an ending.

That's because there is no end. At least for now.

As I write this, I think about Heather desperately trying to take pictures with her aging camera in one hand and a dog in the other, then staying up late to edit them and send to rescues so that another dog doesn't have to die in Franklin County, Tennessee, this month. I think about Laura, her ever-present cellphone functioning as command central and her basement full of dogs in crates, the lucky ones waiting for transport north to rescue. I think of Helen and Sherry in their tiny shelter on the edge of the dismal swamp, trying to find room for one more dog and biting their tongue when another person shows up with a dog tied in the bed of their truck saying he can't keep it anymore. And mostly I think about the Huntingdon dog pound where Fanny should have died and about how many dogs are still there at this very moment, fussing at the flies drawn to the poop they lie in and scratching at the rusted edges of the chain-link fence that imprisons them.

But I also think about Dr. Kim Sanders and Cheyenne and the busy, bustling lobby at P.A.W.S., where dogs find forever homes every day. I think about Kristin at Cheatham and the trails hiding rocks with positive messages luring people to give the dogs a chance. I think about the smile on Dave's face as he talks about his lambs and the shelter SHARK is building. And I think about Morgan and her desire to educate, not simply enforce.

I did end up adopting Fanny. This entire journey started many years ago with another girl dog I adopted who stole my heart—Lucy. We loved that good dog for seventeen years. It was her passing that launched me into the world of dog rescue, and my life has never been the same. Now another dog has changed my life. Fanny is my starfish, and also a daily reminder to focus on the ocean. The only way this changes is if we make it change—you and me. This problem does not belong to rural communities in the South. It does not belong to the big organizations working tirelessly for a no-kill nation. It belongs to all of us. It will take all of us.

Long ago, we domesticated dogs. And while we obviously were not directly involved in making that happen, we humans, as a race, did it. We have an obligation to speak up for them and an obligation to rescue them and give them lives of dignity, but more than anything we have an obligation to fix this fixable problem.

It was Gandhi who said, "The greatness of a nation and its moral progress can be judged by the way in which its animals are treated."

Maybe it speaks volumes that in this country some dogs sleep on $200 memory foam beds and eat organic raw dog food while others starve and die on concrete floors.

I think we're better than that. And I believe in my soul that it doesn't have to be. I remain convinced that thousands of dogs are suffering in our shelters not because people don't care, but because they don't know.

Help me tell them.

Epilogue

I know this book had more than a few sad stories, so let me assure you there were also quite a few happy endings. Sheba, the pit bull puppy our volunteer team met at Oconee Animal Control, was pulled by OPH and renamed Enigma. She was a stellar foster pup who was quickly adopted and now has a forever family. Flannery finally found her family not long after my trip to Alabama, and Houdini (OPH Hot Diggity) traveled north a month after I met him, healthier thanks to his time with Kay, and he became our foster dog. He was still an escape artist, but also an absolute love who starred in several K9&Kds programs before being adopted by his forever family (and then escaping one last time when they got him home—but we found him!). They changed his name to Bob because his disappearing days are over. And Gala? I'm so happy to say that she was finally adopted by the person meant to have her all along: Pam. She is safe and loved and very happy.

Nancy and I did start that nonprofit, Who Will Let the Dogs Out. We created it as an initiative of Operation Paws for Homes. We continue to travel all over our country to raise awareness about the suffering and killing of dogs in our shelters. We have met countless heroes and dogs, taking their pictures and telling their stories on our site, WhoWillLetTheDogsOut.org. We are committed to the idea that awareness is the first step to change.

I won't pretend to have the solution to the problem of so many dogs suffering and dying, because there is no one solution. After visiting nearly fifty shelters* and talking to directors, Animal Control Officers, rescue coordinators, volunteers, and community members, I do have a few ideas.

The solution starts with Dr. Kim Sanders's words: "You just stop killing dogs." Is it that simple? Yes and no. If you start with that premise and work from there, it's much easier to find solutions than if you start with, "We'll stop killing dogs once X happens."

I can't begin to tell you how many times I've heard someone say, "We just have to make spay and neuter a law." Not only is that impossible, impractical, and unenforceable, it's a cop-out. It's a verbal tossing up of the hands, something people say because they don't want to admit that they aren't interested in the details and the work of actually fixing the problem.

I wrote in the book my own explanation for why that kind of law is impractical, but there is a spay and neuter law that I believe would make sense. That law would dictate that animals being adopted or pulled by rescue from public shelters must be spayed or neutered. That's a law that could be enforced. But in order to do that, shelters have to be fully funded and veterinary access has to be available.

In fact, first there have to be shelters. It makes sense (to me) that a law similar to Alabama's law regarding pounds be the law of the land. I would amend it to require that every county either maintain and fund a humane animal shelter or pay their portion to maintain and fund a shelter in conjunction with neighboring counties. That would be a powerful law, but only if it was enforced. In parts of the South, there are counties that simply don't have a shelter. I've asked locals what happens to stray animals there and I get a shrug. Sometimes the animals are cared for by private shelters that pop up (more about this in a minute), sometimes they are shot because they're a nuisance. I've also heard tales and seen evidence of people poisoning strays and much worse. The cost to society of these animals that breed more animals, can carry contagious diseases, kill livestock, and endanger citizens is higher in terms of risk and ultimately fiscal cost than simply maintaining an effective,

---

* . . . At the time of this writing, but by the time you read this it will be dozens more, hundreds if my husband will watch the dogs while I'm gone.

humane shelter. It is our moral responsibility as a country to care for and re-home stray animals.

In too many places where county budgets don't include animal shelters, private citizens with the best of intentions step in. These are animal-loving people who can't bear to see the suffering, but they are not trained animal sheltering professionals. As Rhonda at Brindlee Mountain Animal Rescue told me, "There's a fine line between rescuing and hoarding."

In too many cases, these private rescues with no oversight or inspections too quickly get out of control. Good people with generous hearts do all they can, but they are eventually overwhelmed. Properly sheltering animals and rehoming them is expensive and requires a lot more than best intentions. Private citizens should not be forced into these situations. Every private rescue that I visited started because its founder felt the county government was not doing its job. If the government did its job, many hoarding and cruelty cases could be avoided.

Let's say private rescues are necessary because the government can't/won't operate a humane shelter for its community. If that's the case, then there need to be laws in place to protect these good people with good intentions, laws that monitor and inspect the animals and the conditions they're kept in.

Because I live in York County, Pennsylvania, and foster more than twenty-five animals each year, I'm required by law to have a kennel license. Having this license means that the county dog warden shows up at my house twice a year to inspect my "kennel." She verifies that all my personal dogs and foster dogs are up to date on rabies vaccinations and that my foster dogs that come from out of state have health certificates. She takes a picture of my kennel roster, a form given to me by the county that records where my dogs come from, when they arrive, when they leave, and where they go. She makes sure my kennel license is displayed and that I know where my (at least) two fire extinguishers are (and that they are not expired). She looks over my puppy room, usually meets the fosters, and inspects my fenced area.

While the dog warden's visits can sometimes inconvenience me, I know they are important. I always joke with the warden that she's keeping me from becoming a hoarder. But that's not really a joke because she really is.

So, if we make a law that there has to be a shelter and a law that anyone housing a certain number of dogs each year must have a kennel license and be subject to inspections, and then we make it a law that any animal being adopted from a publicly funded shelter must be spayed or neutered, we're making progress. But I can already hear my father saying, "But how do you pay for that? I don't want my taxes going up!"

I'm no politician and I won't pretend to understand the tax code, but I think an animal shelter is a service to the community like clean water, trash collection, and snow plowing, so it's not ludicrous to expect communities to pay for that service. That said, there are also ways to find that money that don't necessarily raise property taxes. Dog licenses in Pennsylvania help to pay the dog warden's salary. Adding an additional tiny sales tax to animal supplies that are not essential like costumes, toys, beds, strollers, and cat condos could painlessly raise funds. Funding shelters is non-negotiable, so communities need to find a way. To paraphrase Dr. Sanders, "We just start funding the shelters."

Now, let's talk about what the shelters themselves can do. If they are funded adequately, then staff can put into place progressive programs that reduce the stress on the animals, making them easier to manage and more adoptable. Nashville Humane was a great example of little things (pumped in calming pheromones, therapeutic music, built-in obedience training, intentionally designed facilities, daily enrichment activities in their kennels, lots of volunteers, and plenty of foster homes) that are not tremendously expensive but help prevent deterioration from shelter stress.

Activities to involve the community like the trails at Cheatham Shelter or the Doggy Day Out at Greenwood or the dog park at P.A.W.S. are just a few, but there are hundreds of ways to make the shelter a place where the community wants to invest its time. Community ownership is key to the success of any shelter.

Shelters must provide a medical protocol that keeps their population safe. Distemper vaccinations are a no-brainer. Every animal entering a shelter for any reason should be given one. These vaccines are cheap (as little as three dollars each when you buy them in bulk) and are highly effective, providing protection within hours of being given.* On the other hand, a distemper outbreak will cost a shelter thousands in cleanup, plus the devastation of destroying a big part of their animal population and the overtime that will be required of staff and volunteers working to save the dogs they can, not to mention the bad press it is likely to evoke.

Simple procedures like isolating new intakes for a quarantine period, keeping puppies separated from the regular population until they're fully vaccinated, and a deworming schedule will keep everyone healthy and reduce the length of stay. I'm not a shelter expert, but I know there are plenty of best practices that can be game changers. The problem I saw in many shelters was that the staff was working their tails off simply to keep the animals alive long enough to get them out via rescue and had no energy to focus on much else. Plus, their hands were tied by a budget dictated to them by non-animal-sheltering experts. Much of this seems like common sense, and it is, but that doesn't mean it's practiced or even can be practiced.

Heartworm is a huge problem in many of the southern shelters, where mosquito populations flourish. Even if dogs arrive at the shelter heartworm negative, they can easily contract it while in the shelter, as few budgets include heartworm preventatives and so many strays come in heartworm positive. As one director pointed out, there's no point in testing for heartworm (something most shelters do so that they can disclose the status to rescues and adopters) if you aren't going to then give the preventatives. Just this week I saw a veterinary tech in the North griping on Facebook about rescue dogs that arrived heartworm positive even though they originally tested negative before their transport. Without preventatives, living in a shelter in the mosquito-filled South rife with heartworm positive dogs makes the likelihood that an unprotected dog will contract heartworm before they are shipped north a distinct possibility. I purchase heartworm preventatives for my dogs so I know they aren't cheap, but once again, which is cheaper, giving dogs the preventatives

---

* UWsheltermedicine.com/resources/canine-distemper-cdv

and treating heartworm positive dogs or losing the trust of the northern rescue/adopter population?*

I have a thousand thoughts on this, but in the interest of keeping this book a little shorter than *War and Peace*, I'll finish with one more idea.

Reasonably priced veterinary access is critical to the success of solving this crisis. Many of the shelters I visited simply had no access or could not afford the access they had. I would love to see a program like Teach for America put in place for veterinarians. Veterinary school is extremely expensive. I've been told it's harder and more expensive to become a veterinarian than a doctor. Nearly every newly minted veterinarian graduates with a degree and huge debt. If the government developed a program to reduce some of that debt in exchange for a term of service in an underserved community or at a large multi-county shelter, it could be a win-win. New vets get experience and shelter animals get much-needed care. We could call it Vets for Pets. Okay, that's pretty dorky, but you get the idea.

I bet you have a few of your own idea as well. Now is the time to act on them. We need volunteers in the shelters, but we also need them in the political arena developing legislation, advocating for better animal sheltering and laws, and simply raising awareness. This problem is just so darn fixable. Help fix it.

---

* Heartworms are devastating, as without treatment a dog will die a painful death. Treatment can cost upward of $1,000. Heartworms are transmitted by mosquito bite but are completely preventable with a monthly dewormer.

Other Ways to Help

Advocate for shelter and rescue dogs. If you are looking for a dog, choose to rescue, and if you know someone looking for a dog, encourage them to rescue also. As Kim Kavin explains in her excellent book *The Dog Merchants*, it is not a problem of too many dogs and not enough homes; it is a problem of not enough people choosing to rescue. Choose to rescue.

Foster. Taking a shelter dog into your home until it's adopted, for just a weekend, or even a few hours can be the difference between that dog finding a forever family or not. Too much time in a shelter can break dogs down. Dogs who were once someone's pet can forget how to live in a family, and dogs who have never had a home can't learn to trust humans if they don't get consistent positive contact. Fostering bridges the gap between lost and found. [Beware: shameless plug] I wrote a book, *Another Good Dog: One Family and Fifty Foster Dogs*, about our fostering experiences, which shares the good, the bad, and the ugly, but also answers questions about how it all works and will hopefully convince you to be a foster dog family too. If you need a little more convincing or still have questions—read it.

Volunteer. Find a shelter or rescue near you and help. Rescue is hard work, but it is also incredibly rewarding. Human contact is the one item usually most lacking for dogs living in shelters. You can walk a dog, play with a dog, or simply sit with a dog. Shelters and rescues depend on volunteers and are always looking for help. Where do your talents lie? Marketing, fundraising, checking references, processing applications, recruiting volunteers, posting on social media, taking pictures, writing about dogs . . . the list of needs is endless. There is something you can do.

Donate. Obviously, any shelter or rescue can use more money, but you can also donate much-needed items. You can collect treats or toys or dewormers, or whatever is not in the budget of your local shelter. Scout troops or any kind of kids' organizations can make enrichment toys for shelters and rescues.* You can also be an angel for a shelter in need. You can find updated wish lists for shelters on the website, WhoWillLetTheDogsOut.org.

Tell someone. Word of mouth is the most powerful marketing there is, and struggling shelters and rescues desperately need marketing. Talk about the situation in rural southern shelters or even the shelter in your town. Tell them about this book. Share the Who Will Let the Dogs Out blog, Facebook page, and Instagram account, where we post updates on the situation, new ways to help, direct pleas from the shelters themselves, and more stories of the heroes working tirelessly in our shelters.

I think of this situation like that game at the arcade where you drop in your quarter, hoping it will be the one that pushes all the others over the edge and into your hands. You never know which person will be that tipping point in the struggle to end the suffering and killing of adoptable dogs. Awareness is the first step toward change.

Vote intentionally. Local politicians have the power to change the situation for shelter dogs in your community. Get to know the shelter in your community—ask questions about budgets, intake numbers, spay/neuter

---

* There are hundreds of ideas on Pinterest. I almost always have a garbage bag full of bottle sock toys made by my local scout troops to haul with me to the shelters. They are simply an empty water bottle stuffed in a clean sock. Dogs love the crinkly sound they make and moms love the happy ending for the orphan socks that turn up in the dryer. Win-win.

policies, and how many dogs are dying and why. Don't be afraid to ask these questions. I think sometimes the simple fact that no one asks is why outdated, cruel policies persist.

As I was editing this book, I got a message from a reader and shelter worker named Katie in a northern Pennsylvania town four hours from me. The shelter had just taken in a large dog, heavily pregnant. Katie had learned that the dog was scheduled to be spayed and the puppies aborted the next morning, per shelter policy. She asked whether our rescue would pull the dog if she was able to convince the board to make an exception. We agreed to pull the dog, the board made the exception, and the dog, Liberty Bell, gave birth to ten big, beautiful, healthy puppies four days later. They would not be alive today if one person had not chosen to speak up and ask the question.

That experience taught me that it is not only the southern shelters where adoptable dogs are dying. Find out what is happening at your shelter, and if you don't like it, vote for change.

Teach your children how to safely interact with a dog. Many dogs end up in a shelter because they've bitten someone, often a child. And almost always that bite could have been prevented if the child knew how to safely interact with a dog. This is an important life skill, and, just like swimming or crossing the street, one that we must intentionally teach. There is plenty of information on the internet about this topic, but if you live within the reach of OPH (northern Virginia, Maryland, DC, and south-central Pennsylvania), we have a free program called K9&Kds that teaches these skills and will present it for any local group. If you are out of our area or are a shelter or rescue and would like a copy of the program to use, contact me and I'll get it to you.

Love your dog. If you have a rescue dog, care for it and train it well. And when someone asks what breed it is, don't guess or explain the DNA test you had done; tell them your dog's story—this dog is a rescue. You chose to rescue. You are a rescuer.

I can't fix this problem and I realize that I don't have the answers (oh, how I wish I did), but not knowing how has never been any kind of excuse for not trying. I'm learning more about the situation every day, and I believe with all my heart that we will fix this situation in my lifetime, but it's going to take all of us.

Together we rescue, and together we can let the dogs out.

SHELTERS AND RESCUES MENTIONED

Many of these shelters have websites, Facebook pages, and Amazon wish lists. If you'd like to support them in any way, be sure to find them online.

ALABAMA
Brindlee Mountain Animal Rescue
25 County Road 1772
Joppa, AL 35087
brindleemountainanimalrescue.com

Humane Society of Chilton County
139 Shade Tree Drive
Clanton, AL 35045
chiltoncountyhumanesociety.org

Rescuers United For Furbabies (R.U.F.F.)
P.O. Box 453
Oakman, AL 35579
ruffrescuewalkercountyal.org

Safe Haven Animal Rescue and Kennel (SHARK)
P.O. Box 126
Abbeville, AL 36310
Facebook.com/AbbevilleRescue

Walker County Humane and Adoption Center
23470 US-78
Jasper, AL 35501

GEORGIA
Proud Spirit Horse Sanctuary
3495 Elberton Highway
Lincolnton, GA 30817
horsesofproudspirit.org

NORTH CAROLINA
Anson County Animal Shelter
7257 Old US Highway 74
Polkton, NC 28135
Facebook.com/ansoncountyanimalshelter/

Greater Charlotte SPCA
P.O. Box 77491
Charlotte, NC 28271
charlottespca.org

Lenoir County SPCA
2455 Rouse Road Exd
Kinston, NC 28504
lenoircountyspca.org

A Shelter Friend
8100 Twisted Hickory Road
Bladenboro, NC 28320
ashelterfriend.org

SOUTH CAROLINA
Abbeville County Animal Services
79 Calhoun Road
Abbeville, SC 29620
abbevillecountysc.com/animal-services

Anderson County P.A.W.S.
1320 US-29
Anderson, SC 29626
andersoncountysc.org/paws/

Humane Society of Greenwood
2820 Airport Road
Greenwood, SC 29649
gwdhumanesociety.org

Newberry County Animal Control
240 Public Works Drive
Newberry, SC 29108
newberrycounty.net/departments/animal-control

Oconee Humane Society/Oconee County Animal Control
1925 Sandifer Boulevard
Seneca, SC 29678
oconeehumane.org

TENNESSEE
Bedford County Animal Control
205 Lane Parkway
Shelbyville, TN 37160
bedfordcountytn.org/animalcontrol.html

Cheatham County Animal Control
2797 Sams Creek Road
Pegram, TN 37143
cheathamcountytn.gov/animal-control.html

Giles County Animal Shelter
380 Bennett Drive
Pulaski, TN 38478
facebook.com/gilesanimals

Giles County Humane Association
P.O. Box 237
Pulaski, TN 38478
gchumane.webs.com

Greenfield City Pound (c/o Greenfield Police Dept)
222 North Front Street
Greenfield, TN 38230
greenfieldtn.com

Humane Educational Society of Chattanooga
212 N. Highland Park Avenue
Chattanooga, TN 37404
heschatt.org

Huntingdon Dog Pound
(c/o Mayor of Huntingdon)
19810 East Main Street
P.O. Box 668
Huntingdon, TN 38344

Maury County/Columbia Animal Services
1233 Mapleash Avenue
Columbia, TN 38401
Maurycounty-tn.gov/196/animal-services

Nashville Humane Association
213 Oceola Avenue
Nashville, TN 37209
nashvillehumane.org

Red Fern Animal Shelter
1487 Miles Road
Dresden, TN 38225
redfernanimalshelter.org

Rural Animal Rescue Effort (RARE)
1481 Lasea Road
Columbia, TN 38401
rarerescue.org

Shelbyville Animal Control
716 Industrial Parkway
Shelbyville, TN 37160
shelbyvilletn.org/animalcontrol.htm

Williamson County Animal Center
106 Claude Yates Drive
Franklin, TN 37064
adoptwcac.org

VIRGINIA
Scott County Animal Shelter
186 Single Tree Road
Gate City, VA 24251
scottcounty.dogrescues.org

Scott County Humane Society
P.O. Box 1535
Gate City, VA 24251
scotthumane.com

Tappahannock/Essex County Animal Shelter (TECAS)
540 Airport Road
Tappahannock, VA 22560
tecas.rescueme.org

Resource List

There are resources available to shelters and rescues, but it takes motivated staff or volunteers to pursue them. If you're looking for a way to help your local shelter or your favorite rescue, below is a list of resources that you might suggest or pursue on their behalf. This is just a selection of the many organizations in the U.S. committed to animal rescue and a no-kill future, including funding sources, information, and resources.

AmazonSmile is the same as Amazon.com; however, when people purchase through the site, the AmazonSmile Foundation donates 0.5% of the price of eligible products to the charitable organization of their choice. https://www.smile.amazon.com/

Amazon Wish List is a gift registry on Amazon.com, where shelters and rescues create "wish lists" that their supporters can use to buy needed donations. https://www.amazon.com/

American Humane administers: 1) the Meacham Grant for shelter expansion or improvements; and 2) the Second Chance Fund to help offset the costs of rescuing animals who are homeless or the victims of human cruelty. https://www.americanhumane.org/

The American Society for the Prevention of Cruelty to Animals (ASPCA) provides grants to animal welfare organizations and government agencies for natural or other disasters and animal intake from cases involving abuse, neglect, hoarding, animal fighting, and/or puppy mills affecting a minimum of twenty companion animals. https://www.aspca.org/

Animal Farm Foundation, Inc., an organization dedicated to ending breed discrimination toward pit bull–type dogs, provides grants to improve the shelter system and address owner-pet accessible housing. https://animalfarmfoundation.org/

Animal Grantmakers is a funder affinity group focused on animal protection that is comprised of a diverse group of foundations, public charities, corporate giving programs, and individuals working throughout the US and globally. The site includes an animal funding database and resources for grant-seekers. https://animal grantmakers.org/

Banfield Foundation provides grants to nonprofits for programs designed to keep pets and owners together, including funding for veterinary medical equipment, pet-friendly domestic violence shelters, and disaster relief. https://www.banfield.com/

Best Friends Animal Society, a leader in the no-kill movement, provides adoption, spay/neuter, and educational programs, in partnership with nearly 3,000 animal welfare groups, and operates the nation's largest sanctuary for homeless animals. https://bestfriends.org/

Bissell Pet Foundation provides financial support to municipal shelters, rescue groups, and spay/neuter organizations focused on adoption, spay/neuter, and microchipping, and also sponsors Empty the Shelters adoption events in collaboration with their 5,000-member Partners for Pets network. https://www.bissellpetfoundation.org/

Dogs Playing for Life, a program of the Animal Farm Foundation, offers information, plus Shelter Enrichment Seminars and Mentorships to shelter personnel and volunteers to advance skills in handling and training to encourage playgroup programs, which make for happier and less-stressed animals. https://dogsplayingforlife.com/

The Grey Muzzle Organization provides grants to organizations to help senior dogs, focusing on foster and adoption program improvement, owner surrender reduction, medical care and expenses, hospice care, rehoming, and therapy dog training. https://www .greymuzzle.org/

How I Met My Dog custom matches people with their canine soulmate and assists people with rehoming their dogs, working in partnership with dozens of shelters and rescue groups in forty states. https://www.howimetmydog.com/

The Humane Society of the United States (HSUS) runs advocacy campaigns to push for better animal legislation, plus programs designed to ease the burden on local sheltering groups, including the Animal Care Expo; Animal Sheltering magazine; the Pets for Life project, to keep pets with their families; and the Shelter Pet Project, to encourage people to adopt from shelters and rescues. They also provide rescue groups with training and resources. https://www.humanesociety.org/

Maddie's Fund, a family foundation dedicated to building and sustaining a no-kill nation, offers a variety of grants, training opportunities, and resources to shelters and rescues. Since 1994, the fund has awarded $276 million toward increased pet lifesaving, shelter management, leadership, shelter medicine education, and foster care. https://www.maddiesfund.org/

The National Humane Education Society (NHES) offers free humane education programs for schools, churches, clubs, libraries, and other venues serving children. https://www.nhes.org/

The Onyx & Breezy Foundation is a family foundation that provides grants to shelters and rescues for spay/neuter programs, food, medicine and supplies, dogs of veterans suffering from PTSD, puppy mill rescues, and disaster relief. http://www.onyxandbreezy.org/

Pedigree Foundation offers grants to nonprofit shelters and rescues for program development and operations to improve quality of care and adoption rates. Since 2008, the foundation has made 5,300 grants to organizations across the US totaling $7.3 million. https://www.pedigreefoundation.org/

Petco Foundation provides grants to foster-based nonprofits, animal control agencies, SPCA/humane societies, and other nonprofits that operate out of a sheltering facility, in addition to disaster assistance and pet food bank support. https://www.petcofoundation.org/

Petfinder Foundation offers support to municipal and private agencies and Petfinder members for disaster preparation and recovery, enrichment, pet sponsorship, and vaccinations. https://petfinderfoundation.com/

PetSmart Charities, Inc., funds shelters and rescue organizations who become "adoption partners" and hold events in their stores. After becoming a partner, organizations are eligible for general support for vaccinations, spay/neuter, staffing, volunteer support, containment, and supplies. https://petsmartcharities.org/

Pilots N Paws links volunteers engaged in rescuing, sheltering and adopting animals, and volunteer pilots and plane owners to arrange animal transportation, including rescue flights, overnight foster care or shelter, and all other related activities. https://www.pilotsnpaws.org/

Rescue Rebuild, a program of greatergood.org, is a shelter renovation program that recruits volunteers to help shelters in need, including animal shelters, domestic violence shelters, and homeless and veteran housing. http://rescuerebuild.greatergood.org/

Rural Area Veterinary Services (RAVS), a program of The Fund for Animals, an affiliate of the HSUS, is a nonprofit veterinary outreach program that brings free veterinary services to underserved rural communities where regular veterinary care is inaccessible. Each year, six RAVS staff members and more than 350 volunteers provide essential, free veterinary care for more than 7,000 animals, while providing valuable training and experience for hundreds of future veterinary professionals. http://www.fundforanimals.org/rural-area-veterinary-services/

Acknowledgments

I wrote the stories, but so many people made them possible, I couldn't begin to name them all here. So, in no particular order, let me offer a few words of thanks—

Thank you to OPH for trusting me to represent you in the southern shelters, for teaching me what it means to rescue, and for supporting all my efforts big and small. You have become my family and I couldn't do this work without you.

Thank you to the shelter and rescue directors who opened their doors and trusted me to tell their stories. I apologize for whatever I got wrong, but hope you know it was always well intentioned. "Thanks" seems like too small a word to give to the directors, rescue coordinators, ACOs, and volunteers I've met on this journey. You are the ones who are making the real difference. Your commitment, sacrifice, creativity, and belief in saving every animal is what will lead us into a better future, one in which every dog is safe. Thank you for putting the dogs first and your comfort second, for making the hard calls, and for always looking for another way.

Thank you to everyone who traveled the rescue road with me—Lisa Weigard, for holding my hand (and feeding me crackers) on that first trip; Nick Achterberg, for arriving with absolute support and the ability to back up a large vehicle just when I needed it most; and Ian Achterberg, for offering not just his photography skills but his tech knowledge, and great playlists, and for earning me lots of rewards points at Panera. Thanks to the first OPH Rescue

Road Trip team: Nancy Slattery, Jennifer Williams, Jen Kyle, Jessie Godfrey, Matt Liesicki, Erin Fitzgerald, and Leslie Knisley. I'm sure the road looked different to you, so thanks for letting me share my version and for tolerating cheap hotels and too many rushed meals, but mostly for being willing to get your hands dirty and your hearts bruised.

Thanks to Laura Prechel for always being at the ready with advice and friendship, a comfy guest room, the best cheese spread I've ever encountered, the company of Cadence (and other assorted canine guests), and a million rescue connections. But mostly thank you for all you do and sacrifice to save thousands of lives every year.

Thank you to Patty Larson for joining our Who Will Let the Dogs Out team and doing the serious work of finding resources and grants that will help get the dogs out and for putting together the excellent list at the back of this book.

Thank you to Margot Tillitson and Amy Barshinger for your quick reading and your vote of confidence. Thank you to Carly Watters, my agent at P.S. Literary, and Jessica Case, my editor at Pegasus Books, for believing in my ability to tell this story and understanding its importance.

Thanks to Gina Moltz and Ronni Casey for being not only my dog-walking buddies, but also my sounding board as I sifted through the message and purpose of this book. Thanks for your encouragement and your unfailing and possibly misplaced faith in me knowing what I'm doing.

Thanks to the readers of my blog, Another Good Dog, for keeping me accountable each week, celebrating the wins, asking excellent questions, and having my back through the hard parts.

Thanks to Aubrie Kavanaugh for your inspiring passion and belief in no-kill, but even more for your journalistic integrity and the brains you bring to the struggle.

A huge debt of thanks to Nancy Slattery for your friendship, your partnership, your amazing photos, and especially for keeping me on track and helping me be an adult when necessary. I wouldn't want to share a beer at Giant or a hotel room without a bathroom door with anyone else but you.

And, of course, huge thanks to my amazing family, Nick, Brady, Addie, and Ian, who tolerate the dogs and my crazy devotion to them despite the ruined carpets, chewed-up shoes, and endless barking. Thank you for at least pretending to be nose-blind to the smell of puppy poop. But, mostly, thanks for letting me write about you.

Special thanks to Nick for accepting his fate as a dog widow and to Ian for pushing me to go south at a time when my heart didn't think it could and for being my go-to dog babysitter whenever we're away. What will we do when you go away to college?

And big thanks and a thousand treats to all the dogs who teach me again and again that they are so much more than "just a dog," especially Gracie, Gala, Flannery, Edith, and Fanny.

#TogetherWeRescue
#WhoWillLetTheDogsOut?